S0-FPI-853

PRESENTED TO:

Aaron & Miriam

FROM:

Popi & Mimi

DATE:

1-5-2022

Heaven, LIFE, and the RESURRECTION

MyDaily® DEVOTIONAL

COUNTRYMAN
An Imprint of Thomas Nelson Publishers

THOMAS NELSON
Since 1798

Heaven, Life, and the Resurrection

© 2021 Thomas Nelson

All rights reserved. No portion of this book may be reproduced, stored in a retrieval system, or transmitted in any form or by any means—electronic, mechanical, photocopy, recording, scanning, or other—except for brief quotations in critical reviews or articles, without the prior written permission of the publisher.

Published in Nashville, Tennessee, by Thomas Nelson. Thomas Nelson is a registered trademark of HarperCollins Christian Publishing, Inc.

Thomas Nelson titles may be purchased in bulk for educational, business, fundraising, or sales promotional use. For information, please e-mail SpecialMarkets@ThomasNelson.com.

Unless otherwise noted, scripture quotations are taken from the New King James Version®. Copyright © 1982 by Thomas Nelson. Used by permission. All rights reserved.

Scripture quotations marked esv are taken from the esv® Bible (The Holy Bible, English Standard Version®). Copyright © 2001 by Crossway, a publishing ministry of Good News Publishers. Used by permission. All rights reserved.

Scripture quotations marked NASB are taken from the New American Standard Bible® (NASB). Copyright © 1960, 1962, 1963, 1968, 1971, 1972, 1973, 1975, 1977, 1995 by The Lockman Foundation. Used by permission. www.Lockman.org.

Scripture quotations marked NIV are taken from the Holy Bible, New International Version®, NIV®. Copyright © 1973, 1978, 1984, 2011 by Biblica, Inc.® Used by permission of Zondervan. All rights reserved worldwide. www.zondervan.com. The "NIV" and "New International Version" are trademarks registered in the United States Patent and Trademark Office by Biblica, Inc.®

Scripture quotations marked NLT are taken from the Holy Bible, New Living Translation. Copyright © 1996, 2004, 2015 by Tyndale House Foundation. Used by permission of Tyndale House Ministries, Carol Stream, Illinois 60188. All rights reserved.

Any internet addresses, phone numbers, or company or product information printed in this book are offered as a resource and are not intended in any way to be or to imply an endorsement by Thomas Nelson, nor does Thomas Nelson vouch for the existence, content, or services of these sites, phone numbers, companies, or products beyond the life of this book.

ISBN 978-1-4041-1573-6

Printed in China

21 22 23 24 25 DSC 10 9 8 7 6 5 4 3 2 1

Heaven, LIFE, and the RESURRECTION

MyDaily® DEVOTIONAL

Introduction

The devotions in *Heaven, Life, and the Resurrection* were created by fifty-two devoted men of God. We pray God's Word will come alive as you read each devotion through the coming year. May God reveal Himself to you as you learn about heaven, Jesus' life, and His resurrection. May your walk with Him be strengthened as you spend time with Him and meditate on His Word each day.

Johnny M. Hunt

DR. JOHNNY M. HUNT
Senior Vice President of Evangelism
and Pastoral Leadership
North American Mission Board
Alpharetta, Georgia

CONTENTS

WEEK	CONTRIBUTOR	PAGE
Week 1	Dr. Johnny Hunt, North American Mission Board, Alpharetta, GA	4
Week 2	Mark Hoover, NewSpring Church, Wichita, KS	10
Week 3	Dr. Alex Himaya, BattleCreek Church, Broken Arrow, OK	16
Week 4	Dr. Sam Greer, Red Bank Baptist Church, Chattanooga, TN	22
Week 5	Jeremy Morton, First Baptist Church Woodstock, Woodstock, GA	28
Week 6	Cary Schmidt, Emmanuel Baptist Church, Newington, CT	34
Week 7	Dr. Jeff Schreve, First Baptist Church Texarkana, Texarkana, TX	40
Week 8	Tim Sizemore, Lighthouse Baptist Church, Warner Robins, GA	46
Week 9	Mike Stone, Emmanuel Baptist Church, Blackshear, GA	52
Week 10	Dr. Ted H. Traylor, Olive Baptist Church, Pensacola, FL	58
Week 11	Dr. Mike Whitson, First Baptist Church Indian Trail, Indian Trail, NC	64
Week 12	Dr. Brad Whitt, Abilene Baptist Church, Martinez, GA	70
Week 13	Dr. Don Wilton, First Baptist Church, Spartanburg, SC	76
Week 14	H. Marshall Thompson Jr., Riverstone Community Church, Jacksonville, FL	82
Week 15	Dr. Robby Foster, Northside Baptist Church, Valdosta, GA	88
Week 16	Dr. Steven Kyle, Hiland Park Baptist Church, Panama City, FL	94
Week 17	Tim Anderson, Clements Baptist Church, Athens, AL	100
Week 18	Steven Blanton, Ebenezer Baptist Church, Hendersonville, NC	106
Week 19	Marc Pritchett, NorthRidge Church of Thomaston, Meansville, GA	112
Week 20	Chris Dixon, Liberty Baptist Church, Dublin, GA	118
Week 21	Dr. Jim Perdue, Second Baptist Church, Warner Robins, GA	124
Week 22	Dr. Jim Phillips, North Greenwood Baptist Church, Greenwood, MS	130
Week 23	Dr. Robert C. Pitman, Bob Pitman Ministries, Muscle Shoals, AL	136
Week 24	Billy Smith, Christ Chapel Community Church, Zebulon, GA	142
Week 25	Mike Orr, First Baptist Church Chipley, Chipley, FL	148
Week 26	Jamie Altman, Bethlehem Community Church, Laurel, MS	154

Week 27	Chad Campbell, Mount Pisgah Baptist Church, Easley, SC	160
Week 28	Joel Southerland, Peavine Baptist Church, Rock Spring, GA	166
Week 29	Dr. Chris Aiken, Englewood Baptist Church, Rocky Mount, NC	172
Week 30	Dr. Chad Grayson, Life Community Church, Jamestown, NC	178
Week 31	Dr. J. Kie Bowman, Hyde Park Baptist Church, Austin, TX	184
Week 32	Dr. Danny Wood, Shades Mountain Baptist Church, Birmingham, AL	190
Week 33	Dr. Bryan E. Smith, First Roanoke Baptist Church, Roanoke, VA	196
Week 34	Jerry Gillis, The Chapel at Crosspoint, Getzville, NY	202
Week 35	Dr. Frank Cox, North Metro Baptist Church, Lawrenceville, GA	208
Week 36	Tim DeTellis, New Missions, Orlando, FL	214
Week 37	Jeff Crook, Christ Place Church, Flowery Branch, GA	220
Week 38	Dr. Adam B. Dooley, Englewood Baptist Church, Jackson, TN	226
Week 39	Dr. David Edwards, DaveEdwardsSpeaks.com, Oklahoma City, OK	232
Week 40	Dr. Grant Ethridge, Liberty Live Church, Hampton, VA	238
Week 41	Dr. Steve Folmar, Covenant Church, Houma, LA	244
Week 42	Brian Fossett, Fossett Evangelistic Ministries, Dalton, GA	250
Week 43	Roy G. Mack, Grace Fellowship Church, Niles, OH	256
Week 44	Paul Purvis, Mission Hill Church, Temple Terrace, FL	262
Week 45	Dr. William Rice, Calvary Baptist Church, Clearwater, FL	268
Week 46	Rocky Purvis, Northside Baptist Church, Lexington, SC	274
Week 47	Brent Thompson, Heflin Baptist Church, Heflin, AL	280
Week 48	Dr. Kelly Bullard, First Baptist Church Summerfield, Summerfield, NC	286
Week 49	Steven Cox, Peace Baptist Church, Whiteville, NC	292
Week 50	Mark Lashey, LifeHouse Church, Townsend, DE	298
Week 51	Dr. Stephen Rummage, Bell Shoals Baptist Church, Brandon, FL	304
Week 52	Brian Boyles, First Baptist Church, Snellville, GA	310

Contributors *316*

Scripture Index *319*

WEEK 1—MONDAY

He Is My Strength

The LORD is my light and my salvation; whom shall I fear? The LORD is the strength of my life; of whom shall I be afraid? When the wicked came against me to eat up my flesh, my enemies and foes, they stumbled and fell. Though an army may encamp against me, my heart shall not fear; though war may rise against me, in this I will be confident.

PSALM 27:1-3

I have always heard, "if you fear God you will fear no one else." The psalmist has his eyes and heart focused on the Lord. Not only does he see Him as the One who lights his way but as the way itself, his salvation. His intimate relationship with his Lord has given him great confidence and consolation. We are aware of our weaknesses, but he has claimed the Lord as his strength. He speaks with the same clarity as Paul in 2 Corinthians 12:9: "My grace is sufficient for you, for My strength is made perfect in weakness." In Christ, when I am weak, He makes me strong; indeed, He is our Strength.

"Only the strong survive," says an old song. But the Lord says only the weak survive. As the psalmist contemplates the wicked enemies, he sees them through the lens of his Lord's promise, and it's clearly a game changer. His trust is not in his ability but in his relationship with his Lord. May the Lord give us today the capacity to see what is against us through the lens of His promise.

Almighty God, give me the ability today to focus more on You and less on what confronts me or is against me. Praise You that You are enough.

Dr. Johnny Hunt, North American Mission Board, Alpharetta, GA

WEEK 1—TUESDAY

May We Witness Too

And they came to John and said to him, "Rabbi, He who was with you beyond the Jordan, to whom you have testified—behold, He is baptizing, and all are coming to Him!" John answered and said, "A man can receive nothing unless it has been given to him from heaven. You yourselves bear me witness, that I said, 'I am not the Christ,' but, 'I have been sent before Him.'"

JOHN 3:26-28

John the Baptist has always been one of my favorite biblical characters. A forerunner of Jesus, John spoke of One greater than himself—always important for our witness too. John proclaimed Him as "the Lamb of God who takes away the sin of the world" (John 1:29). Others observed John's relationship with Jesus—just as we want people to identify us with Him.

John was faithful to point others to Jesus. He said, "A man can receive nothing unless it has been given to him from heaven." Indeed, salvation belongs to the Lord; only He can lift the veil for us to see our need of Him. "God satisfies the desire that He creates," wrote Oswald Chambers. I am so grateful that He spoke into my heart and made me aware of my need for His salvation.

John went as far as possible to make sure all attention was on Jesus, not himself. May we see ourselves today as John saw himself. He was "sent before Him." Jesus has sent us all into His world with His message, and He *is* the message.

....

Lord Jesus, today is a new day filled with opportunity to represent You in Your world. Help me to make much of You. Thank You for sending me.

WEEK 1—WEDNESDAY

Humility Leads to Service

At that time the disciples came to Jesus, saying, "Who then is greatest in the kingdom of heaven?" Then Jesus called a little child to Him, set him in the midst of them, and said, "Assuredly, I say to you, unless you are converted and become as little children, you will by no means enter the kingdom of heaven."

MATTHEW 18:1-3

Can you imagine asking the exalted Lord such a question? He's the God who humbled Himself and became obedient to death, who modeled humility by washing the disciples' feet, who left heaven to enter our world as one of us so we might be one like Him.

Jesus would often respond to a question by asking a question. In this case, He responded with an illustration. He found an innocent, young child to express an eternal truth. What a picture of grace—God's Riches at Christ's Expense—to realize that what God gives us in Christ is so undeserved and beyond our reach to purchase.

Jesus made the message very personal: "unless you." Everyone who could hear His voice heard what it takes to go to heaven. We must all be "converted," turning from or repenting of our sins, becoming like "little children"—a beautiful picture of humbling ourselves in God's presence. God resists the proud but gives grace to the humble (James 4:6). If you want to be great in God's sight, humble yourself. The less we think of ourselves, the more we think of Him.

....

> Lord, may I humble myself in Your presence today. You promised that if I humble myself, You will lift me up in due time. Throughout this day, may it be all about You.

Dr. Johnny Hunt, North American Mission Board, Alpharetta, GA

WEEK 1—THURSDAY

My Desire for Devotion

"The Son of Man must suffer many things, and be rejected by the elders and chief priests and scribes, and be killed, and be raised the third day." Then He said to them all, "If anyone desires to come after Me, let him deny himself, and take up his cross daily, and follow Me. For whoever desires to save his life will lose it, but whoever loses his life for My sake will save it."

LUKE 9:22-24

One of my favorite verses is in this passage. It can remind me of the day I came to Him in salvation or to continue to come to Him in sanctification.

The Lord spoke of His mission and ultimate sacrifice, then followed with a challenge to those who follow Him. Following Jesus comes with tremendous responsibility in disciplined obedience. Jesus suffered, was rejected by the religious establishment, was killed, and was raised from the dead. Now comes His challenge to us.

It begins with a desire. Question: Where does this desire come from? The Lord creates this desire with His presence and His promises. a sincere craving for the pure milk of the Word (1 Peter 2:2), a hunger and thirst for His righteousness. To come after Jesus means pursuing Him by saying no to self so we can say yes to Him. This is taking up His cross daily. The bottom line is that we must die to our desires and dreams in order to realize His will for our lives. The cross is an instrument of death, and I must die daily to follow Him. That's as good a definition of discipleship as I know.

....

Lord Jesus, here I am again this morning with the same old need for You. Thank You that Your mercies are new each day. I come humbly to receive mine.

Heaven, Life, and the Resurrection

WEEK 1—FRIDAY

Precious in His Sight

For I am the LORD your God, the Holy One of Israel, your Savior; I gave Egypt for your ransom, Ethiopia and Seba in your place. Since you were precious in My sight, you have been honored, and I have loved you; therefore I will give men for you, and people for your life.

ISAIAH 43:3-4

Sometimes we hear someone make a claim and think, "Who do they think they are?" Isaiah wasted no time in making known who was behind the claim: "the Lord your God, the Holy One of Israel, your Savior." Israel belonged to the God of the universe in a covenant relationship with Him. They were His, and He was theirs. They knew Him as Savior, and not just for their souls. He was also their temporal Savior, who protected them from earthly enemies. He promised never to leave or forsakes them—or us.

These great and encouraging words describe how the Lord feels about His own—we are precious, honored, and loved. You are precious to Jesus, and He is so precious to us. Even though He needs nothing to complete Himself, He has endeared Himself to us.

You may be honored by others in this life, but it will never compare to being honored by God. He loves you unconditionally. He first loved us; even when we were yet sinners, He demonstrated His love (Rom. 5:8). What a privilege! Thank Him now for His view of us in Christ.

....

Lord, You are worthy of worship. We praise You for caring so deeply.

Dr. Johnny Hunt, North American Mission Board, Alpharetta, GA

WEEK 1—WEEKEND

Forgiven and Forgotten

He has not dealt with us according to our sins, nor punished us according to our iniquities. For as the heavens are high above the earth, so great is His mercy toward those who fear Him; as far as the east is from the west, so far has He removed our transgressions from us.

PSALM 103:10-12

This psalm emphasizes the benefits of praising and blessing God (Psalm 103:2). Three words—*sins, iniquities,* and *transgressions*—speak of our need for forgiveness. We have all missed the mark (sin), we have all overstepped God's law (transgressions), and we all are filled with ingrained perversity in our soul. We stand in need of being rescued by the Savior.

The wonderful doctrine of substitutionary atonement is in these verses. As we repent and place our faith in Jesus, God deals with Jesus in our place. We have not been punished for our sins; God punished His Son in our place. Jesus is the payment that satisfies God's justice as He extends mercy to us. "Mercy" (v. 11) seems to ring loudest. God has not given us what we deserve but instead has shown mercy in abundance.

As if that's not enough, He then tells us how comprehensive His forgiveness is: He removes our sin "as far as the east is from the west." The two never meet; His forgiveness is forever enough. He has taken it out of the way by nailing it to the cross. From being sluggish in worship, the psalmist is now in step with his Master. His joy returns, and he blesses the Lord with everything within Him. Let's join him now in blessing Him.

Lord, we are overwhelmed by Your mercy and goodness. Amen!

Heaven, Life, and the Resurrection

WEEK 2—MONDAY

Designed for Heaven

Then Solomon stood before the altar of the Lord *in the presence of all the assembly of Israel, and spread out his hands toward heaven; and he said:* "Lord *God of Israel, there is no God in heaven above or on earth below like You, who keep Your covenant and mercy with Your servants who walk before You with all their hearts."*

1 KINGS 8:22-23

Among my favorite Bible verses about heaven is 2 Corinthians 5:5, which says God has designed us for the life to come—a very different message from cultural values that bombard us every day. We're made to feel that if our life experiences don't match up to our dreams, we should be disappointed. But in this broken world, who really lives a dream life?

Years ago, my wife and I went on our first cruise. Every part of it was a new experience. I especially remember a long, rectangular building adjacent to the ship where hundreds of us waited to board. The cruise line did its best to decorate it with a tropical theme. What a mistake it would have been if we assumed the boarding building was the cruise itself, never got on the ship, and judged the whole cruise by that experience.

Just so, God did not design us for this world. He has many purposes for us in this life, but we were built for heaven. As C. S. Lewis said, "If I find in myself a desire which no experience in this world can satisfy, the most probable explanation is that I was made for another world."

Dear Father, if difficulties come today, please remind me I was designed for a perfect world. In Jesus' name, amen.

Mark Hoover, NewSpring Church, Wichita, KS

WEEK 2—TUESDAY

The Person in Heaven You May Not Recognize

To the Son He says: "Your throne, O God, is forever and ever; a scepter of righteousness is the scepter of Your kingdom. You have loved righteousness and hated lawlessness; therefore God, Your God, has anointed You with the oil of gladness more than Your companions." And: "You, Lord, in the beginning laid the foundation of the earth, and the heavens are the work of Your hands."

HEBREWS 1:8-10

"Will I know my loved ones in heaven?" That's probably the question about heaven I've been asked most frequently. It's understandably important. Eric Clapton, in his poignant song "Tears in Heaven," written after the tragic death of his son Conor, asks, "Would it be the same if I saw you in heaven?" The Bible assures us in several places that we will recognize our loved ones, including 1 Corinthians 13:12, which says we will know as we are known.

Just as Peter and John recognized Elijah and Moses at the transfiguration, I'm sure I will know my mom and dad who passed a few years ago. But it occurs to me that there could be one person I'll have a hard time recognizing: me.

I've only known myself as a flawed sinner. Over time, I've experienced unfixable issues in my body due to illness, injuries, and aging. But in heaven, we will be perfect. No sin nature, no limitations, and no weaknesses. Trying to imagine ourselves like that is a challenge. But isn't it glorious?

Heavenly Father, let my heart be excited today with the reality that in heaven, I will be perfectly whole in Your presence. In Jesus' name, amen.

Heaven, Life, and the Resurrection

WEEK 2—WEDNESDAY

The Limitless Jesus

So when Jesus came, He found that he had already been in the tomb four days. . . . Now Martha said to Jesus, "Lord, if You had been here, my brother would not have died. But even now I know that whatever You ask of God, God will give You." Jesus said to her, "Your brother will rise again."

JOHN 11:17, 21-23

As a member of a family of friends of Jesus, Martha would have known Him far better than most people. But she still didn't grasp who He really was. What she said here indicates that she believed God endowed Jesus with great power and that His prayers would likely be answered, but His power had limits. In her mind, that might have put Him on par with Moses, Elijah, and other leaders she'd grown up learning about.

But it's clear she believed He was limited. "If you had been here, my brother would not have died," she said. To her, two things were more powerful than Jesus: time and death. If only He had been there on time, before death took the game clock to zero. So Jesus expanded her understanding by telling her He *is* the resurrection and the life! Then He called her brother out of his grave.

Our Savior truly is limitless. The things that stop us have no authority over Him. Meditate on that today and celebrate what it means.

....

Heavenly Father, please remind me today that my Lord and Savior Jesus Christ has all power in heaven and on earth, and that nothing stops Him. In Jesus' name, amen.

Mark Hoover, NewSpring Church, Wichita, KS

WEEK 2—THURSDAY

Jesus Is There

When all the people were baptized, it came to pass that Jesus also was baptized; and while He prayed, the heaven was opened. And the Holy Spirit descended in bodily form like a dove upon Him, and a voice came from heaven which said, "You are My beloved Son; in You I am well pleased."

LUKE 3:21-22

Any study of heaven presents an interesting dichotomy. On one hand, heaven is certain. On the other, it remains very mysterious. It would seem that our God delights in surprising His children with the awesome glory of His new creation. I believe that when we've been in heaven for a million years, we'll still be discovering new things.

There is one fact about heaven, though, that the Bible presents repeatedly. Jesus is there and is the very centerpiece. Scripture promises us that at death, we will be absent from the body and present with the Lord (2 Corinthians 5:8). It doesn't say we will be with the angels or loved ones who have gone before. We know we will, of course, but Scripture guarantees something even bigger. We will be present with Jesus Himself.

Think about that. It's normal to fear death, but for children of God, it ushers us into the greatest moment of our existence—the moment we open our eyes and look for the first time into the face of Jesus! No wonder the psalmist said, "I will see your face in righteousness; I shall be satisfied when I awake in your likeness."

> Heavenly Father, help me live today with joy, anticipating that moment when I get to see Jesus face-to-face! In His name I pray, amen.

Heaven, Life, and the Resurrection

WEEK 2—FRIDAY

Following Him Right into Heaven

From that time Jesus began to preach and to say, "Repent, for the kingdom of heaven is at hand." And Jesus, walking by the Sea of Galilee, saw two brothers, Simon called Peter, and Andrew his brother, casting a net into the sea; for they were fishermen. Then He said to them, "Follow Me, and I will make you fishers of men." They immediately left their nets and followed Him.

MATTHEW 4:17-20

Christianity is different from other world religions in many ways, perhaps first among them that we weren't called to follow a system but a Person. The Bible teaches that Jesus left us the example to follow in His steps (1 Peter 2:21). In this life, following Jesus is challenging. Our sin nature rebels, and the systems of our world can make us feel like outsiders.

But once we start following Jesus, we can never be separated from Him. Where He goes, we go. That means we will follow Him right into heaven. On the night of His arrest, Jesus comforted His disciples with this truth. He told them about heaven and then added the wonderful truth: "If I go and prepare a place for you, I will come again and receive you to Myself; that where I am, there you may be also" (John 14:3).

> Heavenly Father, when following Jesus gets difficult in this broken world, help me remember where following Him ultimately leads. In Jesus' name, amen.

Mark Hoover, NewSpring Church, Wichita, KS

WEEK 2—WEEKEND

My Favorite "Won't Be" in Heaven

Then I heard a loud voice saying in heaven, "Now salvation, and strength, and the kingdom of our God, and the power of His Christ have come, for the accuser of our brethren, who accused them before our God day and night, has been cast down. . . . Therefore rejoice, O heavens, and you who dwell in them!"

REVELATION 12:10, 12

I have a confession. All my adult life, I've loved a kid's music album. When I was fresh out of college and in my first pastorate, my grandmother passed, and I had to drive all night to preach her funeral. A woman in our church gave my wife and me an eight-track tape to listen to on the trip. It was the Gaithers' 1979 release, "I Am a Promise." We listened to it again and again and fell in love with it.

I especially loved a song called, "Won't Be's in Heaven"—about things that won't be there. It challenged children to make their list, but this isn't just kid stuff. We all need to make that list: pain, sickness, sorrow, death, injustice, abuse, racism, and so many other blights. Today's passage, though, gives us the biggest one of all. Satan, the father of lies and every other scourge of the human race, won't be in heaven. And if you can find that song, give it a listen. You'll enjoy it!

....

Father, when Satan attacks today, encourage me with the reality that his time is limited. In Jesus' name, amen.

Heaven, Life, and the Resurrection

WEEK 3—MONDAY

Blessed Unity

Behold, how good and how pleasant it is for brethren to dwell together in unity! It is like the precious oil upon the head, running down on the beard, the beard of Aaron, running down on the edge of his garments. It is like the dew of Hermon, descending upon the mountains of Zion; for there the Lord commanded the blessing—life forevermore.

PSALM 133:1-3

Unity—is there anything in our culture so elusive? We seem more divided today than ever. Division of all kinds has made its way into the body of Christ.

David describes how good and pleasant unity is—not just any unity, but the unity of those who know God. Not just unity of thought, but the "dwelling" kind of unity that comes together in worship and celebration of God. The writer of Hebrews instructs us to not forsake "the assembling of ourselves together, as is the manner of some" (Hebrews 10:25).

When believers come together in a "dwelling" way, it is not just good and pleasant but also anointed by God. The word "dwell" hints at Psalm 23:6—"I will *dwell* in the house of the Lord forever." Mount Hermon was viewed as the highest place and the throne of God in the region. In both illustrations, the source of all things is God, and His command is a blessing on Christian unity.

> God, I know You are enormously interested in my unity with my brothers and sisters in Christ. I ask that You show me what I can do today to live in that kind of unity.

Dr. Alex Himaya, BattleCreek Church, Broken Arrow, OK

WEEK 3—TUESDAY

No Excuses!

For the wrath of God is revealed from heaven against all ungodliness and unrighteousness of men, who suppress the truth in unrighteousness, because what may be known of God is manifest in them, for God has shown it to them. For since the creation of the world His invisible attributes are clearly seen, being understood by the things that are made, even His eternal power and Godhead, so that they are without excuse.

ROMANS 1:18-20

I don't think I've heard a sermon on the wrath of God in decades. But the wrath of God is mentioned more than six hundred times in the Old Testament alone. Jesus discussed it when He described the rich man begging for someone to dip his finger in water and touch his tongue (Luke 16:19–31). The Good News of the gospel is not really good news without a proper understanding of the bad news it replaces. Paul wrote that sin entered the world when Adam sinned, and death spread to everyone (Romans 5:12). It has become a family tradition in the worst sense.

I am cursed and need a savior, lost and need a shepherd, sick and need a physician. Paul says that God is revealing His light to us in all kinds of ways to the degree that we have no excuse for rejecting it. Even creation itself witnesses to the creator God. Therefore no one is spiritually blind against their will. By nature, we love the darkness more than the light and need eyes to see the truth.

....

> Lord, I ask for the gift of repentance today and eyes to see, not just Your goodness, but also Your holiness.

Heaven, Life, and the Resurrection

WEEK 3—WEDNESDAY

Spiritual House

For we know that if our earthly house, this tent, is destroyed, we have a building from God, a house not made with hands, eternal in the heavens. For in this we groan, earnestly desiring to be clothed with our habitation which is from heaven.

2 CORINTHIANS 5:1-2

We are spirits with souls and bodies—not physical beings with temporary spiritual experiences but spiritual beings with temporary physical experiences. So everything in this world seems to be groaning. We long for something else and believe that this is not all there is. We intuitively know we were made for something else, some other place, and someone else.

A few verses after today's passage, Paul wrote that "to be absent from the body [is] to be present with the Lord" (v. 8). He also said, "To live is Christ, and to die is gain" (Philippians 1:21). Biblical writers from Genesis to Revelation seemed to know that for believers, what comes next will be better than anything this world has to offer today. Sometimes God delivers us *from* the trials of this life, sometimes *by* them, and sometimes *through* them. This is not our home! I am not hoping to cut in line on the way to death, but I do believe what lies ahead is better than what is staring me in the face today.

Father, may I have eyes to see what You have planned for me in the future, and thank You for Your plans designed for good and not for harm.

Dr. Alex Himaya, BattleCreek Church, Broken Arrow, OK

WEEK 3—THURSDAY

Filled then Power

When the Day of Pentecost had fully come, they were all with one accord in one place. And suddenly there came a sound from heaven, as of a rushing mighty wind, and it filled the whole house where they were sitting. Then there appeared to them divided tongues, as of fire, and one sat upon each of them. And they were all filled with the Holy Spirit and began to speak with other tongues, as the Spirit gave them utterance.

ACTS 2:1-4

Pentecost" literally means fifty. Fifty days after Passover, all the believers were meeting together in one place. At the end of Luke's gospel, the disciples were hiding out of fear. Now in Acts, also authored by Luke, they were in quarantine with an expectation of power.

To do what Jesus said we would do—"You shall be witnesses to Me . . . to the end of the earth" (Acts 1:8)—we had to be empowered somehow and from somewhere. As the disciples would experience, we are empowered by the Holy Spirit.

A mighty wind filled the place, and everyone present was filled with the Holy Spirit and began to speak in other languages. There were devout Jews from every nation in Jerusalem for the feast, and when they heard the loud noise, they came running and were shocked to hear their own languages being spoken by the believers.

The point is that the gospel was meant to be understood, not confusing, and it is for all people.

....

Father, fill me and lead me with the power to do ministry by, for, and through the Holy Spirit.

Heaven, Life, and the Resurrection

WEEK 3—FRIDAY

Grow Up

Therefore, leaving the discussion of the elementary principles of Christ, let us go on to perfection, not laying again the foundation of repentance from dead works and of faith toward God, of the doctrine of baptisms, of laying on of hands, of resurrection of the dead, and of eternal judgment. And this we will do if God permits.

HEBREWS 6:1-3

The New Living Translation translates "let us go on to perfection" as "let us move on to mature understanding." Paul and Peter encouraged their readers to move on from milk to solid food (1 Corinthians 3:2; 1 Peter 2:2). Biblical writers believed we are to grow in Christ. As my friend says, "There comes a day when the little boy or little girl must sit down, and the man or woman stands up."

All parents want to see their children advance in maturity. Our heavenly Father is no different. And like good earthly parents, He is not exasperated with us. He is hopeful and excited about what can be ours if we will trust Him and grow in Him.

The writer of Hebrews invites us to dive into the deep end of the pool—the deeper things of God. He invites us beyond doctrines into the actual disciplines of the faith. The "therefore" that begins verse one indicates that we are not abandoning the basic doctrines but, based on them, are invited deeper into the disciplines. Meditation, prayer, fasting, service, solitude, confession, and other disciplines are ours for the taking.

Lord, what spiritual discipline would You permit me to enjoy in this season? I commit to what You will show me.

Dr. Alex Himaya, BattleCreek Church, Broken Arrow, OK

WEEK 3—WEEKEND

The Great Exchange

"If anyone serves Me, let him follow Me; and where I am, there My servant will be also. If anyone serves Me, him My Father will honor. Now My soul is troubled, and what shall I say? 'Father, save Me from this hour'? But for this purpose I came to this hour. Father, glorify Your name." Then a voice came from heaven, saying, "I have both glorified it and will glorify it again."

JOHN 12:26-28

These moments in the life of Jesus are powerful and enlightening. Responding to the request, "Sir, we wish to see Jesus (v. 21)," He seems to summarize the Christian life—the upside-down world of the kingdom of God. It is in "losing" that we win.

What does that mean? I think the bottom line is that we are to be so focused on Jesus and eternity that it seems we are losing here on earth. We are to be so led by the Spirit that our souls are troubled. We are to be focused on God getting the glory. And when He gets all the glory, we get all the joy! God wired us for that kind of life. Come what may, we will glorify Him in heaven.

> As Matthew 6:9-13 says, "Our Father in heaven, hallowed be Your name. Your kingdom come. Your will be done on earth as it is in heaven. Give us this day our daily bread. And forgive us our debts, as we forgive our debtors. And do not lead us into temptation, but deliver us from the evil one. For Yours is the kingdom and the power and the glory forever. Amen."

Heaven, Life, and the Resurrection

WEEK 4—MONDAY

Hoping with Hope

Happy is he who has the God of Jacob for his help, whose hope is in the LORD his God, who made heaven and earth, the sea, and all that is in them; who keeps truth forever, who executes justice for the oppressed, who gives food to the hungry. The LORD gives freedom to the prisoners. The LORD opens the eyes of the blind; the LORD raises those who are bowed down; the LORD loves the righteous.

PSALM 146:5-8

Too many people are hoping without any hope. They place their hopes in success, education, health, wealth, relationships, political parties, lottery tickets, and other fleeting things. The hope of this world is nothing more than wishful thinking, pipe dreams, and pie-in-the-sky feelings. But biblical hope is different. It's confident assurance. As in this psalm, those who are happy are hoping with the hope they have in the LORD.

Psalm 146 reminds us that God helps, makes, keeps, executes, gives, opens, raises, and loves. Just as God helped Jacob, He helps those who place their hope in Him. After wrestling with the LORD, Jacob didn't strut; he limped. A sure way to know if you are hoping in the LORD is whether you walk with a limp or a strut.

Hope in the Lord and, even with a limp, you'll find yourself not only hoping with hope but hopping with hope!

> Father, help us to hope in You alone. Much in this world steals our joy and tries to hinder our hope, but You alone are the hope of the world. Help us point people who are hoping without hope to You.

Dr. Sam Greer, Red Bank Baptist Church, Chattanooga, TN

WEEK 4—TUESDAY

Hail, Heaven!

"We give You thanks, O Lord God Almighty, the One who is and who was and who is to come, because You have taken Your great power and reigned." . . . Then the temple of God was opened in heaven, and the ark of His covenant was seen in His temple. And there were lightnings, noises, thunderings, an earthquake, and great hail.

REVELATION 11:17, 19

What happened to hell? It has all but disappeared in preaching, teaching, thinking, and conversations. We must not dismiss it but tell people how to miss it. We must not attempt to erase it but tell people how to escape it. But just as the horror of hell is often missing, so is the hail of heaven.

When was the last time you were thankful to the God of heaven? The loud voices in Revelation 11 remind us to give thanks to the God who created everything, including heaven. I've heard that there are two times to be thankful: (1) when you feel like it and (2) when you don't feel like it. We should always be thankful to the God who has always been and will always be.

When was the last time you were thankful for heaven itself? We are aliens, exiles on earth, strangers in a strange land, and wanderers in this world. Heaven is not only our hope; it is our home. Heaven is opened in Revelation 11, the ark of the covenant is visible, and Jesus—the very person and presence of God—is there. That's what makes heaven, heaven—and should make us grateful.

> Father, we give You thanks for heaven. Let our thoughts of heaven drive our worship and gospel conversations.

Heaven, Life, and the Resurrection

WEEK 4—WEDNESDAY

Your Walk Talks

When you eat the labor of your hands, you shall be happy, and it shall be well with you. Your wife shall be like a fruitful vine in the very heart of your house, your children like olive plants all around your table. Behold, thus shall the man be blessed who fears the Lord. The Lord bless you out of Zion, and may you see the good of Jerusalem all the days of your life.

PSALM 128:2-5

"Your walk talks and your talk talks, but your walk talks louder than your talk talks," I heard a pastor say. Psalm 128 emphasizes the truths that those who walk with the Lord are satisfied and, whether they say so or not, their satisfaction is seen. People who walk in the ways of the world may say they are satisfied, but their satisfaction is unseen; it doesn't exist. In what ways is our satisfaction seen?

People who walk with the Lord are satisfied with their work. Their focus is more on what they are living for rather than what they do for a living. People who walk with the Lord are satisfied at home because they are "one another" people—serving and submitting to one another. God's design for marriage and the home is work, but it works. People who are walking in the ways of the Lord are willing to do the work to make it work at home, even when it hasn't been working.

....

Father, may we walk in Your ways. Tame our tongue and guard our steps.

Dr. Sam Greer, Red Bank Baptist Church, Chattanooga, TN

WEEK 4—THURSDAY

The End Is Nearer Now Than Ever

"Immediately after the tribulation of those days the sun will be darkened, and the moon will not give its light; the stars will fall from heaven, and the powers of the heavens will be shaken. Then the sign of the Son of Man will appear in heaven, and then all the tribes of the earth will mourn, and they will see the Son of Man coming on the clouds of heaven with power and great glory."

MATTHEW 24:29-30

We are closer to the end of the world than any other time in history. Jesus is coming a second time. His disciples asked him about the timing of His return and the sign of His coming. Jesus' answer—the longest He gave—gives us much to glean about the end times.

First, Jesus' church has not been forsaken. He was forsaken at the cross for the sake of His church. What's more, Jesus is coming back for His church. Through all the tumultuous times surrounding tribulation, we can rest assured that Jesus' church has not, is not, and will not be forsaken.

Second, Jesus' creation will be shaken. Sun darkened, moon dimmed, and stars falling from the sky will put every firework show the world has ever seen to shame.

Third, Jesus' coming will be unmistaken. God has written an executive order that every eye will see, every knee will bow, and every tongue confess that Jesus is Lord.

In light of the end, we must awaken and live with a sense of urgency. Are you ready? Is your family? Are your friends?

....

> Father, help us move our conversations toward the gospel before it's too late.

Heaven, Life, and the Resurrection

WEEK 4—FRIDAY

Rolling Stones

Behold, there was a great earthquake; for an angel of the Lord descended from heaven, and came and rolled back the stone from the door, and sat on it. His countenance was like lightning, and his clothing as white as snow. And the guards shook for fear of him, and became like dead men.

MATTHEW 28:2-4

How easy it is to throw stones, to tear others down, to let that mean-spirited thought exit your mouth. Yet the empty tomb is a strong reminder that Jesus doesn't throw stones; He rolls them. How can the rolling away of the stone at the empty tomb help us to stop throwing stones?

Jesus' resurrection is our receipt proving that He alone forgives sin. If you are unforgiven, the good news means you can be forgiven. And if you are forgiven, the good news means you must forgive. We are not called to forget people as cancel culture tells us; we are called to forgive people as Jesus forgave us.

Jesus was buried in a borrowed tomb. Borrowing is not a foreign concept; people do it all the time. But who has heard of borrowing a tomb? How is the borrower ever going to give the tomb back to its owner? Jesus was buried in a borrowed tomb because He only needed it for three days. He didn't come to condemn by throwing stones; He came to save by rolling stones.

....

Father, thank You for the forgiveness we have in Jesus. We repent from throwing stones of judgment. May we be quick to roll the stones of forgiveness.

Dr. Sam Greer, Red Bank Baptist Church, Chattanooga, TN

WEEK 4—WEEKEND

Trust Is a Must

Who has ascended into heaven, or descended? Who has gathered the wind in His fists? Who has bound the waters in a garment? Who has established all the ends of the earth? What is His name, and what is His Son's name, if you know? Every word of God is pure; He is a shield to those who put their trust in Him.

PROVERBS 30:4-5

You have heard it said, "Don't believe everything you hear!" Sadly, in today's truthless culture, "Don't believe anything you hear!" may be more relevant. What can we believe? Theories are presented as truth while the truth is often not presented at all. Common sense has become uncommon, good is bad, bad is good, and what's posted on social media must be true. Praise the Lord that today's verses hammer home some truths about truth!

First, you *can* trust the truth. Jesus said, "Sanctify them by Your truth. Your word is truth" (John 17:17). Likewise, "Every word of God is pure" (Proverbs 30:5). Truth does exist, and it is trustworthy. It is not of man, of this world, or of social media. Truth is of God alone and therefore can be trusted.

Second, you *must* trust the truth. Every jot and tittle of the Bible is truth. God breathed out every word in His Word—our final authority for what we believe and how we behave. He doesn't merely shield those who trust in the truth; He *is* their shield. Yield to the Word daily so the Word will shield you today.

....

Father, thank You for telling us the truth about truth. May we trust in You alone.

WEEK 5—MONDAY

Jesus Christ—Our Living Hope

Blessed be the God and Father of our Lord Jesus Christ, who according to His abundant mercy has begotten us again to a living hope through the resurrection of Jesus Christ from the dead, [4] to an inheritance incorruptible and undefiled and that does not fade away, reserved in heaven for you.

1 PETER 1:3-4

Our church recently grieved the sudden passing of a beloved, saintly woman named Ruth—a matriarch for her family but also for many members of our congregation. We celebrated her life at her "homegoing" service, but this was not a typical funeral. It was worshipful, inspiring, and encouraging. The highlight was when Ruth's son led a song about our living hope, the Lord Jesus Christ. When he got to a certain stanza, something unexpected happened. Ruth's husband, sitting on the front row, sprang to his feet and lifted his hands in the air, praising God and shouting hallelujah. The moment was riveting. Ruth was gone from earth, but her son was singing a worship song. And her husband was standing and lifting his hands in praise to God.

Who would behave this way at a funeral? Only a Bible-believing, Christian family with sincere faith. My friends knew that through the mercy of God and the resurrection of His Son, something far better is coming for all who believe.

Yes, we were at a funeral. But I witnessed a family who had never felt more alive, all because of Christ!

> Dear Lord, thank You for the empty tomb. We praise You because Your Son, Jesus, lives and reigns. We put our faith in Him today. Amen.

Jeremy Morton, First Baptist Church Woodstock, Woodstock, GA

WEEK 5—TUESDAY

His Kingdom Will Last Forever

"But the court shall be seated, and they shall take away his dominion, to consume and destroy it forever. Then the kingdom and dominion, and the greatness of the kingdoms under the whole heaven, shall be given to the people, the saints of the Most High. His kingdom is an everlasting kingdom, and all dominions shall serve and obey Him."

DANIEL 7:26-27

The anti-God, anti-Christian movement that seems to be happening all around us is nothing new. In fact, it's as old as the garden of Eden. Genesis 1:31 says, "God saw everything that He had made, and indeed it was very good." But by Genesis 3:1, we are told, "The serpent was more cunning than any beast of the field which the Lord God had made." The serpent tempted Adam and Eve, they ate the forbidden fruit, and the human race has been stricken by sin ever since.

Many scholars believe that sometime after the announcement, all creation was good but before the serpent appeared, Lucifer's revolt in heaven occurred, which caused God to banish him and fallen angels from His presence. Since that time, they've been roaming the earth, seeking to destroy God's plan.

But Scripture tells the rest of the story. One day every knee will bow, and every tongue will confess that Jesus Christ is Lord of all (Philippians 2:10-11). John gives a sneak preview of the future: All the kingdoms of earth will become the kingdoms of our Lord (Revelation 11:15).

Dear Father, society may spin out of control, but I look to You. I trust in You, Jesus my King. Amen.

Heaven, Life, and the Resurrection

WEEK 5—WEDNESDAY

Hearing His Holy Word

For in six days the Lord *made the heavens and the earth, the sea, and all that is in them, and rested the seventh day. Therefore the* Lord *blessed the Sabbath day and hallowed it. "Honor your father and your mother, that your days may be long upon the land which the* Lord *your God is giving you."*

EXODUS 20:11-12

In my earliest days as a pastor, the Lord put on my heart to lead our congregation to pray this simple prayer: "Open my eyes, that I may see wondrous things from Your law" (Psalm 119:18). We say this prayer together prior to the Sunday sermon. This is not some perfunctory habit, nor is it another agenda item to fill the time in the worship hour. To the contrary, I am compelled to ask our congregation to join me in this weekly prayer because we desperately need to hear God's Word. A human messenger, even with charisma or knowledge, can only take us so far. But if we experience the living God whose Word is powerful and sharper than a two-edged sword (Hebrews 4:12), we have the opportunity for eternal impact.

God set apart one day as holy unto Himself. The Israelites called it the Sabbath; believers now call it the Lord's Day. It's celebrated by Christians, usually on Sunday, as a testimony to Jesus' resurrection (Acts 20:7).

Are you preparing to honor your heavenly Father this week by gathering with others to hear the Word of God? May we never take this privilege for granted!

> Dear Father, thank You for Your Word. Please give me a heart that is eager to receive Your truth. In Christ's name, amen.

Jeremy Morton, First Baptist Church Woodstock, Woodstock, GA

WEEK 5—THURSDAY

We Need Heavenly Wisdom

If I have told you earthly things and you do not believe, how will you believe if I tell you heavenly things? No one has ascended to heaven but He who came down from heaven, that is, the Son of Man who is in heaven.

JOHN 3:12-13

Many people are smart but not necessarily wise. One of the most extraordinary truths about the gospel of Jesus is that it's simple enough for a small child to embrace it and be saved (Matthew 18:3). Yet the gospel is so profound that a scholar like Nicodemus struggled to grasp the weight of its meaning. Nicodemus had a vast knowledge of the Old Testament, but his eyes had not yet been spiritually opened to embrace Jesus by faith and be born again.

Scripture says the wisest man who ever lived (other than Jesus) was King Solomon. His wisdom was given directly by God because of his sincere, humble request to lead Israel to honor the Lord (1 Kings 3:9). We are fortunate to have the recorded legacy of Solomon's wisdom. His insights have been preserved for us in Proverbs, Song of Solomon, and Ecclesiastes.

One of Solomon's special promises from God tells us that He has put eternity in our hearts (Ecclesiastes 3:11). Everyone wants to believe something better is coming. It's natural and normal to desire a better future. But there is a difference between earthly knowledge and heavenly wisdom.

Take the deepest longing of your heart today and pour it out before Jesus in faith and prayer. He will meet you right where you are!

Dear Lord, please fill my life with heavenly wisdom. For the glory of Christ, amen.

Heaven, Life, and the Resurrection

WEEK 5—FRIDAY

Preparing for His Return

"But of that day and hour no one knows, not even the angels in heaven, nor the Son, but only the Father. Take heed, watch and pray; for you do not know when the time is. It is like a man going to a far country, who left his house and gave authority to his servants, and to each his work, and commanded the doorkeeper to watch."

MARK 13:32-34

For some strange reason, people have often attempted to predict the precise date of Christ's return. These predictions ordinarily occur in conjunction with unusual or tense moments in world history—wars, earthquakes, or natural disasters. This is not a new phenomenon. The disciples asked Jesus, "When will these things be?" (Mark 13:4). Jesus answered quite clearly. No one knows the precise timing, not even the angels or the Son Himself. Only the Father knows when.

So every prediction that has taken place so far has been wrong. We know this because Christ's church is still present on the earth, and the dawning of the new Jerusalem (Revelation 21:10) has yet to occur. This can only mean that God still desires His church to be actively engaged in the mission of making Christ's gospel known to every person in every town, state, and nation.

To "watch and pray" means to be vigilant, to be on high alert, and to live prayed-up and prepared for that glorious day of Christ's triumphant return.

> Dear Jesus, may I live prepared and ready for Your glorious return. In the meantime, help me tell everyone I can about the good news of the gospel. In Your name, amen.

Jeremy Morton, First Baptist Church Woodstock, Woodstock, GA

WEEK 5—WEEKEND

Small Things Become Great Things

Another parable He put forth to them, saying: "The kingdom of heaven is like a mustard seed, which a man took and sowed in his field, which indeed is the least of all the seeds; but when it is grown it is greater than the herbs and becomes a tree, so that the birds of the air come and nest in its branches."

MATTHEW 13:31-32

Some of the best advice I've ever received came years ago from an older, wiser pastor. He encouraged me not to focus on fame, popularity, or success. In fact, he implored me to set my heart in the opposite direction and trust God with the results. "Make it your aim to be small enough, long enough," he said, "and in due season, if God wants to, He can make you big enough, soon enough." Even now I hear his words ringing in my ears.

Though the mustard seed was the smallest seed used by Jesus's audience, it was understood that the tree could grow to a height of eight to twelve feet tall. Jesus used this metaphor as a picture of His coming, glorious kingdom. On some level, the kingdom of God may appear small or insignificant, but we can be assured it is growing. His kingdom will one day come in fullness and grandeur.

This seems to be God's pattern in Scripture. May He give us faith the size of a mustard seed and move mountains all around us for His glory.

....

Dear God, help me be willing to do anything You ask, even if it appears small. I trust my life into Your hands. In Christ's name, amen.

Heaven, Life, and the Resurrection

WEEK 6—MONDAY

The God Who Calls Me Home

"Listen to Me, O Jacob, and Israel, My called: I am He, I am the First, I am also the Last. Indeed My hand has laid the foundation of the earth, and My right hand has stretched out the heavens; when I call to them, they stand up together."

ISAIAH 48:12-13

True love is persistent. It remains even when it is not answered, and it pursues even when it is misunderstood. True love is selfless and sacrificial, always having at its center the wellbeing of the one loved. Such is God's love. Israel was stubborn, prone to rebel and return to pagan practices and idolatry. What was God's response? Chastening, eventually. But His first response was to call again and again.

Today's passage is one of those moments when God called to His rebellious people, inviting them to come to back to Him. He pleaded for Israel to hear and remember Him, to see Him for who He really is—the God who is everlasting to everlasting, who holds the universe together. Why was He calling? Because no one loved them like He did. No false god could care for them and protect them like He would. Apart from Him, they had no hope; in Him, they had all they would ever need.

We're a lot like Israel—prone to wander and turn His blessings into idols. So He calls us to come back home. His arms are always open. His heart is always for us. And because of Jesus, we can always run into His arms. No one will ever love us like He does.

Lord, when I wander from You, help me hear Your voice and return quickly!

Cary Schmidt, Emmanuel Baptist Church, Newington, CT

WEEK 6—TUESDAY

The God Who Fully Satisfies My Soul

How precious is Your lovingkindness, O God! Therefore the children of men put their trust under the shadow of Your wings. They are abundantly satisfied with the fullness of Your house, and You give them drink from the river of Your pleasures. For with You is the fountain of life; in Your light we see light.

PSALM 36:7-9

Have you ever walked the aisles of a store when hungry? As my wife shops, I travel from one sample stand to the next, scrounging up bits of deliciousness. But they only tease me. They never fill me.

Such is life. The world is an anxiety-filled rat race of pursuits, discontentment, consumption, and disappointment. We pursue a dream only to discover it's harder than we imagined and not as fulfilling as we hoped. We realize that our deepest desires are either insatiable or that nothing in life was actually designed to satiate them.

God's many gifts in this life were meant not to completely fulfill us but to point us to the One who can. Only God and His loving heart can actually satisfy us. Through Jesus, He offers us lavish love. His heart is accessible. He is utterly trustworthy and offers fullness in His acceptance and grace. His mercy never runs out, and the life He gives us is bright, full, and flourishing from within.

If you have never placed your trust in Jesus, do it now. Declare your dependence on His grace offered through His cross. If you have, thank God for His gifts but look only to His heart to deeply and abundantly fulfill you.

Lord, thank You for Your gifts, but help me love You more than them all.

WEEK 6—WEDNESDAY

The God Who Gives Good Laws

"For what great nation is there that has God so near to it, as the LORD our God is to us, for whatever reason we may call upon Him? And what great nation is there that has such statutes and righteous judgments as are in all this law which I set before you this day? Only take heed to yourself, and diligently keep yourself, lest you forget the things your eyes have seen, and lest they depart from your heart all the days of your life."

DEUTERONOMY 4:7–9

Over the centuries, across nations and people groups, injustice has been the norm. It's not only that people are corrupt; the systems they build are also corrupt. Laws favor insiders. Power structures tilt toward the power holders. Even the best justice systems are filled with political bias and hidden corruption.

But at times in the ancient world, justice was almost nonexistent. Violence and injustice fell freely from the hands of the world's worst tyrants. It was nearly impossible for common people to experience fair laws, loving leadership, just judges, and systems that helped them flourish.

Israel's God was different. He exposed fake gods, violent kings, and lying legal systems. His heart came near. His ears came close. His laws favored the favorless, and His judgments were just and right. His heart as a ruling Savior was generous and loving. He was like a shepherd, not a dictator. His leadership always served the best interest of those who chose Him.

> Lord, thank You for bringing Your loving authority, gracious guidelines, and merciful justice into my life. Help me to live within that tender care today.

Cary Schmidt, Emmanuel Baptist Church, Newington, CT

WEEK 6—THURSDAY

The God Who Secures Me in a Fallen World

Where can I go from Your Spirit? Or where can I flee from Your presence? If I ascend into heaven, You are there; if I make my bed in hell, behold, You are there. If I take the wings of the morning, and dwell in the uttermost parts of the sea, even there Your hand shall lead me, and Your right hand shall hold me.

PSALM 139:7-10

We live in a fragile world. We anchor our lives to losable and breakable things. We are one breath, one heartbeat, one tragedy away from the house of cards collapsing into a pile of loss and despair. Most things we value are temporary, and we tend to live in secret fear that they will change.

Is there a resolution to this vulnerability—a kind of life that can be fearless, free from anxiety, and confident? The psalmist David discovered durability in a fragile world. He anchored himself to eternity. He tied his hopes and heart to his God and His eternal, changeless qualities. David chose to rest in the ever-present, inescapable care of God. No circumstance or temporal experience could unmoor him from God's ever-watchful, always loving heart. He tied his hopes and heart to the heart of the universe. He buried his hand into the hand that holds it all. He traced his steps in the footprints of the Creator. He followed the One who would never fail him.

Only this God can give us a sense of fearless durability in a fallen, broken world.

....

Lord, direct my steps today! I'm resting in Your hands and following Your lead.

WEEK 6—FRIDAY

The God Whose Promises Are Unfailing

Thus says the LORD: "If heaven above can be measured, and the foundations of the earth searched out beneath, I will also cast off all the seed of Israel for all that they have done, says the LORD. Behold, the days are coming, says the LORD, that the city shall be built for the LORD from the Tower of Hananel to the Corner Gate."

JEREMIAH 31:37-38

Have you ever felt left in the dark by God? Have you ever wondered, *Where did He go? What is He doing? Is He failing me? Is He angry with me?* These are normal experiences for Jesus-followers. God does not follow our script, and sometimes He leads us through dark, wintery seasons. Sometimes His plan carries us through seasons of doubt and distress.

In today's passage, God pronounced discipline—exile to Babylon—on a nation that had fallen far from Him. Yet throughout Jeremiah's prophecy, God continually assured His faithful remnant that He was not forsaking them. His chastening was temporary, and His unfolding plan of redemption was right on schedule.

As God assured Israel, He assures us. His first statement is rhetorical, as if to say, "Just as it is impossible to measure the heavens, so it is impossible for Him to forsake His own." And then He inserts hope: "Behold, the days are coming . . ." He promises renewal and restoration. His good plans will be realized.

If you feel lost in the dark today, look up, cry out, and trust the God who will never forsake His own. Anticipate His good work: "Behold, the days are coming"!

....

> Lord, when You lead me through a chastening work, help me to trust Your heart.

Cary Schmidt, Emmanuel Baptist Church, Newington, CT

WEEK 6—WEEKEND

The God Who Came to Me

He is the image of the invisible God, the firstborn over all creation. For by Him all things were created that are in heaven and that are on earth, visible and invisible, whether thrones or dominions or principalities or powers. All things were created through Him and for Him. And He is before all things, and in Him all things consist.

COLOSSIANS 1:15–17

Have you ever wondered what God is really like? Have you ever wished you could see Him for who He really is? God has answered these questions. Look at Jesus. He is everything God is, wrapped up in a human body. He makes the invisible God visible. He is the Creator, Sustainer, and ultimately Ruler of all things. It all belongs to Him and is all for Him. He has always been and always will be. And in every imaginable way, He holds all things together.

This all-powerful, all-knowing, ever-present Creator broke into time and space, wrapped Himself in flesh, and accomplished redemption's work on our behalf. He made Himself visible, knowable, accessible, and understandable. Why? Because He wants us to know and experience Him, to enjoy a personal relationship with Him through faith in what Jesus accomplished.

He is the accessible God. He knows what life on earth is like and what our hearts feel. His heart is for us, and His grace is inexhaustible. Celebrate Him. Worship Him. Trust Him. Delight in Him. Your Creator came to you and calls you His friend. Talk to Him, walk with Him, and enjoy Him today.

....

> Lord, thank You for coming to this broken planet to save me. Lead me in Your grace today.

WEEK 7—MONDAY

How Near Is the End?

The day of the Lord will come as a thief in the night, in which the heavens will pass away with a great noise, and the elements will melt with fervent heat; both the earth and the works that are in it will be burned up. Therefore, since all these things will be dissolved, what manner of persons ought you to be in holy conduct and godliness?

2 PETER 3:10-11

Most of us have seen "The End Is Near" on social media, street corners, and sandwich boards. But the question that follows that ominous statement is, "How near is the end?" No one knows the exact time of the Second Coming. It is heaven's most guarded secret. But the Bible makes it clear that the Lord's coming will be swift and sudden. When He comes, there will be no time to get ready. We must *be* ready and *live* ready.

To live ready means being certain you have turned from sin and trusted the Savior. It also means living for Jesus in the light of His coming—not being half-hearted in your commitment to Christ but being "all in" and wholly devoted to following Him—no matter what and no matter where.

In these last days, make it your mission to shine for Christ by the way you live and share His story by the way you witness. Stand up for Jesus and speak the truth in love. Let the world know that Jesus is Lord—God's only Son and humanity's only Savior.

> Dear God, I want to live ready. Help me to be "all in" for Jesus and make a difference for Your kingdom. Amen.

Dr. Jeff Schreve, First Baptist Church, Texarkana, TX

WEEK 7—TUESDAY

The Importance of Being Faithful

This is the history of the heavens and the earth when they were created, in the day that the Lord God made the earth and the heavens, before any plant of the field was in the earth and before any herb of the field had grown. For the Lord God had not caused it to rain on the earth, and there was no man to till the ground.

GENESIS 2:4-5

In the beginning of creation and humanity's early days, God did not send rain for irrigation. Instead, a mist would rise up from the ground to provide the needed water for the plants and trees (Genesis 2:6). When we understand this truth, we get a clearer picture of the message of Noah. He claimed that God would destroy the world with a flood because humanity's wickedness was so great. People surely questioned the idea of a flood. Even rain was unknown. Perhaps they dismissed Noah as a religious nut who believed in fairy tales, laughing at his ark and mocking his message.

But Noah remained faithful, and one day, as promised, it started to rain. A few drops turned into a downpour that turned into a deluge. If any had ridiculed Noah's preaching, they would now beat on the ark to find safety. But God had shut the door, and the day of grace was over for that generation.

....

Dear God, help me to be faithful, just like Noah. Help me keep sharing the truth, even when it falls on deaf ears. Help me remember that judgment is coming and that Jesus is the only ark of salvation. Amen.

Heaven, Life, and the Resurrection

WEEK 7—WEDNESDAY

Your Wonderful Job Assignment

Thus says God the Lord, who created the heavens and stretched them out, who spread forth the earth and that which comes from it, who gives breath to the people on it, and spirit to those who walk on it: "I, the Lord, have called You in righteousness, and will hold Your hand; I will keep You and give You as a covenant to the people, as a light to the Gentiles."

ISAIAH 42:5-6

About twenty years ago, my friend Skip called to ask if I would help him with an assignment. A pro basketball player was interested in a Hummer, and the car dealer wanted it delivered to his house. Skip asked me to drive the Hummer and follow him to the player's house. As a big NBA fan then, I jumped at the chance to visit a star.

God's assignment for His children is much more exciting than meeting a sports hero. God has called us to walk with Him in righteousness and be a light to the nations. He has promised His presence and protection as we speak the truth in love to a lost and dying world. Truth may be considered hate to those who hate the truth—the gospel can be offensive in calling sinners to repentance—but it is the message people desperately need to hear. And God has called you to join Him in spreading the word.

Dear God, thank You for calling me to walk in the light with You and share Your love with a fallen world. Help me be a bold witness, knowing that You are holding my hand every step of the way. Amen.

Dr. Jeff Schreve, First Baptist Church, Texarkana, TX

WEEK 7—THURSDAY

When God Ran

"And he arose and came to his father. But when he was still a great way off, his father saw him and had compassion, and ran and fell on his neck and kissed him. And the son said to him, 'Father, I have sinned against heaven and in your sight, and am no longer worthy to be called your son.'"

LUKE 15:20-21

I love the parable of the prodigal son. Charles Dickens called it "the finest short story ever written." It is fast-moving and full of spiritual truth.

We see in this parable the gracious, forgiving heart of God. When the rebellious prodigal finally left the pigsty of his sin to return to his father in humility and confession, he was in for the surprise of his life. Instead of shunning the boy for his insolence and shameful behavior (as the religious leaders would have taught), this father girded up his loins, showed his legs (a scandalous thing then), and ran to receive and embrace his repentant son.

Hang that biblical picture of God in your heart. He runs to repentant sinners to forgive and restore. Throw away the false picture of a harsh God who is quick to write us off and cast us out. Know the truth about who He really is, and rejoice in His love and forgiveness.

....

> Dear God, thank You for not being ashamed to run to me, even when I blow it big-time and return to You in brokenness and repentance. Thank You for Your restoration and complete forgiveness. I love You, Lord, and I am so grateful for a grace that is greater than all my sin! Amen.

WEEK 7—FRIDAY

Working with God

So then, after the Lord had spoken to them, He was received up into heaven, and sat down at the right hand of God. And they went out and preached everywhere, the Lord working with them and confirming the word through the accompanying signs. Amen.

MARK 16:19-20

In the spring of 1988, I flew from Houston to Illinois for a final round of interviews for a job I really wanted. I was very nervous about making a poor showing, but God calmed my fears, helped me present well, and led them to hire me. I was grateful to be part of a first-class company with a wonderful compensation plan.

Can you imagine being hired by God to work for and with Him in His company? Wouldn't that be the best ever? That's what it means to be a Christian in the Lord's service. We are not just hired by God's grace (salvation) but are also given the unfathomable privilege of working with Him (Spirit-filled living) in growing His kingdom.

It is foolish to try to do the work of the Lord without Him. He works with us when we yield to Him, and He authenticates His work with His presence and power when we depend on Him. I tell my church, "I can preach truth, but only the Holy Spirit can impart truth to the human heart." In our zeal to serve Jesus, may we never charge ahead without the Lord of Hosts leading the way.

Dear God, thank You for the great privilege of working with You. May I never foolishly try to go it alone. May I always put You first and follow Your leadership. In Jesus' name, amen.

Dr. Jeff Schreve, First Baptist Church, Texarkana, TX

WEEK 7—WEEKEND

What a Promise!

"Ask, and it will be given to you; seek, and you will find; knock, and it will be opened to you. For everyone who asks receives, and he who seeks finds, and to him who knocks it will be opened. . . . If you then, being evil, know how to give good gifts to your children, how much more will your Father who is in heaven give good things to those who ask Him!"

MATTHEW 7:7-8, 11

Prayer is such a wonderful thing. It links our nothingness with God's almighty hand. It brings us into the throne room of the King of the universe, the God who loves us and can do the impossible.

But prayer can be hard. The devil fights to keep us off our knees. He makes our minds wander and whispers into our ear, "This is doing no good. God is not listening, and He is not going to answer you." Far too often, we believe his lies and throw in the towel.

God really does answer prayer, but not always the first request. *Ask*, *seek*, and *knock* are continual actions in the Greek. We are to ask and keep asking, seek and keep seeking, knock and keep knocking. God delights in persistent prayer; it shows Him we mean business. And He does business with those who mean business!

> Dear God, thank You for this great promise to answer prayer as I commit to calling on Your name. Thank You for being a good Father who gives good things to His children who ask, seek, and knock. What a privilege to be Yours! I love You, Lord. Amen.

Heaven, Life, and the Resurrection

WEEK 8—MONDAY

Focus

For you had compassion on me in my chains, and joyfully accepted the plundering of your goods, knowing that you have a better and an enduring possession for yourselves in heaven. Therefore do not cast away your confidence, which has great reward. For you have need of endurance, so that after you have done the will of God, you may receive the promise.

HEBREWS 10:34-36

In the early church, Christians were often arrested for practicing Christianity, and their houses would be plundered by the soldiers. The author of Hebrews had been imprisoned at some point, and his friends had supported him through that experience. They too had apparently been arrested and had their homes plundered. This was fairly common for Christians at the time.

What may not have been so common was the Christians' response in a time of persecution and false accusations. We could learn much from these early believers. They were focused on heaven, not earthly possessions. We have been going through rocky times, with everyone seeming so divided, which usually comes from fear of losing something—power, control, money, freedom, and more.

What if we remained as vigilant in our pursuit of being more like Christ as we are about politics and social issues? Let's not grow weary in our mission. Let's run with endurance the race that is set before us. As important as politics can be, Jesus did not say, "Go and make good policies." He said to go and make disciples.

Lord, help me to be focused on You alone today. Thank You for the reward that is already prepared for me.

Tim Sizemore, Lighthouse Baptist Church, Warner Robins, GA

WEEK 8—TUESDAY

Reconciled

For it pleased the Father that in Him all the fullness should dwell, and by Him to reconcile all things to Himself, by Him, whether things on earth or things in heaven, having made peace through the blood of His cross. And you, who once were alienated and enemies in your mind by wicked works, yet now He has reconciled in the body of His flesh through death, to present you holy, and blameless, and above reproach in His sight.

COLOSSIANS 1:19-22

When Nathan confronted King David about his sin with Bathsheba and the murder of Uriah, David fell on his knees and confessed that he had sinned against God alone. When I first read that, I could not help but think, "What about Uriah?" I finally recognized that only the one who defines sin could forgive sin. Adultery and murder are not wrong because we say so but because God defined them as sin.

Today's passage acknowledges that God was pleased with Jesus' work; our sins can therefore, be forgiven. To reconcile two accounts means to make them look alike. Our sin causes a debt we cannot pay. Once we sin, no accountant can balance our account. We can never reconcile our righteousness to His. Jesus did that work for us because we could not.

Recognize that your sin caused your account to overdraft. The only way to settle that debt with God is by the sacrifice Jesus made on the cross. Meditate on and thank Him for the price He paid for us.

....

Thank You, Lord, for paying the debt that I could never pay. Help me today to act like I am grateful.

Heaven, Life, and the Resurrection

WEEK 8—WEDNESDAY

What Must I Do?

Now behold, one came and said to Him, "Good Teacher, what good thing shall I do that I may have eternal life?" So He said to him, "Why do you call Me good? No one is good but One, that is, God. But if you want to enter into life, keep the commandments."

MATTHEW 19:16-17

Many people believe that merely recognizing Jesus was who He said He was is enough to receive salvation. When Jesus asked this rich young man why he called Him good, He was asking if the man was confessing that Jesus is God. But He didn't stop at that. He went on to point out that the young man valued his possessions more than following Christ.

There's a big difference between recognizing Jesus as God and making Him Lord of your life. The former means you see Him as the Creator of all things; the latter surrenders control of your life to Him. You cannot call Him Lord when other things are more important to you. Jesus also says, "Not everyone who says to Me, 'Lord, Lord,' will enter the kingdom of heaven, but he who does the will of my Father in heaven" (Matthew 7:21). Salvation is by grace alone, not works, but if you have given your life to Christ, you have surrendered your will and works. What has He asked you to get rid of that you are still holding on to? What are you afraid to let go of that keeps you from trusting in Christ alone? Ask Him. He will show you.

....

Lord, reveal to me what I am placing my trust in today. Help me trust in You alone. Amen.

Tim Sizemore, Lighthouse Baptist Church, Warner Robins, GA

WEEK 8—THURSDAY

I Am

But He kept silent and answered nothing. Again the high priest asked Him, saying to Him, "Are You the Christ, the Son of the Blessed?" Jesus said, "I am. And you will see the Son of Man sitting at the right hand of the Power, and coming with the clouds of heaven."

MARK 14:61-62

For the death penalty to be enforced, Jewish law required at least two witnesses against the defendant. The Sanhedrin had trouble finding two witnesses to tell the same story against Jesus. Jesus didn't argue against their false accusations, maybe because He knew they were irrelevant. Frustrated with his flimsy case, Caiaphas asked a direct question: "Are You the Christ, Son of the Blessed?" Jesus's response is beautiful. Sometimes we get so caught up in doing things that we forget who we are serving. He is the great I Am. He is seated at the Father's right hand and will come again from the clouds of heaven to bring His people home.

It is good to do kingdom work. We should make as much impact as possible and love people and meet needs as long as we are here. But we should not forget why we do those things. It's for a Savior who lives. Christ has not been and never will be dethroned by anything that happens in our lives. Rest assured that at the end of each day, we will be serving a risen Savior. Jesus was very sure about His future. You and I should be too. Stand on that promise today.

....

God, I praise You today for who You are. I am thankful for the reminder that You are in control.

WEEK 8—FRIDAY

The Creator

For thus says the LORD, who created the heavens, who is God, who formed the earth and made it, who has established it, who did not create it in vain, who formed it to be inhabited: "I am the LORD, and there is no other."

ISAIAH 45:18

I am an avid deer hunter. One of my favorite things to do is to sit in a stand at daybreak and listen to the woods come alive. I like to get settled in around thirty minutes before there is any light. There is complete silence. As the sun begins to peek out through the darkness, I begin to hear birds, squirrels, and other animals waking up from their night. It is incredible to experience—a perfect reminder of who God is and the majesty of His creation.

Think about the perfection of the food chain and all of the details required for life to exist here on earth. Some believe that billions of years ago, a tiny blob of matter floating in nothing suddenly exploded without reason, creating everything. They teach that intelligence was created without intelligence. When I consider the wonders of DNA and the various climates of the earth, I can't help but worship the Creator of it all. He formed this planet to be inhabited, and He made us to inhabit it. Over one hundred billion people have lived on earth. Out of all of those, not one (except Jesus) could manage to create life out of nothing. The Lord of creation is the only one worthy to be praised.

> Lord, You alone are worthy of our praise. Help me today, Lord, to recognize Your majesty. Amen.

Tim Sizemore, Lighthouse Baptist Church, Warner Robins, GA

WEEK 8—WEEKEND

Rich Kid

For He will deliver the needy when he cries, the poor also, and him who has no helper. He will spare the poor and needy, and will save the souls of the needy. He will redeem their life from oppression and violence; and precious shall be their blood in His sight.

PSALM 72:12-14

I was not born with a silver spoon. In fact, the one I eat with now may be rusted. When I was young and my dad was attending Bible college, we lived in the projects and pooled our groceries with the neighbor to have a full meal. I vividly remember being embarrassed to wear the clothes I had and to be called to the teacher's desk to pick up my free lunch card. One of my middle school highlights was when my mom scrimped, saved, and came up with enough money to buy me a Members Only jacket.

Pastoring a small church in the south didn't provide for a lot of bling. There have been times when I could be considered poor by the world's standards, but God has provided me with riches not sold at any store. He gave me the best parents, siblings, wife, children, and grandchild anyone could imagine. I would not trade my life or His gift of salvation for the life of the wealthiest person alive. Instead of being disappointed in what you don't have, count the blessings He has provided. God always takes care of His children.

> Lord, thank You for Your many provisions. Thank You for the grace and mercy that You richly give in abundance. Without You, I would be poor; with You, I am a child of the King.

Heaven, Life, and the Resurrection

WEEK 9—MONDAY

Proper Worship Desires a Good Reputation

Therefore concerning the eating of things offered to idols, we know that an idol is nothing in the world, and that there is no other God but one. For even if there are so-called gods, whether in heaven or on earth (as there are many gods and many lords), yet for us there is one God, the Father, of whom are all things, and we for Him; and one Lord Jesus Christ, through whom are all things, and through whom we live.

1 CORINTHIANS 8:4-6

This passage is about Christian liberty. If I am a Christian, do I have freedom to do things that some people think are wrong? Can I be unconcerned about my testimony? Is it enough to know that I am correct in my beliefs if I have no regard for how my life might affect others?

In answering these important questions, Paul makes a profound statement about God. He notes that while there are a lot of "so-called" gods, there is only one true God, the Creator of all things. And that God has only one Son, the Lord Jesus Christ—the only way to true and eternal life.

Each day we should ask, "Am I serving that one true God? Or have I developed a divided allegiance?" It seems that one reason Paul connects these two thoughts is this: if we are truly serving God, we will be very concerned about our testimony for Him before others.

Lord Jesus, help me today to live for You alone. And help me demonstrate that by being concerned about my spiritual reputation and testimony before others. Amen.

Mike Stone, Emmanuel Baptist Church, Blackshear, GA

WEEK 9—TUESDAY

Jesus and the Church

As he journeyed he came near Damascus, and suddenly a light shone around him from heaven. Then he fell to the ground, and heard a voice saying to him, "Saul, Saul, why are you persecuting Me?" And he said, "Who are You, Lord?" Then the Lord said, "I am Jesus, whom you are persecuting. It is hard for you to kick against the goads."

ACTS 9:3–5

Paul's salvation is a compelling story. While there is much to learn from it, one simple truth leaps off the page: Jesus identifies Himself with His church.

Paul had been persecuting the church, but Jesus did not ask, "Why are you persecuting the church?" He asked, "Why are you persecuting Me?" This is both a warning and a reminder. The way we treat the church is the way we treat Jesus, just as the way people treat my wife is the way they treat me, because my wife and I are one.

To neglect or spurn the church is to neglect or spurn the Lord. To assist the church is to minister to the Lord. While Christ and His church are not identical, they are inseparable. We cannot love the Lord without loving the church that wears His name.

Are you involved in a Bible-believing church—faithful in service and devotion through that body of believers? If so, praise the Lord. If not, get involved this week. You will find that the doors of a Christ-following church are as open as the arms of our merciful Lord.

Jesus, I will show my love for You by my love for Your people. I am part of Your body. Help me be faithful to play my part. Amen.

WEEK 9—WEDNESDAY

Christ, Our Sacrifice

Christ came as High Priest of the good things to come, with the greater and more perfect tabernacle not made with hands, that is, not of this creation. Not with the blood of goats and calves, but with His own blood He entered the Most Holy Place once for all, having obtained eternal redemption.

HEBREWS 9:11-12

The role of a prophet was to represent God to the people through a message. The role of the Jewish priest was to represent the people to God through sacrifices and intercession. The Lord Jesus perfectly fulfilled these roles and every other work He came to perform.

Earthly priests would continually offer sacrifices of goats and bulls, a picture and foreshadowing of the greatest sacrifice that was to come: Jesus Himself. The blood of earthly animals never washed away sin. But when Christ shed "His own blood" on the cross, He "obtained eternal redemption" for all who would ever believe on Him in repentant faith.

Salvation and forgiveness were purchased by the blood of Christ. And, as with every other gift, that gift must be received. Have you received the free gift of salvation through Jesus? If so, live today as an expression of thanksgiving. If not, there has never been a better time to be saved than right now.

> Lord Jesus, thank You for Your death on the cross. Your sacrificial death and physical resurrection provided my salvation for all eternity. Please forgive my sin and help me live an obedient life to demonstrate my gratitude. Amen.

Mike Stone, Emmanuel Baptist Church, Blackshear, GA

WEEK 9—THURSDAY

I Can Trust a God Like That

"I form the light and create darkness, I make peace and create calamity; I, the Lord, do all these things. Rain down, you heavens, from above, and let the skies pour down righteousness; let the earth open, let them bring forth salvation, and let righteousness spring up together. I, the Lord, have created it."

ISAIAH 45:7-8

Isaiah 45 prophesies the deliverance of God's people from bondage long before the bondage ever took place. This magnificent description of God's power reminds us that God has always been in control and is still in control today. The God who prophesied their bondage also prophesied their release before either of them occurred.

When we face challenges and difficulty, we can be comforted by God's absolute sovereignty. The same God who spoke light into existence is in control, and He can speak light into our dark circumstance. The same Lord who tells the skies to pour down rain can command the heavens to pour out salvation on our dry and barren situations. The same God who allows calamity to enter our life can also speak peace into the chaos and confusion. The same Lord who created the universe is in total control of the lives of His children. Nothing will touch our lives that did not first pass through His hand. We can trust that if He has allowed it to happen, it has come with great purpose.

> Father, I know You are God and You reign in power. Help me remember today that You are in control of anything and everything I will encounter. I choose to put my trust in Your goodness to me.

Heaven, Life, and the Resurrection

WEEK 9—FRIDAY

The Unchanging Word

So you also, when you see these things happening, know that the kingdom of God is near. Assuredly, I say to you, this generation will by no means pass away till all things take place. Heaven and earth will pass away, but My words will by no means pass away.

LUKE 21:31-33

One day, earth will be no more. The atmosphere ("heaven") will pass away too. Bible scholars often debate when and how that will happen, but one thing is clear: when heaven and earth have passed away, the Word of God will remain.

God's Word is perfect. Jesus calls it "My words." The words of a perfect and blameless God are inevitably perfect themselves. It is a joy to know the Bible is a perfect book without error.

God's Word is powerful. Jesus said that "no means" can overcome it. Sinners have criticized it, skeptics have trivialized it, and scoffers have minimized it. But the living Word of God outlives its harshest detractors.

God's Word is permanent. Almost everything on earth changes—fads, styles, cultures, and opinions. But one thing will never ever change: the Word of the living God.

It is often said that the only two things on earth that will last forever are the Word of God and the human soul. When the end of time comes, God's Word will still be standing. Do you know where your eternal soul will be?

....

Father, Your Word is a sure and constant treasure of truth. I find in it the wisdom of heaven itself. Help me live today in light of its truth and in obedience to its commands. Amen.

Mike Stone, Emmanuel Baptist Church, Blackshear, GA

WEEK 9—WEEKEND

Examining My Priorities

"Again, the kingdom of heaven is like treasure hidden in a field, which a man found and hid; and for joy over it he goes and sells all that he has and buys that field. Again, the kingdom of heaven is like a merchant seeking beautiful pearls, who, when he had found one pearl of great price, went and sold all that he had and bought it."

MATTHEW 13:44-46

These two brief parables speak of the priority we should give to the things of God. The kingdom of heaven is compared to men who find treasure and instantly forsake everything else to pursue it. Oh, that God's will would be a priority for each of us! But how would we determine whether our spiritual priorities are correct? We should consider three questions:

What brings me joy? The first man was filled with joy when he found the hidden treasure. People who prioritize the things of God get excited about spiritual things. Whatever excites me gives me a good idea of my spiritual priorities.

Where do I spend my time? Each of these businessmen immediately rearranged their schedules to buy the field and the pearl. Whatever I'm willing to change my schedule for reveals my priorities.

What do I use my money to buy? There are many responsibilities in life that require the use of our money. But when it comes to disposable income, few things will identify my priorities like watching where I gladly spend money.

> Lord, help me pursue Your will with my heart, my time, and my resources. You are my priority, and I want that to be revealed in the things I do. Amen.

Heaven, Life, and the Resurrection

WEEK 10—MONDAY

Hope of Heaven

And your life would be brighter than noonday. Though you were dark, you would be like the morning. And you would be secure, because there is hope; yes, you would dig around you, and take your rest in safety. You would also lie down, and no one would make you afraid; yes, many would court your favor. But the eyes of the wicked will fail, and they shall not escape, and their hope—loss of life!"

JOB 11:17-20

Zophar was Job's third friend to speak into his life. He called Job to repentance. Believing sin to be the problem leading to Job's trouble, Zophar the legalist brought forth a hollow message. He spoke of hope and then pulled it away (v. 20).

There is hope beyond our last breath. Those in Christ will one day be absent from the body and present with the Lord. Only then will we find rest for souls with no disturbance. Christ is our resting place.

Do not be a judge of your friends. The spirit of Zophar is alive and well. Seek today to have the spirit of Jesus. Be a true friend to a hurting soul. Offer hope eternal in Christ.

> Lord, thank You that my sins are forgiven. Thank You for the hope of heaven. Lead me today to express oneness to my friends. In Jesus' name, amen.

WEEK 10—TUESDAY

The Title Deed

I saw in the right hand of Him who sat on the throne a scroll written inside and on the back, sealed with seven seals. Then I saw a strong angel proclaiming with a loud voice, "Who is worthy to open the scroll and to loose its seals?" And no one in heaven or on the earth or under the earth was able to open the scroll, or to look at it.

REVELATION 5:1-3

John wept. He saw a book he wanted to read. No one was available to open its seven seals. He was in heaven around the throne (see chapter 4 for context), and one of the elders stepped forward with an exhortation: stop weeping!

Jesus was there to open the title deed to the future. He is worthy! The worship began. And the One slain for our sins, the One who purchased us with His blood, the One who made us a kingdom and priests to our God, opened the book.

Dear friend, do not fear the future. Jesus holds the title deed. He knows what is coming, and He has you in His hands. Amen for heaven, hope, and security.

> Lord, today I surrender my future to You. I submit my day into Your hands. You hold the title deed, and I surrender all.

Heaven, Life, and the Resurrection

WEEK 10—WEDNESDAY

Our Inheritance

Whom have I in heaven but You? And there is none upon earth that I desire besides You. My flesh and my heart fail; but God is the strength of my heart and my portion forever.

PSALM 73:25-26

Asaph, the author of Psalm 73, almost lost his faith. His confidence in the Lord had slipped (vv. 2–3). He had allowed the prosperity of the wicked to move his focus from God to the godless. He misdirected his attention.

The singer regained his song. He asked the eternal question, *Whom have I in heaven but you?* (v. 25). He came to desire God alone. The Lord was his portion, a word that speaks of one's part of the inheritance. Jesus is the believer's portion. Our eternal inheritance in the Lord (Psalm 16:5).

Maybe your faith has waned like Asaph's did. Be careful that the glitter of the world does not grab your attention. Come to refocus on the One who is faithful and eternal. Lift your eyes this day to the heavens. All else may fail you, but Jesus never will. He is the strength of your heart. Trust Him for eternity. Trust Him for today!

Thank You, Father, for the assurance of heaven. Today I place all of my focus on and my faith in You. Thank You for being my eternal portion.

Dr. Ted H. Traylor, Olive Baptist Church, Pensacola, FL

WEEK 10—THURSDAY

Praise the Lord

Praise the LORD! Praise the LORD from the heavens; praise Him in the heights! Praise Him, all His angels; praise Him, all His hosts! Praise Him, sun and moon; praise Him, all you stars of light! Praise Him, you heavens of heavens, and you waters above the heavens!

PSALM 148:1-4

Psalm 148 celebrates God as the Creator of all things, calling us to focus our gaze on Him and worship Him. It is difficult to divide, so it must be read as a whole. Take in all fourteen verses. Read them slowly and praise the Lord!

Praise the Lord from the heights of heaven to the depth of the sea and all that is between. Let everyone praise Him—the young and old, rich and poor, male and female, and every created thing. Above all, exalt His name.

Make a list today of God's gifts you are grateful for. Write out your items of praise. Take your eyes off problems and lift them to heaven. Praise registers the power of your God rather than the temperature of your environment.

Go ahead—praise the Lord!

....

Father, today I praise Your name. I exalt You. For being the Creator, I praise You. For being my Savior, I praise You. For being my strength, I praise You. Amen.

Heaven, Life, and the Resurrection

WEEK 10—FRIDAY

Up, Up, and Hurray

And He led them out as far as Bethany, and He lifted up His hands and blessed them. Now it came to pass, while He blessed them, that He was parted from them and carried up into heaven. And they worshiped Him, and returned to Jerusalem with great joy, and were continually in the temple praising and blessing God. Amen.

LUKE 24:50-53

The ascension of Jesus Christ marks His victory over sin, death, and the earthly grave. He is risen and reigns. He is our great Intercessor. Our Victor occupies the throne. Nothing gives us more hope than knowing Jesus is eternally alive. Glory to God!

Jesus' role as Victor changes and energizes our worship. When we gather with others, we glorify His name and give praise to God.

Our Victor emboldens our prayer life. He instructs us to come boldly to the throne of grace. He is our Priest, and we need no other. Call out to Him.

Our Victor is preparing a place for us in eternity, and He will come again and receive us unto Himself. Where He is, we will be also.

Our Victor teaches us that earthly death is not our end. There is so much more. One day we will rise to meet Him. What a day that will be when our Jesus we shall see. We will take our crowns and cast them at His feet, for He is the Victor!

Thank You, Jesus, for being the overcomer. Today I turn my eyes toward heaven. Thank You for my eternal assurance. Glory to God!

Dr. Ted H. Traylor, Olive Baptist Church, Pensacola, FL

WEEK 10—WEEKEND

The Most High God

I even found an altar with this inscription: TO THE UNKNOWN GOD. Therefore, the One whom you worship without knowing, Him I proclaim to you: God, who made the world and everything in it, since He is Lord of heaven and earth, does not dwell in temples made with hands. Nor is He worshiped with men's hands, as though He needed anything, since He gives to all life, breath, and all things.

ACTS 17:23-25

Paul was at Mars Hill, looking into the face of man-made religion. He saw the religion of the worlds manifested in the Parthenon. On the rocky ledges of the Acropolis, there were countless idols. The most revered Greek sculptors had been employed for the work of making a god for everyone and everything. There was even an altar for the unknown god in case one was missed.

Religion is a death trap. It can challenge the mind and soothe the emotions, but man-made religion cannot breathe life into the dead spirit of a person. It takes the living and Most High God to do that. Only Jesus can give eternal life.

Be very careful today when you look at spiritual things. Make certain you bow before the living God. Not everything that glitters is gold, and not everything religious is God.

You may attend a large church with a tall steeple or a country church with only a few rows of pews. But remember that you are the temple of the Holy Spirit. The Most High God lives in you.

> Thank You for my church. I love the people I gather with on a regular basis. Teach us to be grateful for our manmade structures. And remind me that I am Your temple. Live in me this day. Amen.

Heaven, Life, and the Resurrection

WEEK 11—MONDAY

You Can Make a Difference!

"For what will it profit a man if he gains the whole world, and loses his own soul? Or what will a man give in exchange for his soul? For whoever is ashamed of Me and My words in this adulterous and sinful generation, of him the Son of Man also will be ashamed when He comes in the glory of His Father with the holy angels."

MARK 8:36-38

Being ashamed of Jesus is not always demonstrated by what people say but by what they don't say. The fear of being rejected or not knowing what to say has led to a generation of silent Christians and an "adulterous and sinful generation" around them.

A story adapted from Loren Eisely makes a powerful point: "One day a man was walking along the beach when he noticed a boy picking something up and gently throwing it into the ocean. Approaching the boy, he asked, 'What are you doing?' The youth replied, 'Throwing starfish back into the ocean. The surf is up, and the tide is going out. If I don't throw them back, they'll die.'

"'Son,' the man said, 'don't you realize there are miles and miles of beach and hundreds of starfish? You can't make a difference!' After listening politely, the boy bent down, picked up another starfish, and threw it back into the surf. Then, smiling at the man, he said. . . . 'I made a difference for that one.'"

Father, give me the boldness and courage to share the story of how Your goodness and mercy have changed my life. Help me never shy away from the opportunities You give me. I pray Your Holy Spirit would enable me to make a difference in someone's life. In Jesus' name, amen.

Dr. Mike Whitson, First Baptist Church Indian Trail, Indian Trail, NC

WEEK 11—TUESDAY

Listen and Understand

Then they departed from there and passed through Galilee, and He did not want anyone to know it. For He taught His disciples and said to them, "The Son of Man is being betrayed into the hands of men, and they will kill Him. And after He is killed, He will rise the third day." But they did not understand this saying, and were afraid to ask Him.

MARK 9:30-32

Jesus took His disciples on a private road trip toward Jerusalem, away from the crowds, to pour into them an important message of warning and of hope. Imagine hearing that their teacher would be betrayed and killed, holding their ears because they didn't want to hear any more!

But don't condemn their lack of understanding; they were new at this. We have 2,000 years of history and the Word of God to enable us to figure out what was being said. Jesus gave them this message because they would be the ones to carry the gospel to a lost and dying world.

God has a strong message to deliver through you, a message of warning and hope, a gospel message that Jesus died for our sins and rose again so we too can live. Don't be afraid to ask Him how He can use you. His plan is not to harm you but to prosper you and secure your future. Ask Him to expand your influence so others may know of His love.

> Father, we do not understand so many things. We do ask for wisdom and the power to carry this message of hope to those who do not know You.

Heaven, Life, and the Resurrection

WEEK 11—WEDNESDAY

Gossip the Gospel

As you go, preach, saying, "The kingdom of heaven is at hand.' Heal the sick, cleanse the lepers, raise the dead, cast out demons. Freely you have received, freely give. Provide neither gold nor silver nor copper in your money belts."

MATTHEW 10:7-9

One of the tasks of God's children is to gossip the gospel, to tell others about the kingdom of God. The commission in today's passage is to go through our lives, whether at work or play, being intentional about sharing with those who may not be a part of God's kingdom—to tell how we came into it and how they can too.

The disciples were gifted to carry out miracles in order to validate their claims and draw people to Jesus. They did not hem or haw but went straight to the point: "The kingdom of heaven is at hand."

With very few physicians and no hospitals, these itinerant preachers were a welcome sight to the infirmed. Every miracle legitimized their message. Jesus said, "Freely you have received, freely give"—in other words, "Give away what I gave *you*." They were able to do what they did because of what Jesus had done for them.

The greatest miracle is a changed life. Jesus changed you so you can carry the kingdom of heaven wherever you go. The kingdom of heaven is wherever the will of God is being done—in your home, on the job, at school, in all of life. Share that miraculous story of your changed life with someone today.

Father, thank You for saving my soul. Send someone my way today to hear my story. In Jesus' name, amen.

Dr. Mike Whitson, First Baptist Church Indian Trail, Indian Trail, NC

WEEK 11—THURSDAY

Sought, Saved, and Sent

Paul, a bondservant of Jesus Christ, called to be an apostle, separated to the gospel of God which He promised before through His prophets in the Holy Scriptures, concerning His Son Jesus Christ our Lord, who was born of the seed of David according to the flesh, and declared to be the Son of God with power according to the Spirit of holiness, by the resurrection from the dead.

ROMANS 1:1-4

Paul said he was called by God to bear witness of the truth of the gospel—the good news of Jesus Christ. Have you ever thought about the miracle of this gospel? Fifty-five Old Testament prophecies fulfilled in Jesus Christ have been counted. The likelihood of even eight of those being fulfilled in Jesus would be like covering the state of Texas with silver dollars two feet deep and asking a blind person to pick up the only one that was marked. That is the odds of one man fulfilling all those prophecies, but Jesus did. What a miracle He is!

Jesus was born of a virgin in a little town called Bethlehem. He lived sinlessly until He was crucified on a cross outside Jerusalem. He was buried in a borrowed tomb, and three days later rose triumphantly from that grave, overcoming death for you and me. Hallelujah! What a Savior! Now we are called by this same God to publish the good news of Jesus Christ.

....

Father, thank You for Your Son, Jesus. I pray that I will forever be a gossiper of the gospel. In Jesus' name, amen.

Heaven, Life, and the Resurrection

WEEK 11—FRIDAY

Our Ascended Lord

For You meet him with the blessings of goodness; you set a crown of pure gold upon his head. He asked life from You, and You gave it to him—length of days forever and ever. His glory is great in Your salvation; honor and majesty You have placed upon him. For You have made him most blessed forever; you have made him exceedingly glad with Your presence.

PSALM 21:3-6

Many psalms, like this one, have dual meanings. They may carry a historical significance while simultaneously pointing to a future event. Here David had just come from a major battle in which the Lord went before him "with the blessings of goodness." The Lord goes before us with the supply to our needs before the need ever arises. The goodness of God chases after His children throughout our lives—"length of days forever and ever." Isn't it wonderful to know that we have a companion who anticipates every need and can provide everything we will ever need in the battles of this life?

The passage also indicates events that were to transpire. When the King of kings fought the battle of Calvary, He defeated death, hell, and the grave and paid the debt for all our sins. When "it is finished" reverberated throughout human history, our Lord and Savior ascended back into glory, robed with "honor and majesty" and crowned with a "crown of pure gold."

Father, thank You for Calvary. I know that the power of the cross can meet every need in my life.

Dr. Mike Whitson, First Baptist Church Indian Trail, Indian Trail, NC

WEEK 11—WEEKEND

From Heaven's Point of View

When I consider Your heavens, the work of Your fingers, the moon and the stars, which You have ordained, what is man that You are mindful of him, and the son of man that You visit him? For You have made him a little lower than the angels, and You have crowned him with glory and honor.

PSALM 8:3-5

Imagine the young shepherd lying under the stars, taking in all the majesty of God's creation. He looked up and saw many stars that he likely knew by name. He saw the reflective light of the moon and gasped in amazement that the God who created such overwhelming magnificence would dare want a relationship with him!

Isn't it wonderful to know that in the midst of all His creative works, sovereign God declares that we take precedence over all of it? God loves *you*. He cares about *you*. Jesus died, not for the heavens or the animal kingdom, but for *you*. One day He intends to take us home to be with Him, where we will no longer be "a little lower than the angels" but raised beyond the highest archangels in glory!

Jesus took on the form of flesh, but after His death, God raised Him and crowned Him with glory, honor, and majesty. He sits on the throne of heaven, interceding for you and me. Oh, what a Savior! This same Jesus loves and cares for you.

....

Father, thank You for giving me life. Thank You for loving me enough to die for me. Please help me live for You. In Jesus' name, amen.

Heaven, Life, and the Resurrection

WEEK 12—MONDAY

The Wonder of Heaven

"I will show wonders in heaven above and signs in the earth beneath: Blood and fire and vapor of smoke. The sun shall be turned into darkness, and the moon into blood, before the coming of the great and awesome day of the Lord. And it shall come to pass that whoever calls on the name of the Lord shall be saved."

ACTS 2:19-21

Peter preached up a storm on the day of Pentecost. Like every good Bible preacher, he quoted this passage from Joel's prophecy, explained it, and then applied it to those who heard him. This well-known prophecy was originally given after a terrible calamity that caused Israel to look to heaven for help. Peter used it to call men and women to cry out to Jesus to be saved.

Though Joel was talking about supernatural disasters that will come at the end of the age, it's interesting how natural disasters are often used in our day by the Lord to get people's attention so they will call out to Jesus to be saved. If you've never trusted Christ, don't wait for something drastic to get your attention. Look at the wonder of heaven and the beauty of the heavens, and realize how good and glorious He is. Call on Him to save you today.

Lord, You are the Creator and Controller of everything, and You work out all things for our good. May we look to the heavens today and put our trust in You, the Wonder of Heaven. Amen.

Dr. Brad Whitt, Abilene Baptist Church, Martinez, GA

WEEK 12—TUESDAY

The Mystery of Heaven

Having made known to us the mystery of His will, according to His good pleasure which He purposed in Himself, that in the dispensation of the fullness of the times He might gather together in one all things in Christ, both which are in heaven and which are on earth—in Him.

EPHESIANS 1:9-10

I don't know about you, but I've always loved a good mystery. I especially love that moment when it all comes together and you understand what happened—when, where, and why. Up until that point, it's secret, hidden, not yet understood.

The mystery Paul mentions here isn't a secret beyond our ability to understand. It is a mystery that can only be comprehended when revealed by God. In the prophetic sense, there is coming a day when the Lord will open up the heavens and reveal His will, work, and plan for the end of the age. On a personal level, this revealing happens when the Spirit of God removes the blinders from our eyes and allows us to see our sinful condition and personal condemnation and call out to Christ for salvation. In the end, as Paul says, it's all about Him!

....

Lord, will You reveal Yourself today? Will You show Yourself strong and able to handle whatever situation we face today? And, will You draw men and women to Yourself so they will be saved today and understand just how great You are? Amen.

Heaven, Life, and the Resurrection

WEEK 12—WEDNESDAY

The Bread of Heaven

"He who eats My flesh and drinks My blood abides in Me, and I in him. As the living Father sent Me, and I live because of the Father, so he who feeds on Me will live because of Me. This is the bread which came down from heaven—not as your fathers ate the manna, and are dead. He who eats this bread will live forever."

JOHN 6:56-58

This is one of my favorite "I am" statements of Jesus. Seven times in John's Gospel, Jesus gave us critical insight into who He is and what He came to do with these two powerful words: "I am the light of the world" (8:12); "I am the resurrection and the life" (11:25); "I am the good shepherd" (10:11). Here Jesus declared that He is "the bread which came down from heaven" (v. 41). He drew people's attention back to when the children of Israel were facing starvation in the desert and God miraculously met their greatest physical need.

Jesus used that picture to show how He, the bread of life from heaven, could meet their greatest spiritual need. Their fathers ate manna in the desert and later died. Those who receive Him, who eat this bread "will live forever." Have you come to Jesus? Have you received Him? Have you feasted on the bread that came down from heaven? Those who do will never die.

> Lord, help us find sustenance in our Savior, Jesus Christ. Help me find satisfaction in Him. Jesus, You truly are the bread of life that came down from heaven. Thank You for the strength and security You give me in these uncertain, fearful days. Amen.

Dr. Brad Whitt, Abilene Baptist Church, Martinez, GA

WEEK 12—THURSDAY

The Reward of Heaven

"Blessed are you when men hate you, and when they exclude you, and revile you, and cast out your name as evil, for the Son of Man's sake. Rejoice in that day and leap for joy! For indeed your reward is great in heaven, for in like manner their fathers did to the prophets."

LUKE 6:22-23

What an unusual statement. Jesus said we are "blessed"—literally, "happy"—when people hate us, exclude us, revile us, and cast us out. Why should this make us happy? It certainly doesn't work that way naturally, but Jesus was talking about the supernatural. The reason we can be happy and feel blessed is because of the reward that awaits us in heaven.

What makes the difference? Our names? No, His name. When we face all of these horrible things for the sake of the name of Jesus, we can be happy because we don't face anything Jesus didn't face for us. This truth doesn't mean we provoke others to treat us this way, but when the Jesus in us stirs up the devil in them, we can take comfort in the fact that we are serving and living in the name of Jesus. We are not better than Jesus and as His followers can't expect to live without many of the things our Savior endured. For that, we should consider ourselves to be "blessed."

>Lord, thank You for enduring the scorn, ridicule, abuse, and ultimately death on the cross for me. I know You loved me so much that You suffered and died for me. Help me live my life for You today. Amen.

Heaven, Life, and the Resurrection

WEEK 12—FRIDAY

The Kingdom of Heaven

The kingdom of heaven is like a dragnet that was cast into the sea and gathered some of every kind, which, when it was full, they drew to shore; and they sat down and gathered the good into vessels, but threw the bad away. So it will be at the end of the age. The angels will come forth, separate the wicked from among the just, and cast them into the furnace of fire. There will be wailing and gnashing of teeth."

MATTHEW 13:47-50

Jesus loved to use metaphors to help us understand the nature of heaven. This one isn't very familiar today but would have been then. The kingdom of heaven is like a dragnet—a net dragged through the water to collect all kinds of fish. On shore, the fishermen go through the net to see which ones should be kept or discarded.

At the end of the age, people to be ushered into heaven will be separated from those to be cast into hell—a real place of eternal torment that awaits those who reject Jesus and His salvation. If you have never trusted Christ, won't you trust Him today? If you have, won't you commit to be more intentional in taking more family members and friends to heaven with you by sharing the good news of the gospel with them?

> Lord, help me be aware of the kingdom of heaven's glory and the reality of hell's terrors. May I be ready, willing, and able to share with those You bring across my path today. You love them and paid the price for them to be able to enjoy heaven by placing their faith in You. Amen.

Dr. Brad Whitt, Abilene Baptist Church, Martinez, GA

WEEK 12—WEEKEND

The Lord of Heaven and Earth

Bless the Lord, O my soul! O Lord my God, You are very great: You are clothed with honor and majesty, who cover Yourself with light as with a garment, who stretch out the heavens like a curtain.

PSALM 104:1-2

This wonderful psalm reveals two characteristics of the Lord of heaven's relationship with the universe He created. First, contrary to pantheism, the true God is distinct from His creation. He's not the rocks, and rocks aren't God. He's not a mystical force that comes from and connects all trees and flowers. The true God of the Bible is separate from and sovereign over His creation.

But that doesn't mean He is removed from it or doesn't care about it. He didn't set the universe in motion, walk away, and stop caring about it. He delights in and endues His creation with the power of His presence. It is like His robe, His tent, His palace, and His chariot.

Jesus demonstrated His dominion over creation through His miracles in the Gospels. There is great comfort in knowing that our God is intimately aware of every aspect of His creation and is powerful enough to oversee every aspect of it. This is always true in whatever circumstances you are wrestling with today.

> Lord, You are the Lord of heaven and earth. Nothing happens in Your creation that You are not aware of and sovereignly overseeing. I may not always understand why You allow certain things to happen, but I trust that You are a good God who loves us and is working out all things for our good and Your glory. Amen.

Heaven, Life, and the Resurrection

WEEK 13—MONDAY

The God of Covenant

For You, O God, have heard my vows; you have given me the heritage of those who fear Your name. You will prolong the king's life, his years as many generations. He shall abide before God forever. Oh, prepare mercy and truth, which may preserve him! So I will sing praise to Your name forever, that I may daily perform my vows.

PSALM 61:5-8

David understood how much he depended on God. He knew God did more for him than he could ever do for God. Writing in the middle of some of his most depressing struggles, this servant of the Lord cried out to God for help.

The confidence with which David affirmed his need for God is clearly seen in his prayer for himself as he faced his struggles with Absalom, his own son. The vows God had made guaranteed His covenant relationship with his people. God would be merciful and faithful, not only with David but also with His people as a nation. In response, David expressed thanksgiving to God, pledging to sing praises to His name forever. His obedience to the call and commands of the Lord would continue to be seen and heard every day of his life.

Dear God, how thankful we are for Your faithfulness to us. How grateful I am to stand upon Your promises. I renew my pledge to serve and obey You all the days of my life. In Jesus' name I pray, amen.

WEEK 13—TUESDAY

The God of Life

If we have been united together in the likeness of His death, certainly we also shall be in the likeness of His resurrection, knowing this, that our old man was crucified with Him, that the body of sin might be done away with, that we should no longer be slaves of sin. For he who has died has been freed from sin. Now if we died with Christ, we believe that we shall also live with Him.

ROMANS 6:5-8

How wonderful it is to know of our eternal hope in and through the sacrifice of the Lord Jesus. In this passage, Paul points to our greatest hope—every believer's regeneration in Christ. Our salvation in Christ is the means by which we have become united with Him.

Our former life was not only worn out but totally useless. We were lost in our sins. We had no hope in life and no hope after death. But when we gave our lives to Christ, our old self died with Him, and the life we now have is the life of Christ Himself. God's purpose is for every inclination of sin in the flesh of our bodies to be set free through the redemptive power of Jesus' life and death. While sin is still held in our flesh, our union with Jesus frees us from its dominion and control. Because we died with Christ, we have guaranteed hope of eternal life with Him.

> Dear God, thank You for the hope I have in Jesus Christ—even when I am sad and grieve. Because I belong to You, I am able to live with You forever. In Jesus' name I pray, amen.

Heaven, Life, and the Resurrection

WEEK 13—WEDNESDAY

The God of Creation

Let the heavens rejoice, and let the earth be glad; let the sea roar, and all its fullness; let the field be joyful, and all that is in it. Then all the trees of the woods will rejoice before the Lord. For He is coming, for He is coming to judge the earth. He shall judge the world with righteousness, and the peoples with His truth.

PSALM 96:11-13

God created the heavens and the earth and all that is in them. He also created human beings. Genesis tells us that God looked upon all of His creation and considered it "good." It was perfect in every way. But sin interrupted the perfection of all God had made. As a result, creation was blemished and spoiled. Humanity was separated from God by falling short of His holiness.

Praise the Lord for Jesus Christ. Through His death, burial, and resurrection, people can now be reconciled to a holy and righteous God by repenting of their sin and placing their faith and trust in Jesus. But we still live in a fallen world. Creation suffers and groans as a consequence of sin. This is why the psalmist expresses such joy and confidence related to the heavens, the sea, the fields, and the trees. The rule he describes is not the present universal kingdom but one that Christ will establish when He returns. The God of creation is the God of our re-creation!

> Dear God, thank You for the joy of knowing we have been made new creatures in Christ Jesus. We look forward to Jesus coming again, and to the new heaven and the new earth forever. In Jesus' name I pray, amen.

Dr. Don Wilton, First Baptist Church, Spartanburg, SC

WEEK 13—THURSDAY

The God of Consideration

Lord, what is man, that You take knowledge of him? Or the son of man, that You are mindful of him? Man is like a breath; his days are like a passing shadow. Bow down Your heavens, O Lord, and come down; touch the mountains, and they shall smoke.

PSALM 144:3-5

Any study of human history reveals truths that are irrefutable. We are evidently unable to solve our own problems. Differences of opinion leave people exhausted with one another, while the court of public opinion never provides the peace people want. Nations are divided among themselves as people jostle for positions of authority and urge others to join them. The results are everywhere. Wars, famines, civil strife, racial divisions, injustice, and political deadlocks seem to permeate most countries and people.

In many ways, the psalmist looks into the face of God and asks a question that draws attention to this predicament. Why would God have any regard for the futility of sinful humanity? Why would our God, sovereign and mighty in all His ways, have any cause to deal with us? The psalmist places eternal God in His rightful position while contrasting Him with sinful human beings. The brevity of our existence, compared to God, is nothing more than a momentary breath and a passing shadow. As a result, the psalmist cries out to hasten the coming of the Lord so the whole earth would be redeemed.

Dear God, thank You for Your gracious and kind consideration of all people in our weakness and sinfulness. We long for Your second coming. In Jesus' name I pray, amen.

WEEK 13—FRIDAY

The God of Commission

Jesus came and spoke to them, saying, "All authority has been given to Me in heaven and on earth. Go therefore and make disciples of all the nations, baptizing them in the name of the Father and of the Son and of the Holy Spirit, teaching them to observe all things that I have commanded you; and lo, I am with you always, even to the end of the age." Amen.

MATTHEW 28:18-20

Jesus' disciples had followed Him everywhere and been taught many things. They had watched Him heal the sick and make the blind see. They had seen Him respond to opposition and deal with demon possession. Most of all, they knew He loved them. They were convinced He was exactly who He said He was: the Son of the living God, the Messiah.

Now it was time for Jesus to leave them. Most of them heard what He said about His departure. They remembered that He would send His Comforter to walk with them. Perhaps few really understood, but they believed Him. They were willing to take Him at His word.

So Jesus gave the disciples their ultimate commission to go into the vast world with the same message He had taught them. The sweeping scope of their commission is consummate with His unlimited authority as Father, Son, and Holy Spirit. All the power of the triune God would be brought to bear on those who obey His commission to go. And the kind of evangelism called for in this commission does not end with the conversion of the believer. It involves all things.

Dear God, I will go! In Jesus' name I pray, amen.

WEEK 13—WEEKEND

The God of Forgiveness

"And whenever you stand praying, if you have anything against anyone, forgive him, that your Father in heaven may also forgive you your trespasses. But if you do not forgive, neither will your Father in heaven forgive your trespasses."

MARK 11:25-26

The disciples had heard so much. From the time Jesus confounded many by turning water into wine at the wedding in Cana, they witnessed His unspeakable and unexplainable power. Gradually, these followers had tried to "connect the dots" of their amazement and understanding. And they did this as sinful men—jostling for position, arguing among themselves, dealing with a vast array of emotions, and constantly getting in each other's way.

We can only imagine the great times they had together, but we can also imagine them fighting one another regularly. When they asked Jesus to teach them how to pray, they may not have expected the issue of forgiveness to come up any more than the need to ask for daily bread. But they heard Him talk of His Father, and they knew the connection was crucial to their well-being.

Jesus knew what they needed most. He loved His followers and knew that an unforgiving heart is a detriment to spiritual happiness and joy. This instruction was not a suggestion; it was a mandate. Forgive others. If you do not, you do not understand grace, and God will not forgive you.

....

> Dear God, just as You have forgiven me, please help me forgive those who have deeply hurt and offended me. I cannot, but You can do this in and through me. I pray this in Jesus' name, amen.

Heaven, Life, and the Resurrection

WEEK 14, MONDAY

Never Break!

Bondservants, be obedient to those who are your masters according to the flesh, with fear and trembling, in sincerity of heart, as to Christ; . . . knowing that whatever good anyone does, he will receive the same from the Lord, whether he is a slave or free. And you, masters, do the same things to them, giving up threatening, knowing that your own Master also is in heaven, and there is no partiality with Him.

EPHESIANS 6:5, 8–9

I started my first job in the warehouse of my family's grocery business. My first assignment was to unload 400,000 pounds of Campbell's Soup from a rail car. Mr. Mike gave the order: "Stack sixty cases on a pallet. Every fifteen minutes or so, someone will scoop it up and take it away. When you run out of pallets, press the buzzer and we'll bring you another stack." I was twelve, and I would see many more rail cars over the next thirteen years.

The day I left to answer the call to ministry, Mr. Mike found me and said, "Young man, I want to shake your hand! You may not remember this, but on your first day, I had you unloading rail cars all by yourself. Your father and grandfather told me to do everything in my power to break you in half. I tried for thirteen years, and you never broke."

As an employee or employer, we have a tremendous responsibility to be faithful, diligent, hardworking, and most of all, "as to the Lord," *never break!*

> Dear Lord, I pray that I will serve others and work, just as You served and worked to bring honor and glory to the Father. In Jesus' name I pray, amen.

H. Marshall Thompson Jr., Riverstone Community Church, Jacksonville, FL

WEEK 14—TUESDAY

Sealed with a Handshake

He who has prepared us for this very thing is God, who also has given us the Spirit as a guarantee. So we are always confident, knowing that while we are at home in the body we are absent from the Lord. For we walk by faith, not by sight.

2 CORINTHIANS 5:5-7

Mark McCormack was a bored attorney in the late 1950s working cases of little interest, wishing he could find a way to combine his law skills with his love for golf. He had been keeping up with Arnold Palmer and knew that his "made for television" looks, his "swashbuckling" swing, and his cavalier attitude would make Palmer a star. So McCormack, already managing a few other athletes, pitched his idea of representing Arnie. Palmer agreed, but with one condition. McCormack had to drop everyone else and only represent him. McCormack agreed, and with a handshake, IMG (International Management Group) was born. It has since become a global multibillion-dollar sports, events, and talent management company.

If two people can have such faith and trust to commit the rest of their professional lives to each other with a handshake, how much more can we trust in our blessed Lord? His handshakes are the precious promises of His Word, the Holy Spirit, the redemption He provided on the cross, and the eternal home He is preparing for all who have taken hold of His hand. Alleluia, what a Savior!

....

Dear heavenly Father, thank You that I am sealed unto the day of redemption because of the price You paid for me, and for coming into my life and saving my soul! In Jesus' name I pray, amen!

Heaven, Life, and the Resurrection

WEEK 14—WEDNESDAY

I Know This!

Jesus spoke these words, lifted up His eyes to heaven, and said: "Father, the hour has come. Glorify Your Son, that Your Son also may glorify You, as You have given Him authority over all flesh, that He should give eternal life to as many as You have given Him. And this is eternal life, that they may know You, the only true God, and Jesus Christ whom You have sent."

JOHN 17:1-3

Sometimes I hear people say, "The older I get, the less I know." I know it's true of me. Former Secretary of Defense Donald Rumsfeld put it this way: "There are known knowns; there are things we know we know. There are known unknowns; that is to say, we know there are some things we do not know. But there are also unknown unknowns—the ones we don't know we don't know."

I don't know what all of that means but, I know this: At Calvary's cross, the Father glorified the Son, and the Son glorified the Father. He is all-powerful. He gives eternal life to *everyone* who will come to Him. Through the Holy Spirit, I know the only true God. I know this: Jesus was sent for us!

If you and I had only a minute or two in life to talk with one another, I would only be interested in one thing. I would hope to ask you the only question that matters: "Do you know that you know Jesus?" *I know this!*

Dear heavenly Father, thank You for saving me and knowing me. I pray that You would put people in my path who need to know You. In Jesus' name I pray, amen.

H. Marshall Thompson Jr., Riverstone Community Church, Jacksonville, FL

WEEK 14—THURSDAY

The Greatest Arrival!

So it was, when the angels had gone away from them into heaven, that the shepherds said to one another, "Let us now go to Bethlehem and see this thing that has come to pass, which the Lord has made known to us." And they came with haste and found Mary and Joseph, and the Babe lying in a manger.

LUKE 2:15-16

Once when I was making a hospital visit, I saw a young couple on the elevator. The expecting mom looked at me with a big smile and said, "We are having a baby today!" I was almost as excited as they were! They welcomed a beautiful little girl into their family. I can't think of anything more exciting than the arrival of a newborn.Such was the case for the Greatest Arrival. Just before this scene, a multitude of angels was praising God and saying, "Glory to God in the highest, and on earth peace, good will toward men" (Luke 2:14). The shepherds received the next word. Two things about them should speak to our hearts: (1) They heard from God, which means they were watching and listening for His voice, and (2) they "came with haste" (v. 16). I love what "haste" implies in Greek: "to jump over fences." In other words, the shepherds didn't allow any obstacle, any entity, any situation, to keep them from Jesus! We must follow suit on both counts. The Greatest Arrival is Jesus!

....

Dear heavenly Father, thank You for Jesus!

Heaven, Life, and the Resurrection

WEEK 14—FRIDAY

Why Worry?

Then He said to His disciples, "Therefore I say to you, do not worry about your life, what you will eat; nor about the body, what you will put on. Life is more than food, and the body is more than clothing. Consider the ravens, for they neither sow nor reap, which have neither storehouse nor barn; and God feeds them. Of how much more value are you than the birds? And which of you by worrying can add one cubit to his stature?"

LUKE 12:22-25

There is no such thing as a "respectable" sin. But have you ever noticed that there's one sin we can not only commit but might even brag about? We would never brag about being up all night robbing convenience stores, but I've heard many people say, "I was up all night worrying." When we worry, we are actually not trusting our Lord or living by faith, and "without faith it is impossible to please Him" (Hebrews 11:6). Our Lord has a much better plan and solution for the people, places, and things we tend to worry about.

The master Teacher told His disciples not only to not worry about what you might eat or wear (v. 22) or how tall you may be (v. 25) but to seek the most important thing in life, the kingdom of God. When we pursue the kingdom, not only is there no time to worry; there is also little opportunity to mistrust our Lord! Why worry?

> Dear heavenly Father, I pray that I would lean not on my own understanding today but trust You with every situation I face. In Jesus' name I pray, amen.

H. Marshall Thompson Jr., Riverstone Community Church, Jacksonville, FL

WEEK 14—WEEKEND

The Holy Trifecta!

Not unto us, O LORD, not unto us, but to Your name give glory, because of Your mercy, because of Your truth. Why should the Gentiles say, "So where is their God?" But our God is in heaven; He does whatever He pleases.

PSALM 115:1-3

A couple of years ago, I had the privilege of meeting a former professional gambler. God had saved him from that life and has greatly used him to touch many lives, including mine. He knew all too well the term "trifecta"—to pick the three top finishers of an event.

There may be no greater trifecta than the one we find in today's verses: *glory* to display magnificence and beauty; *mercy* to demonstrate compassion and forgiveness; and *truth* to convey what is accurate and right. Our Lord is the only one worthy of this Holy Trifecta and the only source of it. And we alone are in great need of this Holy Trifecta. Why would we gamble on our future and our eternity with anyone other than the living, eternal God?

The psalmist lets us know with certainty that our Lord is not only alive but cares for us, considers us, and desires the best for us. You can bet your soul on His priceless promises. There is only one "lock" in this world: that our God is the only one to be glorified. He alone is merciful. He is the source of all truth. Glory, mercy, and truth—the Holy Trifecta!

> Dear God, thank You for loving and saving me. Thank You for giving me what I do not deserve and what I could never repay. I glorify Your name. In Jesus' name I pray, amen.

Heaven, Life, and the Resurrection

WEEK 15—MONDAY

The Advantages of United Prayer

Then Daniel went to his house, and made the decision known to Hananiah, Mishael, and Azariah, his companions, that they might seek mercies from the God of heaven concerning this secret, so that Daniel and his companions might not perish with the rest of the wise men of Babylon. Then the secret was revealed to Daniel in a night vision. So Daniel blessed the God of heaven.

DANIEL 2:17-19

Have you ever found yourself in a very difficult situation when you desperately needed help in prayer? This is where Daniel and his companions found themselves when the demand of the king of Babylon came. It was altogether unreasonable to expect someone to tell the king his dream without any knowledge of it. But if they could not discern the dream and interpret it, they would be cut to pieces.

Sometimes people say, "The least I can do is pray." But prayer is the best we can do. There is power and encouragement when we gather as believers to pray. Daniel and his companions had agreed to serve God no matter what, so when the crisis came, they immediately went to the throne room of grace, and God revealed the dream.

There are many advantages of united prayer. I encourage you to be a part of a prayer group, have a prayer partner, pray together through difficult situations, and know that the power of God moves to reveal and work in these times.

....

Father, thank You for the body of Christ and the power of prayer as we gather together. We know You are the God who answers, so we unite to pray through our circumstances.

Dr. Robby Foster, Northside Baptist Church, Valdosta, GA

WEEK 15—TUESDAY

The Sense of God's Presence

Then Jacob awoke from his sleep and said, "Surely the LORD is in this place, and I did not know it." And he was afraid and said, "How awesome is this place! This is none other than the house of God, and this is the gate of heaven!"

GENESIS 28:16-17

Jacob had outwardly been a wordly man in his character. But here he identified the presence of the Lord and became a spiritual man. When God awakens us to a sense of the spiritual life, things begin to change. I believe Jacob marked this place on his spiritual journey because he knew something significant had happened. He could sense a real change, a fresh presence of God. This vision represents Jacob's conversion, and his conduct afterward gives evidence of great change.

Wherever God reveals himself impacts our lives, our thoughts, and our actions. We belong to God, and our Bethels become places where we worship and honor Him and where we value our spiritual growth. Sometimes when I enter the door of God's church on Sunday morning, I like to think, "How awesome is this place!" The church is not the only place to experience the presence of God; we should know that daily. But a Bethel, a place we identify as a marker in our spiritual journey, encourages us to continue growing and being transformed in Christ.

....

Jesus, thank You for Your abiding presence and the impact Your presence makes in my daily life.

Heaven, Life, and the Resurrection

WEEK 15—WEDNESDAY

This Life Is Real

"For as the Father has life in Himself, so He has granted the Son to have life in Himself, and has given Him authority to execute judgment also, because He is the Son of Man. Do not marvel at this; for the hour is coming in which all who are in the graves will hear His voice and come forth—those who have done good, to the resurrection of life, and those who have done evil, to the resurrection of condemnation."

JOHN 5:26-29

None of us has life in ourselves. Our life is derived from our parents and the fragile environment around us. Jesus claimed that His life was derived from no one; it is inherent and uncreated. The life of God comes forth from itself. He is the object of all dependent life.

But also know that Christ has all authority to execute judgment. A believer's life is now in Christ. I am thankful that Christ judged my sin and paid for it in full at Calvary. Real life that is eternal and can never die again is found in Christ, the Giver of life. It is amazing that Jesus came not to condemn the world but to save it (John 3:17), yet many miss the life God offers in Christ. We know we have all sinned and that the wages of that sin is death (Romans 3:23; 6:23). My desire is to see all come to the saving knowledge of Christ and have real life.

Lord Jesus, thank You for Your gift of real life and for judging my sin at Calvary. May many turn to Christ today to have real life forever.

Dr. Robby Foster, Northside Baptist Church, Valdosta, GA

WEEK 15—THURSDAY

The Baptism of Jesus

It came to pass in those days that Jesus came from Nazareth of Galilee, and was baptized by John in the Jordan. And immediately, coming up from the water, He saw the heavens parting and the Spirit descending upon Him like a dove. Then a voice came from heaven, "You are My Beloved Son, in whom I am well pleased."

MARK 1:9–11

To baptize means to immerse, symbolizing purification or regeneration. John came baptizing in the wilderness and preaching a baptism of repentance for sin. Baptism identifies believers in Christ who have repented of their sin and trusted Jesus as their Savior.

So why was Jesus baptized? He was not a sinner and did not need cleansing from sin. We know He was thirty and beginning His public ministry, and all priests were ceremonially washed at the beginning of their ministry. Christ was baptised because He chose obedience to fulfill all things (Matthew 3:15).

Baptism shows obedience to Christ and identifies with Him in death, burial, and resurrection. To repent of our sin by trusting Christ as our Savior and following His example of being baptized is scriptural baptism. It should follow conversion. Some have been baptized, sprinkled, or confirmed but never saved. If you were baptized at an early age and later saved, I pray this would encourage you to be baptized scripturally, as a believer. It is an important part of our spiritual journey.

Jesus, may truth prevail and help someone today who needs to trust Christ and be baptized.

Heaven, Life, and the Resurrection

WEEK 15—FRIDAY

Family Matters

He answered and said to the one who told Him, "Who is My mother and who are My brothers?" And He stretched out His hand toward His disciples and said, "Here are My mother and My brothers! For whoever does the will of My Father in heaven is My brother and sister and mother."

MATTHEW 12:48-50

We were all born into an earthly family. I was born to Dwayne and Myrtice Foster in Gainesville, Georgia., in 1964. I have two brothers and two sisters. My wife, Laura, was born to Bill and Jerry House in Gainesville, and she has four older brothers. Our families have grown through marriages and children. We love all of our family members and would love to see them be very blessed. We have wonderful memories, great times together, and appreciate our time we spend at Christmas together or family events. Laura and I especially love our family time with our children and grandchildren. We are proud of them and love every minute with them. Family is very important to us.

Our spiritual family is very important to us and a significant part of our spiritual journey because it will last forever. Jesus emphasized our eternal relationships. He loved Mary and his brothers, but His mission was His Father's business to rescue humanity. While the body of Christ has its earthly struggles, it is always good to remind ourselves that we belong to the family of God that will last forever. May we pray that our families will belong to the family of God.

....

Lord Jesus, we are blessed and favored to be a part of the family of God.

Dr. Robby Foster, Northside Baptist Church, Valdosta, GA

WEEK 15—WEEKEND

Be Ready

"But of that day and hour no one knows, not even the angels of heaven, but My Father only. But as the days of Noah were, so also will the coming of the Son of Man be." . . . Then two men will be in the field: one will be taken and the other left. Two women will be grinding at the mill: one will be taken and the other left. Watch therefore, for you do not know what hour your Lord is coming."

MATTHEW 24:36-37, 40-42

Jesus refers here to the question in verse 3: "What will be the sign of your coming?" The answer was unexpected: "Of that day and hour no one knows." Jesus did not identify the day but did say what the days would be like. He warned His disciples not to be deceived. There will be many false religions, wars and rumors of wars, famines, pestilences, and earthquakes. Jesus also made a reference to great tribulation, abominations that were spoken by Daniel, and days like Noah's. Then Jesus said some will be taken and others will be left.

We must not escape Jesus' emphasis at the end of these warnings. We must be ready. The world will carry on as usual. It will be marked by violence and demonic oppression. Judgment will eventually come, just as in Noah's days. We may be living in the last days. The church should be ready, faithful, and watching for Jesus's return. What would happen if we put our eyes on Jesus and saw the opportunities to minister that Jesus sees?

Lord, let us be ready today to do Your business.

Heaven, Life, and the Resurrection

WEEK 16—MONDAY

The Suffering Savior

Now Jesus, going up to Jerusalem, took the twelve disciples aside on the road and said to them, "Behold, we are going up to Jerusalem, and the Son of Man will be betrayed to the chief priests and to the scribes; and they will condemn Him to death, and deliver Him to the Gentiles to mock and to scourge and to crucify. And the third day He will rise again."

MATTHEW 20:17-19

The sufferings of Jesus Christ were no accident or miscalculation. They were no surprise or shock to Him. He gave precise details about what was going to happen. He knew why He was on earth. In His omniscience, being able to conceive all that suffering would entail, He must have suffered through it a thousand times before He actually got there.

So Jesus' suffering was not a bad turn in a nice revolution. It was foretold by many Old Testament prophets. People who accuse Jesus of being some misguided patriot or well-meaning peacemaker whose revolution went awry not only misunderstand Him but don't understand the Old Testament either. This was the culmination of God's redemptive plan. It is the gospel—what we call the "good news."

The good news is good, but bad news came with it—that the Messiah suffered. But we must understand the reason for His suffering—"The just for the unjust, that He might bring us to God" (1 Peter 3:18). We couldn't get there any other way.

....

> Jesus, thank You for finishing the work of salvation through the cross and the empty tomb!

Dr. Steven Kyle, Hiland Park Baptist Church, Panama City, FL

WEEK 16—TUESDAY

The Broken Can Become Beautiful

Then He took the five loaves and the two fish, and looking up to heaven, He blessed and broke them, and gave them to the disciples to set before the multitude. So they all ate and were filled, and twelve baskets of the leftover fragments were taken up by them.

LUKE 9:16-17

After Jesus looked to heaven and blessed the food, He broke it. It was in the breaking that the bread began to multiply. In our materialistic culture, a broken object becomes less valuable, but in God's economy, brokenness only increases the value. The bread had to be broken before it could multiply. Mary's alabaster box had to be broken before the perfume could be poured out (John 12:1-3). Gideon's clay pots and had to be broken before the light could shine (Judges 7:16-22). The roof above Jesus had to be broken before the paralyzed man could be lowered to Jesus (Mark 2:1-12). Jesus' body had to be broken before our sins could be forgiven.

Would you come to Jesus today with the little bit you have and say, "Here, Lord. It's not much, but I place it in your hands." If you think you don't have much to offer Him, I remind you that the best ability is availability. Maybe you feel broken, worthless, and useless. Jesus loves and uses the broken. It's not about who we are and what we have; it's all about Him. We may feel like insignificant biscuits and sardines, but in the hands of the Master, our lives can become something beautiful and lasting.

Father, here am I. Break me. Make me. Use me for Your glory! Amen.

Heaven, Life, and the Resurrection

WEEK 16—WEDNESDAY

He Is a Good Father

"If a son asks for bread from any father among you, will he give him a stone? Or if he asks for a fish, will he give him a serpent instead of a fish? Or if he asks for an egg, will he offer him a scorpion? If you then, being evil, know how to give good gifts to your children, how much more will your heavenly Father give the Holy Spirit to those who ask Him!"

LUKE 11:11-13

My dad wasn't perfect, but he was a great dad who coached my little league teams, took me to church, and never missed a ball game. So when Jesus says God is like a perfect father, I have a good frame of reference. Some people who were abused or abandoned by their earthly fathers have trouble seeing God like a father. But if you imagine the most ideal earthly dad possible and multiply that concept by infinity, you can begin to understand just how much God cares for you.

God is good and wants to answer your prayers. One of the greatest promises in the Bible is in Romans 8:32—"He who did not spare his own Son, but delivered Him up for us all, how shall He not with Him also freely give us all things?" God is such a loving, caring Father that He has already given you the most valuable asset in heaven: His precious, only Son to die for your sins. Since God has already done that, would He have any trouble giving you anything else?

> Dear heavenly Father, thank You for being a good Father and providing for me both physically and spiritually. Amen.

Dr. Steven Kyle, Hiland Park Baptist Church, Panama City, FL

WEEK 16—THURSDAY

His Plans Will Be Fulfilled

"Therefore behold, the days are coming that I will bring judgment on the carved images of Babylon; her whole land shall be ashamed, and all her slain shall fall in her midst. Then the heavens and the earth and all that is in them shall sing joyously over Babylon; for the plunderers shall come to her from the north," says the LORD.

JEREMIAH 51:47-48

God does not take the worship of idols lightly. He judged the false idol worship of Babylon, revealing that these carved images were unable to prevent Babylon's destruction. As a result, the heavens would sing for joy over what was to happen to them.

People on earth would have rejoiced because Babylon's iron grip had been broken and nations would be freed from its dominance. The Medo-Persian Empire would sweep in and capture Babylonian cities. What Babylon had sown it would reap, especially because of what it had done to God's people. Babylon had caused the Israel to fall; now it would itself suffer the same fate.

God is mindful of what happens to His people. Although His retribution may be delayed, we can be sure that in the end it will certainly be fulfilled. The greatest fulfillment of His judgment will be on sin. Humanity will one day be condemned because of our sin. But thanks be to God, even in His righteous judgment, He graciously offers a pardon for those who will trust in Jesus.

God, I praise You in all Your works. Thank You for the hope of grace. Amen.

Heaven, Life, and the Resurrection

WEEK 16—FRIDAY

The Mercy of Discipline

Then the L*ord* *God said, "Behold, the man has become like one of Us, to know good and evil. And now, lest he put out his hand and take also of the tree of life, and eat, and live forever"—therefore the* L*ord* *God sent him out of the garden of Eden to till the ground from which he was taken.*

GENESIS 3:22-23

Adam and Eve were forcibly evicted from Eden. The serpent told Eve she would become like God when she knew good and evil. That was a half-truth. By sinning, Adam and Eve knew evil personally. Sometimes personal knowledge leads to destruction; by sinning, they entered a realm of experience that cost them dearly.

So God cast them out for their own good. If they had stayed in Eden and eaten from the Tree of Life, they would have lived forever in sin, separated from God. Eden would have become like hell. Paradise would not only have been lost but would have become a prison. It may have been humiliating, but it was also merciful. If God let them stay, they would have been doomed and damned. They were sent "out of Eden," to the hard earth now filled with danger on every side.

Our sin has likewise separated us from God, and we deserve the harshest penalty. But God offers mercy and grace through Jesus. It is sin that separates. It is salvation by grace through faith that reconciles.

....

Lord, thank You for Your love that covers a multitude of sins. Amen.

Dr. Steven Kyle, Hiland Park Baptist Church, Panama City, FL

WEEK 16—WEEKEND

Am I Ready?

"Whoever seeks to save his life will lose it, and whoever loses his life will preserve it. I tell you, in that night there will be two men in one bed: the one will be taken and the other will be left. Two women will be grinding together: the one will be taken and the other left. Two men will be in the field: the one will be taken and the other left."

LUKE 17:33-36

Jesus will come for you in one of two ways. Either you'll meet Him in death, or He will return before your death. Either way, you need to be prepared. Your death may happen suddenly or slowly; His return will be sudden and surprising.

God wants everyone to be saved, but only those who accept His grace enter into His family. When Jesus comes for His church, some will be taken and others left. Two men may be working together in a field. Two women may be working next to each other in an office. In each case, one may be taken and the other left.

There is no question about whether Christ is going to come. The only remaining question is whether you will be ready. And only you can answer that question. Jesus said, "Therefore you also be ready, for the Son of Man is coming at an hour you do not expect" (Matthew 24:44). Have you ever turned from your sins and placed your faith in Jesus? That's the only way to know for certain you'll be ready to meet Jesus.

Lord, thank You for making a way of salvation through Jesus. In His name, amen.

Heaven, Life, and the Resurrection

WEEK 17, MONDAY

God's Forward Blessing

"Blessing I will bless you, and multiplying I will multiply your descendants as the stars of the heaven and as the sand which is on the seashore; and your descendants shall possess the gate of their enemies. In your seed all the nations of the earth shall be blessed, because you have obeyed My voice."

GENESIS 22:17-18

What Abraham and Isaac did on the altar that day brought blessing and change to the entire world. Abraham found that God's name that day was Jehovah-Jireh, "the Lord will provide." The Jewish temple was built on Mount Moriah, and during the Lord's ministry, He could be found there. He was the true Lamb of God provided for the sins of the world.

Sufferings brought about by God's will always bring about His blessings. Abraham would have been very discouraged if all he had seen on Mount Moriah was a sacrifice. But with eyes of faith, he saw a blessing. He believed God's promise that his descendants would be as numerous as the stars in the sky and the sand on the sea.

Abraham came away from his trial with a deeper love for the Lord than ever. In the words of an old song by John Henry Sammis, "When we walk with the Lord in the light of His Word, what a glory He sheds on our way. While we do His good will, He abides with us still and with all who will trust and obey. Trust and obey, for there's no other way, to be happy in Jesus, but to trust and obey."

Jesus, thank You for Your many blessings! Amen.

Tim Anderson, Clements Baptist Church, Athens, AL

WEEK 17, TUESDAY

A Martyr's Vision

When they heard these things they were cut to the heart, and they gnashed at him with their teeth. But he, being full of the Holy Spirit, gazed into heaven and saw the glory of God, and Jesus standing at the right hand of God, and said, "Look! I see the heavens opened and the Son of Man standing at the right hand of God!"

ACTS 7:54-56

The human heart has not changed, nor will it ever apart from the grace of God. Stephen preached a great, Spirit-filled sermon, but he did not receive any accolades from the religious leaders that day. He was stoned to death for his faithfulness. It was the Word of God that upset the people, and it's still that way today; people get upset when God's Word is preached. Stephen's message "cut to their hearts," and the Word revealed the unbelief of the people.

Notice the difference in their responses. Stephen's accusers were so angry that they gnashed their teeth at him; meanwhile, he was full of the Holy Spirit. Prior to his stoning, he had a vision of the glory of God. The Father was preparing him for his death. He saw the heavens opened and Jesus waiting at His Father's right hand. What a vision!

God did something for Stephen that He will still do for us today. He will give us the grace to forgive our persecutors and the ability to pray for them (Acts 7:59–60). That's kingdom living at its best.

Jesus, please help me always to practice the power of forgiveness. Amen.

Heaven, Life, and the Resurrection

WEEK 17, WEDNESDAY

Jesus, the Bread of Life

"This is the bread which comes down from heaven, that one may eat of it and not die. I am the living bread which came down from heaven. If anyone eats of this bread, he will live forever; and the bread that I shall give is My flesh, which I shall give for the life of the world."

JOHN 6:50-51

Into this fallen world of disappointment, despair, and desperation came the Lord Jesus Christ. He is the bread of life, the only One who can satisfy the human soul's deepest longings. Our Lord loved to use words to paint eternal pictures and metaphors. He called Himself the bread of life (John 6:35, 51); the light of the world (John 8:12); the door of the sheep (John 10:7); the resurrection and the life (John 11:25); the good shepherd (John 10:11); the way, the truth, and the life (John 14:6); and the vine (John 15:1, 5).

When Jesus called Himself the living bread, He wasn't claiming to be exactly like the manna in the wilderness. He was claiming to be even greater. The manna sustained life, but Jesus gives life to the world. Israelites ate the daily bread and eventually died, but we live forever when we trust in Jesus. Manna was an earthly gift; Jesus is an eternal gift. Israelites had to eat the manna every day, but as sinners who come to Jesus once, we are given eternal life.

It isn't hard to see the parallel between Jesus and manna. He is not far from sinners, who only must humble themselves and take the gift God offers.

Jesus, thank You for feeding me with Your life. Amen.

Tim Anderson, Clements Baptist Church, Athens, AL

WEEK 17—THURSDAY

Suffering, Death, and Resurrection

From that time Jesus began to show to His disciples that He must go to Jerusalem, and suffer many things from the elders and chief priests and scribes, and be killed, and be raised the third day. Then Peter took Him aside and began to rebuke Him, saying, "Far be it from You, Lord; this shall not happen to You!" But He turned and said to Peter, "Get behind Me, Satan! You are an offense to Me, for you are not mindful of the things of God, but the things of men."

MATTHEW 16:21-23

I often find myself just like the disciples, not fully understanding what the Holy Spirit tells me. Or perhaps I simply don't listen. Jesus often told His disciples of His coming death, but they did not fully understand until the resurrection. On the other hand, the disciples understood Jesus' words all too well. Otherwise, why would Peter have tried to discourage Jesus from this way of thinking? The problem was not their understanding of the words but that suffering did not fit into their idea of what Jesus should do. Beware of advice like, "Surely God doesn't want you to do this." Often our most difficult temptations come from those who try to protect us the most.

Jesus' rebuke of Peter teaches us an important principle: that true discipleship always involves a cost. Without the cost of the cross, there would be no salvation because there would be no Savior. It is easy to limit Jesus' impact on our lives when we are so preoccupied with our earthly goals.

Lord, I am so guilty; help me always to count the cost of following You. Amen.

Heaven, Life, and the Resurrection

WEEK 17—FRIDAY

Finding Refuge in Our God

The LORD is in His holy temple, the LORD's throne is in heaven; His eyes behold, His eyelids test the sons of men. The LORD tests the righteous, but the wicked and the one who loves violence His soul hates. . . . For the LORD is righteous, He loves righteousness; His countenance beholds the upright.

PSALM 11:4–5, 7

It's so important to remember that the eyes of the Lord search the whole earth in order to strengthen those who are fully committed to Him (2 Chronicles 16:9). He tests the righteous to confirm their dependence on Him. There are many examples in the Bible of people fleeing: Adam and Eve, Saul, Jonah, Israel, Judah, and Peter. But how should the church respond to the current evils we are facing? The Bible gives us two choices: either we can flee to the hills or take refuge in God.

When the pressures of life come rolling in, Scripture calls us to hide ourselves in God. Only our Lord can offer us true refuge from what we are facing in today's world. But simply taking our heavenly seat beside the Lord does not shield us from all pain and suffering. It does mean God is concerned with what concerns us. He is always carrying out His perfect plan in our lives. We should therefore always take our worship seriously. We should proudly sing with John Newton, "Through many dangers, toils, and snares I have already come. 'Tis grace that brought me safe thus far and grace will lead me home."

Jesus, I need Thee every hour, every hour I need Thee. Amen.

Tim Anderson, Clements Baptist Church, Athens, AL

WEEK 17—WEEKEND

Joy Does Eventually Come

O LORD, You brought my soul up from the grave; You have kept me alive, that I should not go down to the pit. Sing praise to the LORD, you saints of His, and give thanks at the remembrance of His holy name. For His anger is but for a moment, His favor is for life; weeping may endure for a night, but joy comes in the morning.

PSALM 30:3-5

Our world is in a very challenging time—fights against disease, injustice, and numerous other threats that have brought fear, uncertainty, sickness, and even death. The night can seem long, but joy is always coming for the child of God.

Jesus experienced long nights too—especially in the Garden of Gethsemane, where He was arrested before being beaten, broken, and placed upon an old, rugged cross to die. He brought joy to the world with the dawning of the first Easter Sunday morning, when He rose from the dead. Through His resurrection, our Lord announced that not even death gets the final word. Jesus does, and He brings the joy of eternal life to those who have placed their faith and trust in him.

In the words of an old pastor and hymn writer, Edward Mote: "My hope is built on nothing less than Jesus Christ, my righteousness; I dare not trust the sweetest frame, but wholly lean on Jesus' name. On Christ, the solid rock, I stand; all other ground is sinking sand."

Jesus, thank You for the joy You always bring. Amen.

Heaven, Life, and the Resurrection

WEEK 18—MONDAY

What Would It Require?

"This is the interpretation, O king, and this is the decree of the Most High, which has come upon my lord the king: They shall drive you from men, your dwelling shall be with the beasts of the field, and they shall make you eat grass like oxen. They shall wet you with the dew of heaven, and seven times shall pass over you, till you know that the Most High rules in the kingdom of men, and gives it to whomever He chooses."

DANIEL 4:24–25

What is required of God to help you recognize who He is? We can convince ourselves that it was our skill, our ability, and our personal aptitude that brought about great successes and accomplishments. It has been said that the greatest test is not in how people respond to adversity but in how they handle success. We would be wise to quickly recognize the Lord as the one who blesses us with the gifts and skills needed to experience success and overcome the challenges we face.

The Lord has a way of bringing us to this recognition when we swell in pride and conceit. An extended season living among oxen in the field was what Nebuchadnezzar needed to understand the Lord whose "kingdom is from generation to generation" (Daniel 4:34). When the goodness of God blesses us, let's be quick to recognize Him as the Giver of every good and perfect gift (James 1:17).

> Father, I pray that my heart would always recognize You alone as the Most High, the Giver of every good and perfect gift. In Jesus' name I pray, amen.

Steven Blanton, Ebenezer Baptist Church, Hendersonville, NC

WEEK 18—TUESDAY

What Will Be Said of Me When I'm Gone?

And behold, the word of the Lord *came to him, saying, "This one shall not be your heir, but one who will come from your own body shall be your heir." Then He brought him outside and said, "Look now toward heaven, and count the stars if you are able to number them." And He said to him, "So shall your descendants be." And he believed in the* Lord, *and He accounted it to him for righteousness.*

GENESIS 15:4-6

Have you ever considered what will be said of you when you have passed into eternity? It's a sobering question. In today's passage, we read one of the best descriptions that could be written of someone's life.

Abraham and Sarah had hoped for a child, but a barren womb prevented that dream from becoming reality—until the day God promised them a son who would be their heir. They were both old—"as good as dead," as Paul said of Abraham (Romans 4:19). But the Lord made a promise, and while the promise would require a miracle, He would indeed give them a son. But that's not the most important detail of Abraham's life. Perhaps the greatest phrase from Scripture concerning his life is in verse 6: "And he believed in the Lord." When our life comes to an end, may people describe our lives by that simple phrase: "[your name] truly believed in the Lord."

Father, when my life on earth is over, please let it be said of me that I believed in You. For Your glory I ask this in Jesus' name, amen.

Heaven, Life, and the Resurrection

WEEK 18—WEDNESDAY

Will I Be Ready?

For as the lightning that flashes out of one part under heaven shines to the other part under heaven, so also the Son of Man will be in His day. But first He must suffer many things and be rejected by this generation. And as it was in the days of Noah, so it will be also in the days of the Son of Man.

LUKE 17:24-26

A lightning bolt can travel at an amazing speed—by some estimates, up to 270,000 miles per hour or 3,700 miles per second. To say that's fast would be an understatement. The Lord Jesus used this meteorological fact to describe His return to earth.

There is much debate about when the Lord Jesus will return to gather His church to Himself. But one thing is for certain: He is coming back. In the days of Noah, all of humanity was eating, drinking, and giving in marriage as if life would go on as usual. But when God's mercy shifted to judgment, the earth's population, save Noah and his family, was destroyed in His wrath. For some, the lightning-like return of Christ will mean immediate separation from God, but for genuine believers, it will mean the "glorious appearing of our great God and Savior Jesus Christ" (Titus 2:13). As sure as the flood in Noah's day began with a single drop of rain, Jesus will also come in a flash of glory to receive His church unto Himself. Today could be the day! Will you be ready?

> Father, I pray Your grace and kindness would move my heart to readiness for the imminent return of Your Son. I pray this in Jesus' name, amen.

Steven Blanton, Ebenezer Baptist Church, Hendersonville, NC

WEEK 18—THURSDAY

How Will I Respond?

Then Jesus, looking at him, loved him, and said to him, "One thing you lack: Go your way, sell whatever you have and give to the poor, and you will have treasure in heaven; and come, take up the cross, and follow Me." But he was sad at this word, and went away sorrowful, for he had great possessions.

MARK 10:21-22

With many stories in Scripture, I wonder how would I have responded if I had been there. If I were the "rich young ruler," would I have obeyed the Lord and abandoned all or gone away sorrowful because I "had great possessions"? We all have to face the question: will I take up my cross and follow Christ?

Having possessions may not be a sin, but this young man's possessions had become an idol, an extension of his identity. He needed to learn that his heart was not capable of worshipping both God and his possessions. There is room for only one master in the heart (Matthew 6:24). The text reveals his decision, but the encounter he had with Jesus is one we all must face.

Maybe as you read this, the Spirit is reminding you of a prompting you would rather have ignored today. Please hear Him saying, "Follow Me." God is writing your story, and you're one of two key characters in the narrative. How will you respond?

> Father, help me put away the fear of abandoning all to follow You. The cross is scary, but the grace You give is greater than the cost of following You. Desiring a closer walk with You, I ask this in Jesus' name, amen.

Heaven, Life, and the Resurrection

WEEK 18—FRIDAY

Where Are You Lord?

Now a certain man was sick, Lazarus of Bethany, the town of Mary and her sister Martha. . . . Therefore the sisters sent to Him, saying, "Lord, behold, he whom You love is sick." When Jesus heard that, He said, "This sickness is not unto death, but for the glory of God, that the Son of God may be glorified through it."

JOHN 11:1, 3–4

Life can be hard. Any day can present us with challenges we find difficult to understand or explain. When Jesus' delay resulted in Lazarus' death, Martha and Mary were in the depths of grief and despair. But when Jesus called Lazarus from the tomb, they would quickly understand why all of this happened.

When we're tempted to scream, "Where are You, Lord?" it is usually because we don't know why we're suffering or understand God's plan in the moment. When we feel abandoned, we would do well to remember two principles. First, God will not waste a trial or difficulty in our life; He will use the struggle for our good and His glory. Second, when the Lord allows things we don't understand, we must surrender the "why" to Him. Until He chooses to answer the "why," we must rest in the hope that He knows exactly what He is doing and will make sense of the senseless in time or eternity.

> Father, I believe You are in total control, even in my suffering. Help me not forget what I know to be true of You when I don't understand what is happening in or around me. Resting in Your grace, I ask this in Jesus' name, amen.

Steven Blanton, Ebenezer Baptist Church, Hendersonville, NC

WEEK 18—WEEKEND

Will I Acknowledge Him?

Sing to the Lord *with thanksgiving; sing praises on the harp to our God, who covers the heavens with clouds, who prepares rain for the earth, who makes grass to grow on the mountains. He gives to the beast its food, and to the young ravens that cry. . . . The* Lord *takes pleasure in those who fear Him, in those who hope in His mercy.*

PSALM 147:7-9, 11

Praise and thanksgiving pour out of an attentive heart. Some of the most ungrateful people we know are those who just can't seem to see the bountiful blessing of what they already have. Covetousness, the lust and desire for more, springs from an ungrateful heart.

In today's text, the psalmist praises and thanks God because of what he has come to recognize about Him. He acknowledges that it is the Lord who provides rain for harvests and the beauty of the mountains. It is God who feeds the beasts of the field and the birds of the air. As we recognize the authority and work of God, it is faith-building to see the psalmist's description of how God acknowledges us: "The Lord takes pleasure in those who fear Him, in those who hope in His mercy." May He help us recognize the One who crafted the mountains, fashioned the heavens, and provides for the earth. He takes pleasure in the joy we find in Him.

Father, You are the only God, Creator and Sustainer of all things. Today I acknowledge You as my God. I pray that the joy I find in You would continually increase and fill my soul. I ask this in Jesus' name, amen.

Heaven, Life, and the Resurrection

WEEK 19—MONDAY

He Will Do It Again!

"Behold, God works all these things, twice, in fact, three times with a man, to bring back his soul from the Pit, that he may be enlightened with the light of life. "Give ear, Job, listen to me; hold your peace, and I will speak. If you have anything to say, answer me; speak, for I desire to justify you. If not, listen to me; hold your peace, and I will teach you wisdom."

JOB 33:29-33

Elihu reminded Job that God had rescued him before, and as the Maker of heaven and earth, He would do it again. The same God is mindful of you, even to the point of numbering the hairs on your head (Luke 12:7).

Henry Ford is thought to have said, "If I asked people what they wanted, they would have said faster horses." God doesn't want us merely to believe He can make us a better, faster, version of ourselves. He wants to make us new, and sometimes that happens in times of suffering. Like Ford, Job had to look beyond being made better to being made over, a new creation. The master Potter spins the clay on his wheel, seeing not what is currently there but the potential being fashioned in his hands. And when He does see imperfections in you, He doesn't throw you away; He makes you new. You are a vessel of honor just waiting to be made or remade, especially in suffering.

God, thank You for not throwing away the clay! I am in a difficult time right now, but I pray I'm being shaped into Your image. Help me rest well tonight, that I may be a reflector of Your tender mercies. Amen.

Marc Pritchett, NorthRidge Church of Thomaston, Meansville, GA

WEEK 19—TUESDAY

Forging New Trails

He who overcomes, I will make him a pillar in the temple of My God, and he shall go out no more. I will write on him the name of My God and the name of the city of My God, the New Jerusalem, which comes down out of heaven from My God. And I will write on him My new name. "He who has an ear, let him hear what the Spirit says to the churches."

REVELATION 3:12-13

What Jesus promised the church in Philadelphia, He also promises to us, New Testament Christians, if we love the Lord with all our hearts. Our love for Jesus prompts us to love other believers with the same godly love. With God's name written on our hearts, we become "pillars"—literally "unshaken ones"—of the church.

Are you unshaken by current events, or are you moved by every wind of change? It's time to stop following the leader. Christians must forge new trails and take higher ground in order to live for Jesus. The world is screaming for us to follow their leader or to align with the status quo. You may feel as if you have to dredge through the briars and vines of this chaotic world, but know that believers are setting new examples—the ones we want our children and grandchildren to follow as we navigate them to Jesus. Do not follow where the path may take you. Go instead where there is no path and leave a new trail—the right one!

....

Jesus, thank You for giving me the guidance in Your Word to follow Your example, to walk in the paths of Your righteousness! Amen.

Heaven, Life, and the Resurrection

WEEK 19—WEDNESDAY

Dreaming Big for His Glory!

The heavens declare the glory of God; and the firmament shows His handiwork. Day unto day utters speech, and night unto night reveals knowledge. There is no speech nor language where their voice is not heard. Their line has gone out through all the earth, and their words to the end of the world. In them He has set a tabernacle for the sun, which is like a bridegroom coming out of his chamber, and rejoices like a strong man to run its race.

PSALM 19:1-5

I have heard it said, "If people aren't laughing at your dreams, your dreams aren't big enough!" I love that because I dream big. Do you? Or do you just live out a "come what may" existence? David's psalm assures us that God is too vast for you just to survive; it's time to start thriving for His glory! He really does want to do "exceedingly abundantly above all that we ask or think" (Ephesians 3:20).

Aside from knowing Christ, however, our dreams are just lofty pursuits. But *in* Jesus, our dreams can have historic consequences. The passage goes on to say, "according to the power that works in us, *to Him be glory* in the church by Christ Jesus to all generations" (vv. 20–21). This great "work" Jesus wants us to dream about will be life changing, and it will *all* be about Him and for His glory. Now, that's a big dream!

God, tonight as I lay my head upon my pillow, fill my heart with the joy of knowing You have used me to accomplish all You've place in my heart this day, for Your glory, in Jesus' name, amen!

Marc Pritchett, NorthRidge Church of Thomaston, Meansville, GA

WEEK 19—THURSDAY

Be Glorified in Me

God came from Teman, the Holy One from Mount Paran. His glory covered the heavens, and the earth was full of His praise. His brightness was like the light; He had rays flashing from His hand, and there His power was hidden. . . . He stood and measured the earth; He looked and startled the nations. And the everlasting mountains were scattered, the perpetual hills bowed. His ways are everlasting.

HABAKKUK 3:3-4, 6

How often have you tried to pray yourself out of extreme difficultly? If you're like most, every time you face a struggle. But what if God brought you to this desolate place to make you stronger and to make Him known? Would it be worth it? Would it change your prayer?

Habakkuk prayed for revival and began praising the God of revival. That's what God wants for us—to embrace the uncertainty, trust Him in the wait, and enjoy the beauty of the storm. That's where we listen to Him best. He allows for times of extreme difficulty, knowing He will have our full attention, and only His glory remains. In Gethsemane, Jesus, in His humanity, would rather not have taken the path of flogging and crucifixion but was more concerned about bringing glory to His Father, no matter what. I challenge you today to be more interested in the Father's will than your momentary inconvenience. After all, He is Lord over the storm too.

> Jesus, thank You for using me to further Your kingdom. Thank You for allowing me to move past my own convenience for the sake of another. Tonight, I will rest in You. Amen.

Heaven, Life, and the Resurrection

WEEK 19—FRIDAY

He Alone Is Worthy!

While the word was still in the king's mouth, a voice fell from heaven: "King Nebuchadnezzar, to you it is spoken: the kingdom has departed from you! And they shall drive you from men, and your dwelling shall be with the beasts of the field. They shall make you eat grass like oxen; and seven times shall pass over you, until you know that the Most High rules in the kingdom of men, and gives it to whomever He chooses."

DANIEL 4:31-32

Nebuchadnezzar took credit for the glory of his kingdom when all glory belonged to God. The same is true for our salvation; God deserves all the glory. Since we can't save ourselves, all honor in the redemption Jesus gained for us by His sinless life, atoning death, and resurrection belongs to Him.

Paul, acknowledging his perseverance rather than striving for some spiritual utopia, went on to say that "Jesus Christ has laid hold of me" (Philippians 3:12), giving purpose to everything he did to take the gospel to others in spite of opposition. We too must realize that our salvation and daily perseverance are not based on what we've been through and overcome but what Jesus has been through and overcome for us to live eternally secure in Him. Our fuel is to be more like Him and live out audacious faith, acknowledging the hold He has on our lives—never forgetting that He alone deserves all the glory!

....

> Jesus, help me walk in the assurance of what Your salvation has granted me, to share the gospel with everyone I can, as You hold me close in my own salvation. Jesus, be glorified in me. Amen!

Marc Pritchett, NorthRidge Church of Thomaston, Meansville, GA

WEEK 19—WEEKEND

It Will Be as He Said . . . Do Not Fear

For this they willfully forget: that by the word of God the heavens were of old, and the earth standing out of water and in the water, by which the world that then existed perished, being flooded with water. But the heavens and the earth which are now preserved by the same word, are reserved for fire until the day of judgment and perdition of ungodly men.

2 PETER 3:5-7

"Fear is a liar." It sounds like a great title for song, but it's also a truth we need to learn. Fear of a snake, a housefire, or a shark is completely normal. In fact, *not to fear any of those in the moment may be insanity!* But when fear of a pandemic, election, social unrest, or any other problem keeps you from living in peace, it's not of God. The earth is being preserved by God's Word.

We live in a fear-mongering culture, and we are taking the bait—hook, line, and sinker. But "God has not given us a spirit of fear, but of power and of love and of a sound mind" (2 Timothy 1:7). We need to stop being afraid of everything that could go wrong and start be excited about what could go right. "Do not fear" appears numerous times in Scripture because God knows the enemy uses fear to diminish our confidence and limit our victories. Fear is real, but faith is stronger. Tap into God's power and love, and you'll gain a sound mind. Let's make fear an afterthought!

> Thank You, Jesus, for the gift of Your power and love! Today, I choose to combat my fear with Your truth! Help me rest in that same confidence tonight and wake up tomorrow and face my faith. Amen.

Heaven, Life, and the Resurrection

WEEK 20—MONDAY

The Prayer Request of Jesus Christ

Now the multitude of those who believed were of one heart and one soul; neither did anyone say that any of the things he possessed was his own, but they had all things in common. And with great power the apostles gave witness to the resurrection of the Lord Jesus. And great grace was upon them all.

ACTS 4:32-33

Jesus Christ asked for oneness among His followers (John 17:21). He taught that the second greatest commandment is to "love your neighbor as yourself" (Mark 12:31). Paul defined what this looks like: "Do nothing from selfishness or empty conceit, but with humility consider one another as more important than yourselves" (Philippians 2:3, NASB). Love, sacrifice, generosity, and service are the foundational for those who follow Jesus.

We will never make an impact on every life God wants us to impact unless we have this attitude of love and service. We will not be able to forgive, sacrifice, and be generous toward others unless we have first been filled with the love of our living God. I love today's verses about God empowering the apostles to witness to Jesus' resurrection and "great grace" coming upon all believers. When our hearts are full of God's love and grace for us, we will reveal love and grace toward others "with great power." Seek to know God in His great love toward you today and then allow that love to shine through you. Go out and act in love toward the people around you.

> Lord, help me show boundless love and grace to others. I want to be the person that others can count on. Amen.

Chris Dixon, Liberty Baptist Church, Dublin, GA

WEEK 20—TUESDAY

Without God, We Cannot, Without Us, God Will Not

"For behold, I create new heavens and a new earth; and the former shall not be remembered or come to mind. But be glad and rejoice forever in what I create; for behold, I create Jerusalem as a rejoicing, and her people a joy. I will rejoice in Jerusalem, and joy in My people; the voice of weeping shall no longer be heard in her, nor the voice of crying."

ISAIAH 65:17-19

Isaiah prophesied of a time when the people had returned to their land from exile in Babylon. But they had returned to devastated communities and empty homes, a culture in ruins. Everything had to be rebuilt. But to people beaten down by years of oppression, God had already spoken a fresh and powerful word.

God plays the crucial role in rebuilding a nation, but He does not work alone. He and the people worked together. God would "create new heavens and a new earth" (v. 17), but the people would "build houses and . . . plant vineyards" (v. 21).

We all desire better days in our homes and nation, but we too often allow selfish desires and past experiences to distract us from becoming the people God wants us to be and doing what He wants us to do. It is tempting to wait for God to rebuild everything around us. But as Augustine said, "Without God, we cannot. Without us, God will not." We face obstacles and challenges, but we are strengthened by God's promises as we work in returning sinful, separated people to Him through His Son.

Lord, help me stay strong and have faith despite the challenges our country faces. Amen.

Heaven, Life, and the Resurrection

WEEK 20—WEDNESDAY

The Priorities of Prayer

So He said to them, "When you pray, say: Our Father in heaven, hallowed be Your name. Your kingdom come. Your will be done on earth as it is in heaven. Give us day by day our daily bread. And forgive us our sins, for we also forgive everyone who is indebted to us. And do not lead us into temptation, but deliver us from the evil one."

LUKE 11:2-4

Prayer that turns God's promises into performance. I am convinced that Christ followers believe in the importance of prayer but don't have confidence that their prayers will be answered. This disconnect happens because we do not hold our prayers accountable to Jesus' teachings and the conditions of prayer.

Our first priority in prayer is seeking God's will over our own ("Your kingdom come"). The second priority is acknowledging God's sufficiency in supplying all of our needs ("our daily bread"). The third is to get right with others in order to be right with God ("Forgive us . . . for we also forgive"). The fourth is righteousness ("Do not lead us into temptation"). In order to accomplish things around us, prayer must accomplish some things in us. If we become obedient, God will lead us to pray according to His plans because we are now His people. When we prioritize these things, God will answer our prayers in powerful and mighty ways!

Lord, I know You are always listening. I trust Your plans and have faith that You will always provide. Amen.

Chris Dixon, Liberty Baptist Church, Dublin, GA

WEEK 20—THURSDAY

The Heart of God

Then little children were brought to Him that He might put His hands on them and pray, but the disciples rebuked them. But Jesus said, "Let the little children come to Me, and do not forbid them; for of such is the kingdom of heaven." And He laid His hands on them and departed from there.

MATTHEW 19:13-15

This is a beautiful picture of the heart of God. We often feel that He is inattentive to our circumstances and needs, but nothing could be further from the truth. God's response to us is, "Let the little children come to Me."

Whenever we come to Jesus, He is attentive, available, and able. He wants us to trust Him with our daily cares and concerns. Mark wrote that Jesus was "displeased" with the disciples for hindering the children (Mark 10:14). Why? God desires a close, intimate walk with us.

Jesus is calling you to come to Him. Bring your burdens, cares, dreams, and plans. Spend time with Him, listen to His voice, and experience His love for you. Do not allow the hindrances of life to keep you from experiencing the joy, peace, and direction that only comes from time in His presence. "Come to Me, all who are weary and burdened, and I will give you rest. . . . I am gentle and humble in heart, and you will find rest for your souls" (Matthew 11:28-29, NASB). Only in His presence is fullness of joy! (Psalm 16:11).

....

Lord, when I am discouraged help me stay positive and find peace. I know You will lead me on the right course. In Christ's name, amen!

Heaven, Life, and the Resurrection

WEEK 20—FRIDAY

Faith Is the Key to Victory

When Jesus heard it, He marveled, and said to those who followed, "Assuredly, I say to you, I have not found such great faith, not even in Israel! And I say to you that many will come from east and west, and sit down with Abraham, Isaac, and Jacob in the kingdom of heaven."

MATTHEW 8:10-11

If Jesus came back today, how many people of faith would he find? God is looking for faithful people—"those whose heart is completely His" (2 Chronicles 16:9). He wants to bless us and use our lives to bless others, and faithfulness is the key to unlocking His blessings in our lives. If you have faith in our great God, you will see God do great things (Matthew 9:29).

Faith is so powerful that when you place a little in a big God, you get big results. Faith turns dreams into reality, the basis for any miracle. God still does miracles through prayer and faith. But truly faithful people who trust God and live for Christ can be hard to find.

God's great desire for us is faithfulness. Faith is the key to victory. The greater our faith, the more victory we will experience. "For whatever is born of God overcomes the world; and this is the victory that has overcome the world—our faith" (1 John 5:4, NASB). Faith is belief with legs on it. Everything we truly believe, we obey. Everything else is just religious talk.

> Lord, I am a faithful follower and believe in Your miracles. I will always place my trust in You. Amen.

Chris Dixon, Liberty Baptist Church, Dublin, GA

WEEK 20—WEEKEND

God Is Watching

Blessed is the nation whose God is the Lord, the people He has chosen as His own inheritance. The Lord looks from heaven; He sees all the sons of men. From the place of His dwelling He looks on all the inhabitants of the earth; He fashions their hearts individually; He considers all their works.

PSALM 33:12-15

These powerful words remind us of the blessings that come from aligning with God's priorities. But we are also reminded of God's watchful eye over our lives. One day, there will be an audit of your life. You will give an account for how you used everything God gave you—your gifts, relationships, opportunities, mind, money, and time. It doesn't matter how much or little you have. God is watching and testing you and wants to see how you handle what you have been given.

You can decide what you want your life to be about and start making choices that show God you want to live for what really matters. Today is the day you have been given. We all need to make the most of what we have with the time He has given us. Do not spend your life thinking about what you want to do "one day" or wishing you could do more. Do something today that will matter tomorrow. Invest your time, talents, resources, words, and love in others today. When you use your resources to make an eternal difference, you will be rewarded and will hear God say to you, "Well done" (Matthew 10:42; 25:21).

> Lord, show me how to share and invest my gifts with others. I want to use the gifts You have given me. Amen.

Heaven, Life, and the Resurrection

WEEK 21—MONDAY

Treasure Hunters

Of this salvation the prophets have inquired and searched carefully, who prophesied of the grace that would come to you. . . . To them it was revealed that, not to themselves, but to us they were ministering the things which now have been reported to you through those who have preached the gospel to you by the Holy Spirit sent from heaven—things which angels desire to look into.

1 PETER 1:10, 12

My wife's favorite movie is the 2004 action-adventure *National Treasure*. Nicholas Cage plays a historian and amateur cryptologist searching for an immense treasure hidden during the Revolutionary War. In the end, Cage finds the fortune by stealing the Declaration of Independence, cracking the code, and overcoming impossible obstacles along the way.

The word "search" means to seek diligently for something, especially something hidden, like miners digging for precious metals in the depths of the earth. It was first used to describe a dog sniffing out something with his nose.

In 1 Peter 1:10, we find the prophets of old searching for the great treasure of grace and salvation through the coming Messiah. The gospel is a treasure of eternal importance. We should search out the truths of the Word of God like those who search for buried treasure. The tragedy is that people too often show more zeal in acquiring material wealth than spiritual treasures.

....

Gracious Father, help me remember the true value of the gospel of Jesus Christ. By God's grace, may I value eternal rewards more than earthly treasure. In Christ's name, amen.

Dr. Jim Perdue, Second Baptist Church, Warner Robins, GA

WEEK 21—TUESDAY

Coming to Your Senses

And at the end of the time I, Nebuchadnezzar, lifted my eyes to heaven, and my understanding returned to me; and I blessed the Most High and praised and honored Him who lives forever: For His dominion is an everlasting dominion, and His kingdom is from generation to generation. All the inhabitants of the earth are reputed as nothing; He does according to His will in the army of heaven and among the inhabitants of the earth. No one can restrain His hand or say to Him, "What have You done?"

DANIEL 4:34-35

Legendary boxer Muhammad Ali was once asked by a flight attendant to fasten his seat belt. Ali, known for his claim to be the greatest boxer in history, turned to her and said, "Superman doesn't need a seat belt." She calmly replied, "Superman doesn't need an airplane either."

Nebuchadnezzar thought he was Superman. After being warned by Daniel about his pride, the Babylonian king was struck with insanity. The Lord restored his mind, but only after he had spent seven years in a field, acting like a wild animal. He went from being full of himself to being full of gratitude to God.

At the time God appointed, Nebuchadnezzar came to the end of himself and his selfish pride. When he came to his senses, he saw God for who He is and himself for who he was. The Bible tells us, "God resists the proud, but gives grace to the humble" (James 4:6; 1 Peter 5:5) When we get our eyes off of ourselves and fix our eyes on Jesus, we begin to understand just how truly amazing God is.

Lord, help me remember that You are the highest God. Your dominion is an everlasting dominion, and Your kingdom is from generation to generation.

WEEK 21—WEDNESDAY

The City of God

But you have come to Mount Zion and to the city of the living God, the heavenly Jerusalem, to an innumerable company of angels, to the general assembly and church of the firstborn who are registered in heaven, to God the Judge of all, to the spirits of just men made perfect, to Jesus the Mediator of the new covenant, and to the blood of sprinkling that speaks better things than that of Abel.

HEBREWS 12:22–24

A Philadelphia law firm sent flowers to an associate in Baltimore upon the opening of its new offices. Through an embarrassing mix-up, the note on the floral arrangement read, "Deepest sympathy." When the florist was informed of his mistake, he was horrified. "Good heavens!" he exclaimed. "Then the flowers that went to the funeral said, 'Congratulations on your new location!'"

Heaven will be a wonderful new location. Hebrews 12 gives us a glimpse into our heavenly destination made possible only by grace and not by the law. The author contrasts the covenant God made with Moses and the covenant made possible through Jesus. He symbolizes these two covenants by contrasting two mountains. Mount Sinai symbolizes the Law; Mount Zion symbolizes grace.

At Mount Sinai, the Israelites received the Law from God with fear and trembling. At Mount Zion, believers in Christ can boldly approach their heavenly Father through a "new and living way." Jesus is the mediator of a new covenant, and through His blood we are promised a "new location" that will be our eternal home in heaven.

> Lord, thank You for the promise of grace offered through the blood of Jesus Christ. Help me live in the power of grace and not under the burden of the law.

Dr. Jim Perdue, Second Baptist Church, Warner Robins, GA

WEEK 21—THURSDAY

Leaning on the Everlasting Arms

"Ah, Lord God! Behold, You have made the heavens and the earth by Your great power and outstretched arm. There is nothing too hard for You. You show lovingkindness to thousands, and repay the iniquity of the fathers into the bosom of their children after them—the Great, the Mighty God, whose name is the Lord of hosts."

JEREMIAH 32:17-18

Most of us can relate to being in confusing, seemingly hopeless situations. If we're not there now, we have been and we will be again. But facing an impossible situation can actually be good. It can remind us of our weakness and reveal God's strength. His "strength is made perfect in weakness" (2 Corinthians 12:9).

A lady facing troubling circumstances came to her pastor at the close of a sermon and said, "I'm very much afraid I might fall." The pastor replied, "Well, why don't you do it?" She protested, "But preacher, where would I fall to?" He replied, "You would fall down into the everlasting arms of God." Then he said, "I have read in the Bible that His everlasting arms are underneath His children. And you know, I believe that if you fall down upon those everlasting arms, it is sure and certain that you will never fall through them."

An "outstretched arm" clearly pictures God's power and strength, especially His power to deliver from bondage or oppression. It reminds us of His power in creation. Remembering God's love and power are vital in making it through tough times.

....

> Heavenly Father, thank You that I can rest safely and securely in Your everlasting arms. Help me trust in Your power and grace.

Heaven, Life, and the Resurrection

WEEK 21—FRIDAY

The Pay Scale of Heaven

"For the kingdom of heaven is like a landowner who went out early in the morning to hire laborers for his vineyard. Now when he had agreed with the laborers for a denarius a day, he sent them into his vineyard. And he went out about the third hour and saw others standing idle in the marketplace, and said to them, 'You also go into the vineyard, and whatever is right I will give you.' So they went."

MATTHEW 20:1-4

In this parable, Jesus deals with our motives and rewards when we are working in God's kingdom. He addressed Peter's question in 19:27—"See, we have left everything and followed you. Therefore what shall we have?" The answer is grace. When you get grace, you get more than you deserve. The Lord is a Master who values His laborers on the basis of His supreme grace rather than on human merit.

It's a privilege to be invited to labor for the Lord's kingdom. There is work to be done in advancing the cause of Christ. It is eternal work that outlasts anything the world has to offer. And we get the privilege of working for a Master who rewards those who faithfully serve Him.

We should be warned and encouraged by this parable—warned not to think of ourselves too highly and encouraged that we have been called to serve in God's kingdom. The Master determines the pay scale of heaven. And He offers us all far more than we deserve.

Lord, thank You for calling me to labor for Your kingdom work. Help me remember what an incredible privilege it is to serve You.

Dr. Jim Perdue, Second Baptist Church, Warner Robins, GA

WEEK 21—WEEKEND

Why We Praise

Let them praise the name of the Lord, for His name alone is exalted; His glory is above the earth and heaven. And He has exalted the horn of His people, the praise of all His saints—of the children of Israel, a people near to Him. Praise the Lord!

PSALM 148:13-14

A little girl visiting her grandfather crawled into his lap and said, "Grandpa, did God make you?" He said, "Oh, yes, my dear. God created me a long time ago." She said, "Did God make me, too?" He said, "Oh, yes, my dear, God created you a little while ago." She thought about it for a moment, then said, "God's been doing better work more recently, hasn't He?" That's a girl who appreciates the way God made her!

The message of Psalm 148 is simple—everything and everyone in heaven and on earth should praise the Lord. The term "praise" appears thirteen times in these fourteen verses. The Lord's name refers to all that He is in the perfection of His being. Since He is the only eternal being, the all-powerful Creator of everything, "His name alone is exalted; His glory is above earth and heaven" (v. 13).

The psalm describes the people of Israel as "a people near to [God]." This is the beauty of the gospel. In Christ, those who were far off and separated because of sin have now been brought near through Jesus Christ. If you are near to God through the blood of Christ, the final exhortation is appropriate: "Praise the Lord!"

....

Lord, Your glory is above the earth and the heavens. I praise You for Your grace, salvation, and faithfulness. In Jesus' name, amen.

Heaven, Life, and the Resurrection

WEEK 22—MONDAY

God on My Side

Behold, God is my helper; the Lord is with those who uphold my life. He will repay my enemies for their evil. Cut them off in Your truth. I will freely sacrifice to You; I will praise Your name, O LORD, for it is good. For He has delivered me out of all trouble; and my eye has seen its desire upon my enemies.

PSALM 54:4-7

A "superscription" at the beginning of a psalm describes the context of that psalm, often the situation the psalmist is facing. According to the superscription in this one, David was on the run from Saul and in hiding, yet Saul's warriors knew exactly where he was. It prompted David to declare his faithfulness to God regardless of his potential capture.

If you've ever known a bully who sought to hurt or intimidate you, you know exactly what David was experiencing. You go to bed at night and get up the next day thinking about how that "enemy" is seeking to undermine you. It can lead to many a sleepless night and can often tie you in knots throughout the day.

But what if you had the confidence that God was in your camp and on your side and was already looking out for your welfare? You know that to be true because He has been so faithful before. That confidence changes everything. You face the day and night in complete awareness that with God on your side, your enemies are always going to be outnumbered.

Lord, help me always recall Your past faithfulness when facing current obstacles. May I find perfect peace in that awareness. Amen.

Dr. Jim Phillips, North Greenwood Baptist Church, Greenwood, MS

WEEK 22—TUESDAY

Just Wait Until Your Daddy Gets Home

He shall call to the heavens from above, and to the earth, that He may judge His people: "Gather My saints together to Me, those who have made a covenant with Me by sacrifice." Let the heavens declare His righteousness, for God Himself is Judge.

PSALM 50:4-6

Growing up in a home with two older sisters, we had plenty of opportunities for unrest. I can recall a number of occasions when I had to defend myself in light of being outnumbered. Before or after school, our mom was often faced with trying to keep the peace since my dad left for work early and returned late.

If there was ever one of those days when I pushed my mom too far, she would clearly announce, "Just wait until your daddy gets home." It didn't take me long to realize that I had best straighten up or it would not be pleasant.

Looking around at our fallen world, it's easy to become discouraged at so many who think so little about the welfare of others and who often behave as if there is no one to whom they will be held accountable. The psalmist reminds us, however, that a day is coming when our God will return to His world, and He will judge all people and all sin that has not been placed under the blood of His Son.

Are you frustrated at our fallen world? Just wait until our Father comes home!

....

God, thank You that I can know in advance that I won't have to face judgment because I've placed my faith in Your Son. Amen.

Heaven, Life, and the Resurrection

WEEK 22—WEDNESDAY

How Will You Be Remembered?

Then Samson called to the LORD, saying, "O Lord GOD, remember me, I pray! Strengthen me, I pray, just this once, O God, that I may with one blow take vengeance on the Philistines for my two eyes!" And Samson took hold of the two middle pillars which supported the temple, and he braced himself against them, one on his right and the other on his left. Then Samson said, "Let me die with the Philistines!" And he pushed with all his might, and the temple fell on the lords and all the people who were in it.

JUDGES 16:28-30

Mention the name Samson, and almost everyone will recall a man who had great strength. Some people remark about an unusually strong athlete that "he has the strength of Samson." That is stated as a compliment.

Not everyone would recall that Samson's life ended in a pile of rubble created by his own actions, or that he got himself into that situation by not controlling his own lusts. He did not live nobly, but he died a noble death. The story ends with, "Thus he killed many more when he died than while he lived" (v. 30).

The Bible hides nothing. Samson could have been remembered for how many lived under his leadership, but the story concludes with the opposite. May it bring conviction to us, reminding us that God allows us to finish our own story. May we finish well.

God, may our prayer to You today find us desiring to be used of You to bless and not to bring shame upon Your holy name. Help us to be remembered well.

Dr. Jim Phillips, North Greenwood Baptist Church, Greenwood, MS

WEEK 22—THURSDAY

Into His Loving Arms

Blessed be the LORD, *who has not given us as prey to their teeth. Our soul has escaped as a bird from the snare of the fowlers; the snare is broken, and we have escaped. Our help is in the name of the* LORD, *who made heaven and earth.*
PSALM 124:6-8

According to the "fine print" at the start of this psalm, it is "A song of ascents. Of David." That means it was used by Jewish pilgrims "going up" to worship at the temple in Jerusalem. It reflects praise from grateful hearts for God somehow intervening on behalf of Israel and delivering it from an enemy. It underscores their awareness of the fact that "if the Lord had not been on [their] side," they would not have survived.

When we "go up to church" on Sunday, how often are we aware of how many potential pitfalls the Lord has delivered us from throughout the week? There are times when I could testify to His faithfulness, knowing I had done battle with the enemy in recent days and did indeed sense Him pulling me safely into His arms. But I think the Lord might inform us in heaven of many other "close calls" we had on earth with no idea He was standing near.

Peter reminds us that "the devil prowls around like a roaring lion looking for someone to devour" (1 Peter 5:8, NIV). Have you been in his clutches lately? Have you sensed him breathing down your neck? Run to the arms of the Great Shepherd. He will hold you close.

Lord, thank You for always watching out for us. Bless Your holy name.

Heaven, Life, and the Resurrection

WEEK 22—FRIDAY

Raising the Standard

"You have heard that it was said, 'You shall love your neighbor and hate your enemy.' But I say to you, love your enemies, bless those who curse you, do good to those who hate you, and pray for those who spitefully use you and persecute you, that you may be sons of your Father in heaven; for He makes His sun rise on the evil and on the good, and sends rain on the just and on the unjust."

MATTHEW 5:43-45

When Jesus spoke these words, He was addressing followers and prospective followers gathered around Him. Some in that crowd had already indicated their allegiance to Him, while others were still pondering His words. They were quite familiar that the Law affirmed "loving your neighbor," but blessing those who cursed or hated you was a new concept. Jesus made it clear that His followers were to be much different than ever thought possible.

Many of us have had to think back to our Lord's words when faced with threats, hatred, and criticism. Perhaps you can think of times when you were taken advantage of by so-called friends or enemies. Our natural tendency is to strike back with equal or greater force.

Jesus asks us to be prepared, in the power of His Spirit, to respond just as He did to those who threaten us. We are commanded to love, bless, and do good to others regardless of their favor toward us. It will not be easy, but neither was it for Him.

Jesus, may others see You in how I treat them today. Amen.

Dr. Jim Phillips, North Greenwood Baptist Church, Greenwood, MS

WEEK 22—WEEKEND

He Knew and He Knows

Saying, "Father, if it is Your will, take this cup away from Me; nevertheless not My will, but Yours, be done." Then an angel appeared to Him from heaven, strengthening Him. And being in agony, He prayed more earnestly. Then His sweat became like great drops of blood falling down to the ground.

LUKE 22:42-44

It all had come down to this: Would He and could He remain faithful? Being God in the flesh, Jesus knew this was it. He had stated at other times that only the Father knew when and if something was going to happen. But that night in the Garden of Gethsemane, He knew. The shadow of the cross was falling across Him. He also knew that Judas Iscariot and others were coming to arrest Him. He knew that the night ahead would be painful and unfair as they placed Him on trial. He knew it all.

Wasn't it just like the Father to send an angel to His Son in His deepest hour of need? And why did the angel arrive? To strengthen and shore Him up, to prepare Him for these final hours. If Jesus had not stood the test of the flesh to avoid the cup of suffering, He could have walked away. But He also knew something more. He knew that the Father's love for us was about to be expressed through His death and that our sins could be forgiven.

The same Father who knew His own Son's needs, knows all of ours as well. If necessary, He will send angels to our side. Be comforted today because He knew, and knows, our every need.

....

Jesus, be by my side today.

Heaven, Life, and the Resurrection

WEEK 23—MONDAY

Reconciled to God

And you, who once were alienated and enemies in your mind by wicked works, yet now He has reconciled in the body of His flesh through death, to present you holy, and blameless, and above reproach in His sight—if indeed you continue in the faith, grounded and steadfast, and are not moved away from the hope of the gospel which you heard, which was preached to every creature under heaven, of which I, Paul, became a minister.

COLOSSIANS 1:21-23

In this passage, the apostle covers the past, present, and future of every Christian. In the past, we were alienated from God and were His enemies. In the present, we are reconciled to Him—no longer separated but joined to Him, and no longer enemies but His friends. In the future, we will be presented to God as holy, unblameable, and above reproach in His sight.

Do you know what made the difference? The death of the Son of God. We were reconciled in the body of His flesh through death. We did not become members of God's family or His friends by self-effort or good works. Only through the blood of Jesus are we reconciled to our heavenly Father.

The evidence of real salvation is a changed life. It has been correctly said that "a faith that fizzles before the finish had a flaw from the first." Genuine salvation produces a longing in the heart of the believer to "continue in the faith, grounded and steadfast."

Father, thank You for loving us when we did not love You, and thank You for giving Your Son to die on the cross that we might be reconciled to You. Amen.

Dr. Robert C. Pitman, Bob Pitman Ministries, Muscle Shoals, AL

WEEK 23—TUESDAY

The Sufficiency of the Cross

For it is impossible for those who were once enlightened, and have tasted the heavenly gift, and have become partakers of the Holy Spirit, and have tasted the good word of God and the powers of the age to come, if they fall away, to renew them again to repentance, since they crucify again for themselves the Son of God, and put Him to an open shame.

HEBREWS 6:4-6

Some think these verses teach that it is possible for truly saved people to lose their salvation. In reality, it teaches the opposite. Look at the fourfold description of a saved person: enlightened; having tasted the heavenly gift; a partaker of the Holy Spirit; and having tasted the good word of God and the powers of the age to come. Those are the settled facts and legacy of every Christian.

If it were possible for a genuinely saved person to be lost again, the only way they could be saved a second time would be for Jesus to leave heaven once again, return to the earth, and be humiliated, beaten, and crucified all over again. That is not going to happen. His death at the cross was sufficient for all people for all time. That doesn't mean that all people will be saved, but they could be. When people go to hell, it is not because of the insufficiency of the precious blood of Christ. It is because they refuse to repent and they reject the provision made by the Lord on the cross. The cross is sufficient for us in every way.

....

Father, today we gladly proclaim, Hallelujah for the cross! Amen.

WEEK 23—WEDNESDAY

What a Mighty God We Serve

He has made the earth by His power; He has established the world by His wisdom, and stretched out the heaven by His understanding. When He utters His voice—there is a multitude of waters in the heavens: "He causes the vapors to ascend from the ends of the earth; He makes lightnings for the rain; He brings the wind out of His treasuries."

JEREMIAH 51:15-16

These two verses are repeated from Jeremiah 10:12–13. If God says something once, it is enough. If He says something twice, it is more than enough. Jeremiah speaks of God's power, wisdom, and understanding. There is nothing God cannot do, nothing He does not know, and nothing He does not understand. He is truly a mighty God. He has no flaw or weakness, no need to be taught how to act, and no need for counsel to help Him understand any situation. He is an all-sufficient God.

This powerful, wise, and understanding God is not passive but active. He speaks, He oversees, and He is at work in His creation, both in heaven and earth. He has everything He needs to bless your life. His resources from His treasuries are limitless. If you are in darkness, He has light. If you are groping in indecision, He has guidance. If you are weak, He has strength. If you have failed, He has forgiveness. If you are discouraged, He has hope. Cling to Him!

> Father, we praise You today for being a mighty God who dares to invest Your life in human beings. Amen.

Dr. Robert C. Pitman, Bob Pitman Ministries, Muscle Shoals, AL

WEEK 23—THURSDAY

Lessons Along the Way

Then He took the twelve aside and said to them, "Behold, we are going up to Jerusalem, and all things that are written by the prophets concerning the Son of Man will be accomplished. For He will be delivered to the Gentiles and will be mocked and insulted and spit upon. They will scourge Him and kill Him. And the third day He will rise again."

LUKE 18:31-33

Jesus and the twelve disciples were on their way to Jerusalem, and He was teaching them some very important life lessons that every Christian needs to know. First, God is in charge of history. He prophesied the end from the beginning, and it will all be accomplished. Nothing surprises Him or catches Him off guard.

Second, salvation is free, but it is not cheap. It cost God a very high price to provide salvation for lost sinners—His Son, Jesus Christ. Look at the sad verbs that describe what awaited Him in Jerusalem: mocked, insulted, spit upon, scourged, and killed. He was no murderer, thief, or child molester. He is God's Son. He did not endure all those things because of His sin but because of ours. He took our sins to the cross so we might be saved.

Third, there is victory in the Christian life. Jesus said He would rise again the third day, and thank God, He did! God's design for history did not end at the cross or in the tomb. Up from the grave He arose! Our victory does not rest in our physical strength or mental acumen. We have victory because of His resurrection power.

....

Lord Jesus, may Your resurrection power fill me this hour. Amen.

Heaven, Life, and the Resurrection

WEEK 23—FRIDAY

All in the Family

"Take heed that you do not despise one of these little ones, for I say to you that in heaven their angels always see the face of My Father who is in heaven. For the Son of Man has come to save that which was lost."

MATTHEW 18:10-11

A man once told me, "I have been a Christian all my life." Some people come to Christ at an early age, but none have been a Christian all their life. Before salvation people are lost—the saddest word in the Bible. It refers to those who have never been saved or forgiven and have no hope of heaven.

The good news is that lost people can be saved because Jesus stepped out of heaven and came to earth to save them. While He was on earth, He walked on water, healed the sick, and raised the dead, but that was not why He came. He came to save lost people.

When lost people receive Christ, they become members of God's family. In God's family, some are old and some are young, some are strong and some are weak, some are mature and some are spiritual babes. No believer is to lord over another. We are to respect and encourage one another. The "little ones" are in the family and should be loved, not despised.

Do Christians have guardian angels? This verse teaches that we do. Whether it is one particular angel or many, it is good to know that these heavenly messengers are on our side.

Father, thank You for saving me and placing me in Your family. May I be an encourager to my brothers and sisters. Amen.

Dr. Robert C. Pitman, Bob Pitman Ministries, Muscle Shoals, AL

WEEK 23—WEEKEND

Citizens of Heaven

Brethren, join in following my example, and note those who so walk, as you have us for a pattern. . . . For our citizenship is in heaven, from which we also eagerly wait for the Savior, the Lord Jesus Christ, who will transform our lowly body that it may be conformed to His glorious body, according to the working by which He is able even to subdue all things to Himself.

PHILIPPIANS 3:17, 20-21

Christians are citizens of two worlds. First, we are citizens of this present world. As earthly citizens we obey laws, pray for our leaders, serve in the military, salute the flag, vote on Election Day, and pay taxes.

Second, we are citizens of another world. That world is not of this earth; it is in heaven. That's where our Savior now resides bodily, but one day He will return to gather His followers and take them to heaven.

Of course, Jesus will have to change us before we can enter heaven. Our earthly bodies are corruptible and mortal, subject to decay and death. In heaven, there is no decay or death. At His coming, He will give Christians a new body just like His resurrection body.

What a joy to know the best is yet to come. This world is not our final home. We are just passing through, waiting for the time we shall stand in the presence of the King.

> Father, as we wait for the coming of Your Son, may we be good citizens of our present kingdom. At the same time, we are looking forward to the future You have for us. Amen.

WEEK 24—MONDAY

Repentance

We acknowledge, O Lord, our wickedness and the iniquity of our fathers, for we have sinned against You. Do not abhor us, for Your name's sake; do not disgrace the throne of Your glory. Remember, do not break Your covenant with us. Are there any among the idols of the nations that can cause rain? Or can the heavens give showers? Are You not He, O Lord our God? Therefore we will wait for You, since You have made all these.

JEREMIAH 14:20-22

Jeremiah prayed an honest and sincere prayer of repentance on behalf of the people. A drought in the land had become a matter of life and death. Sadly, many people only seek God and repent during a "drought," an extremely difficult season in life. Thank God He still hears us and answers prayers, even though He is often our last resort rather than our first choice.

True repentance is not merely being sorry for our sins. It leads to change and a more God-focused future. It involves regret and deep remorse. The proof of repentance is put on display by our future choices and actions. Two Hebrew words help us understand the process of repentance. The first is *nacham*, which means to turn around or change one's mind. The second is *sub*, used often in the Old Testament, and it means to turn around, restore, seek out, and return.

....

Father, as we pray and seek Your forgiveness, let us walk out repentance. Help us change our behavior in areas that do not please You. Restore us unto You.

Billy Smith, Christ Chapel Community Church, Zebulon, GA

WEEK 24—TUESDAY

A Name Change and an Assignment

Jesus answered and said to him, "Blessed are you, Simon Bar-Jonah, for flesh and blood has not revealed this to you, but My Father who is in heaven. And I also say to you that you are Peter, and on this rock I will build My church, and the gates of Hades shall not prevail against it. And I will give you the keys of the kingdom of heaven, and whatever you bind on earth will be bound in heaven, and whatever you loose on earth will be loosed in heaven."

MATTHEW 16:17–19

Name Change. In this passage, Jesus refers to Simon and then to Peter. He was addressing the same person but called him two different names. People in the Bible often have a name change after a life-changing encounter. Saul the persecutor of Christians, for example, was known as Paul the preacher after meeting Jesus. Jesus renamed Simon and called him Peter, which means stone or rock. Jesus was waking Peter up to his potential and branding him as the leader of the church.

An Assignment. Jesus wanted Peter to know he would play a crucial role in the founding of the church. Yes, Peter the follower of Christ who often acted before thinking; Peter the disciple who might be considered obnoxious at times; Peter the one who denied Christ three times.

We often think we have been disqualified because of our mistakes too, but Jesus uses us in spite of those past mistakes!

....

Lord, give us a name change and an assignment. After our encounter with You, none of us is ever the same again. We have a desire to make a difference in our world. Use us!

Heaven, Life, and the Resurrection

WEEK 24—WEDNESDAY

Where Do You Place Your Trust?

Now I know that the LORD *saves His anointed; He will answer him from His holy heaven with the saving strength of His right hand. Some trust in chariots, and some in horses; but we will remember the name of the* LORD *our God. They have bowed down and fallen; but we have risen and stand upright. Save,* LORD*! May the King answer us when we call.*

PSALM 20:6-9

Often in Scripture, David and the kingdom of Israel found themselves in perilous circumstances. David had a rich history with the Lord. He was aware of God's presence when he killed the lion, the bear, and ultimately the giant. Each one of those battles was preparation for bigger ones. Every time he found success, his trust in God grew stronger. David made it clear that our chariots and horses will not be enough, but we have a secret weapon in our God.

We often place our trust in people or things that will ultimately disappoint. Our money can evaporate after one bad investment. Our friends may walk away after a conflict. Careers can be shaken and taken when a company decides to reorganize. It is critical for believers to place their trust and future in the hands of God. Our talents, resources, and connections will sooner or later fail us, but our God is faithful and completely trustworthy.

....

God, we trust in You. You are our source and strength. You have never lost a battle!

Billy Smith, Christ Chapel Community Church, Zebulon, GA

WEEK 24—THURSDAY

Good Will Prevail

War broke out in heaven: Michael and his angels fought with the dragon; and the dragon and his angels fought, [8] but they did not prevail, nor was a place found for them in heaven any longer. So the great dragon was cast out, that serpent of old, called the Devil and Satan, who deceives the whole world; he was cast to the earth, and his angels were cast out with him.

REVELATION 12:7-9

Good and evil are always at odds. The devil wants to create confusion, division, and hatred everywhere. His power on earth is apparent. He divides groups based on race, political affiliation, gender, and much more. He is the author of confusion. But he will not have the last word! Just as he was cast out of heaven, his efforts on earth will have a final day. His days are numbered.

God will reign supreme. The earth continues to decay morally and spiritually, but do not be dismayed. The future for believers and the church is very much intact and destined for success. We will fight against evil until our last breath, but we do not fight alone. We have a huge advantage because we serve and fight alongside the One who will stand on the final day. Our Lord was, is, and will be the winner. He has a perfect record. He has never lost a battle, and He never will.

....

> God, thank You for providing us with adequate cover. We may be attacked, but we have not suffered defeat. You are the conquering King. We trust in You to sustain us in perilous times.

Heaven, Life, and the Resurrection

WEEK 24—FRIDAY

Esther–A Woman of Courage

Then Queen Esther answered and said, "If I have found favor in your sight, O king, and if it pleases the king, let my life be given me at my petition, and my people at my request. For we have been sold, my people and I, to be destroyed, to be killed, and to be annihilated. Had we been sold as male and female slaves, I would have held my tongue, although the enemy could never compensate for the king's loss."

ESTHER 7:3-4

Queen Esther knew something had to be done to save her people. She made a bold request to the king, and he listened and responded. She was not sure how the king would react, but she was willing to lose her life, if necessary, to right a wrong. In our lives, crucial matters will break our hearts to the point that we have to do something. Esther put on a display of remarkable courage.

Stories of courage like Queen Esther's can infuse you with a dose of courage. The enemy loves to steal your boldness. He wants you to be timid and unassertive with your faith. He loves to see you doubtful and fearful. But "God has not given us a spirit of fear, but of power and of love and of a sound mind" (2 Timothy 1:7).

God, bless us today with courage. When we doubt ourselves, remind us that the Spirit of the living God is inside us. Grant us boldness to walk out our faith.

Billy Smith, Christ Chapel Community Church, Zebulon, GA

WEEK 24—WEEKEND

The Greatness of Our Lord

The LORD is high above all nations, His glory above the heavens. Who is like the LORD our God, who dwells on high, who humbles Himself to behold the things that are in the heavens and in the earth? He raises the poor out of the dust, and lifts the needy out of the ash heap, that He may seat him with princes—with the princes of His people.

PSALM 113:4-8

How can we accurately describe our God? The psalmist does a good job of creatively painting a picture of God, but there is so much more. Words fail us in our efforts to describe the God of the universe adequately. Poets and song writers have tried. Pastors have preached messages that attempt to capture the majesty of our Lord. All of them fall short of accurately portraying His greatness.

God created everything in the universe, according to Genesis. He created galaxies, planets, the earth, and humanity, to name just a few of His works. It is amazing what He is limitlessly capable of doing. Everything He does is spectacular. Average and status quo do not exist in His thoughts. Look in the mirror at how wonderfully you are made. You have ears to hear, eyes to see, a nose to smell, and the list goes on. You are a custom product from the hands of the Father. There is not another you! God does good work.

......

God, I don't ask for anything today. I just wanted You to know that I know just how amazing You are.

Heaven, Life, and the Resurrection

WEEK 25—MONDAY

The Power of Resurrection

There is also an antitype which now saves us—baptism (not the removal of the filth of the flesh, but the answer of a good conscience toward God), through the resurrection of Jesus Christ, who has gone into heaven and is at the right hand of God, angels and authorities and powers having been made subject to Him.

1 PETER 3:21-22

Baptism is an extremely important act for Christians. All believers are to be baptized to be obedient to our Lord. He established the ordinance of baptism as an indication that He is our Lord and we will therefore obey Him. The symbolism of baptism is rich; believers have died and are raised new in Christ.

Peter was inspired to write about baptism with a typological emphasis. He compared baptism's symbolism with Noah's rescue from the wrath of God (v. 20). As Noah and his family were saved through the flood waters by being on the ark, Christians are saved through Christ's death and resurrection. The physical act of baptism doesn't save. It is the work of Christ and His resurrection that saves.

Our Lord is now at the right hand of God in a place of sovereign authority. All powers are subject to Him. All who have applied this gospel are saved from God's just and eternal wrath, to life eternal in Christ. His resurrection brings us life and the future experience of resurrection and transformation to live in His eternal kingdom. There is no wrath for the saved, but a magnificent future. Praise Him for the power of His resurrection to save!

Lord, help me depend upon Your resurrection power today.

Mike Orr, First Baptist Church Chipley, Chipley, FL

WEEK 25—TUESDAY

In the Beginning God

In the beginning God created the heavens and the earth. The earth was without form, and void; and darkness was on the face of the deep. And the Spirit of God was hovering over the face of the waters.

GENESIS 1:1–2

The first time I stood at the rim of the Grand Canyon and took in the view, I was in awe. I thought, *Is this real?* The radiant blue sky touched the mountains, the mountains dropped off into a colossal gorge, and a tiny green river flowed at the canyon floor. The heavens and earth truly declare God's glory. At night when it is clear, the sparkle of the stars reveals another level of the canyon that is God's great handiwork. The apostle is clear in Romans 1 that all people are without excuse because God has truly revealed Himself through creation.

There is another place revealed in Scripture called heaven—the abode of God. It was from this place God spoke the heavens and earth into being. Before anything existed, God always existed. His power is extreme. His majesty is above all. This one and only God made it so we can be with Him forever. He loves us. Through our Lord, He has made the way to be with Him. Sit and take that in for a moment and praise Him.

....

Lord, help me reflect on Your greatness today and to praise You.

WEEK 25—WEDNESDAY

True God

He has made the earth by His power, He has established the world by His wisdom, and has stretched out the heavens at His discretion. When He utters His voice, there is a multitude of waters in the heavens: "And He causes the vapors to ascend from the ends of the earth. He makes lightning for the rain, He brings the wind out of His treasuries."

JEREMIAH 10:12-13

The prophet Jeremiah delivered the truth that the true God, the God of Israel, is superior to all the false gods represented in idol worship. What can these false gods do? Nothing!

God is all powerful. Proof of His power is in the fact that He made heaven and earth. He is all-wise; His wisdom is perfect. The one true God holds all things in the universe together and controls the thunder and lightning.

We need this reminder. Even Christians easily fall into this trap of idolatry. We often place higher value and trust in things, resources, authorities, powers, and possessions than we do in the true God. I've seen Christians on all sides put more trust in their political party and leader than in God. They feel safer and more secure with their particular party in control than trusting in the fact that God is in control. We mustn't put anything above Him. Trust, worship, and magnify our God. He alone is worthy.

....

Lord, help me depend on nothing but You.

WEEK 25—THURSDAY

Worth the Cost

Then Jesus said to His disciples, "If anyone desires to come after Me, let him deny himself, and take up his cross, and follow Me. For whoever desires to save his life will lose it, but whoever loses his life for My sake will find it. For what profit is it to a man if he gains the whole world, and loses his own soul? Or what will a man give in exchange for his soul? For the Son of Man will come in the glory of His Father with His angels, and then He will reward each according to his works."

MATTHEW 16:24-27

Satan has been using the same strategy with humans from the beginning. He convinces people that if they follow the Lord, their lives will not be as rich, fun, or good. It's a diabolical lie. People hear the gospel, and many want to receive this great gift, but they choose to give in to the deception that it will cause them to miss a pleasurable life. Even Christians find themselves in this trap.

Instead of pursuing holiness and laying up treasure in heaven, they choose to pursue worldly pleasures. They do not pursue fulfillment in Christ, and lives are wasted. As the Lord said, what profit is there in gaining the world and losing one's soul? To be saved, one must repent and by faith surrender to Christ. Once saved, we are to deny self and follow Christ. The riches and pleasure found in Him far exceed those of the world. Don't be deceived. Follow the Lord Jesus.

Lord, help me daily to pursue fulfillment from Christ.

Heaven, Life, and the Resurrection

WEEK 25—FRIDAY

Rubbish Compared to Christ

What things were gain to me, these I have counted loss for Christ. Yet indeed I also count all things loss for the excellence of the knowledge of Christ Jesus my Lord, for whom I have suffered the loss of all things, and count them as rubbish, that I may gain Christ and be found in Him, not having my own righteousness, which is from the law, but that which is through faith in Christ, the righteousness which is from God by faith.

PHILIPPIANS 3:7-9

Two houses stand in my home county in Georgia that were built in the nineteenth century. One was built prior to the Civil War, the other five years after the war ended. Two of my ancestors lived in these houses. Both had significant lands and were considered well off. They were able to experience quite a bit from a material perspective in their world. Both left it all behind. Though the two houses still stand, one day they will not—a reminder that life must be lived from an eternal perspective.

Paul left cultural prestige, material goods, and possible position as a community leader when he followed Christ. He faced hardships, trials, and difficulties in obedience to the Lord. Did he regret leaving everything else behind for Jesus? Not at all. In fact, he considered all he lost as "rubbish" in exchange for knowing Christ.

The Lord has an amazing future in store for those who are His. We will regret nothing if we live a devoted life for Christ. Nothing compares to Him.

Lord, help me not to be in love with the things of this world but to seek the things above.

Mike Orr, First Baptist Church Chipley, Chipley, FL

WEEK 25—WEEKEND

Death Has No Power

The rest of the dead did not live again until the thousand years were finished. This is the first resurrection. Blessed and holy is he who has part in the first resurrection. Over such the second death has no power, but they shall be priests of God and of Christ, and shall reign with Him a thousand years.

REVELATION 20:5-6

TV icon Larry King recently died. I've watched and read about two interviews in which he expressed a fear of death. I don't think Larry ever publicly professed Christ as Lord and Savior. Those who are truly Christ's don't have to fear death. In Him, death is defeated. At death, we experience life.

Today's text describes the first resurrection, which I believe happens in a couple of stages. It is the resurrection of the saved. When Christians die, we immediately depart to be with the Lord. We are alive and functioning in heaven. One day when the Lord returns for His people, the dead in Christ will be raised. Resurrection will occur, and we will each receive a body like the Lord's, one made for the eternal kingdom. Death has no power over us because our Lord defeated death for us at His resurrection.

The most feared thing among most humans is death. The Lord Jesus gives us victory over death. Praise Him!

......

Thank You, Lord, for overcoming death for me and giving me eternal life to look forward to.

Heaven, Life, and the Resurrection

WEEK 26—MONDAY

How to Fear God

Come, you children, listen to me; I will teach you the fear of the Lord. *Who is the man who desires life, and loves many days, that he may see good? Keep your tongue from evil, and your lips from speaking deceit. Depart from evil and do good; seek peace and pursue it.*

PSALM 34:11-14

Fearing things of this world unfortunately seems to come naturally for us. But the fear of God does not come naturally. We must learn the fear of the Lord, and God desires to teach it to us—if we'll come to him and listen. The reason this kind of fear must be taught becomes obvious as our relationship with God grows. This relationship progresses as we follow through in our surrender to God by conforming to His way of life. In our obedience to Him, we begin to taste His goodness and desire the life only He can give us.

Charles Spurgeon's definition of fearing God was, "Pay to him humble child-like reverence, walk in his laws, have respect to his will, tremble to offend him, hasten to serve him." However, David's focus here in these verses is not on the meaning of fearing the Lord but on how to fear Him. The formula is simple. If God is good, as Psalm 145:9 reminds us, and we want to enjoy what is good, then we are to do what is right.

Lord, I love You and I thank You for teaching me your ways! Help me fear You more. Give me the wisdom to avoid evil and the strength to do what is right!

WEEK 26—TUESDAY

The Importance of Family

"Hear, O Israel: The LORD our God, the LORD is one! You shall love the LORD your God with all your heart, with all your soul, and with all your strength. And these words which I command you today shall be in your heart. You shall teach them diligently to your children, and shall talk of them when you sit in your house, when you walk by the way, when you lie down, and when you rise up."

DEUTERONOMY 6:4-7

This passage, along with verses 8–9, is known as the *Shema*, the Hebrew word that begins verse 4. It literally means to "hear" or "listen." For Jews, it taught how education should work and how they were to commend the works of God to the next generation. Here Moses was calling the people to sit up and listen because of the importance of these words—so important that Jesus would later call it "the greatest commandment" (Matthew 22:37–39).

It was essential for Israelites to get this right if they were going to thrive and survive in the promised land. The family was to become the primary place where faith in and love for the Lord would be modeled and passed on. This responsibility remains essential in today's society. It should not be placed on the government, the school system, or even the church, but must rest on the family. Spiritual training within the family unit is the only way for a proper biblical worldview to be handed down from one generation to the next.

Lord, help me stay committed to the spiritual training of my family. Take me deeper in my relationship with You so they can learn from me.

Heaven, Life, and the Resurrection

WEEK 26—WEDNESDAY

Calling All God-Seekers

God looks down from heaven upon the children of men, to see if there are any who understand, who seek God. Every one of them has turned aside; they have together become corrupt; there is none who does good, no, not one.

PSALM 53:2–3

Do you desire to do good? Do you long to worship God? Are you searching for Him? Not many seem to be. History teaches us that God has not found many God-seekers, especially in times of wickedness or prosperity. But seeking Him does matter to Him because "He is a rewarder of those who diligently seek Him" (Hebrews 11:6). He is looking for worshippers (John 4:23). Our God longs to walk with us and reveal Himself to us—so much so that He declares, "You will seek Me and find Me, when you search for Me with all your heart" (Jeremiah 29:13).

Romans 3:10–12 echoes Psalm 53:2 in pointing to the fact that, due to our fallenness, we have become corrupt and lost. Have you ever found yourself being thankful that your child found you when you were unable to find him or her? That is the story of the human race: "The Son of Man has come to seek and to save that which was lost" (Luke 19:10). John Newton said it this way: "Amazing grace, how sweet the sound, that saved a wretch like me. I once was lost, but now am found, was blind, but now I see."

Lord, I'm grateful that You love me and search for me. I want to be a God-seeker! Help me seek You with all my heart.

Jamie Altman, Bethlehem Community Church, Laurel, MS

WEEK 26—THURSDAY

Christ Be Lifted Up

And as Moses lifted up the serpent in the wilderness, even so must the Son of Man be lifted up, that whoever believes in Him should not perish but have eternal life. For God so loved the world that He gave His only begotten Son, that whoever believes in Him should not perish but have everlasting life.

JOHN 3:14-16

God commanded Moses to make a brass snake so whoever looked at it would be healed from their snakebite (Numbers 21:4-9). Jesus used that event as an illustration of God's plan for redemption. Just as the snake was lifted up for all to see, Christ must be lifted up so that all suffering from the poison of sin might be healed and have eternal life.

Has Christ been lifted up in your life? This question needs to be answered both personally and corporately. It should be addressed on a personal level because there is no salvation in any other, no other name by which we must be saved (Acts 4:12). But we also have an obligation to lift Christ up corporately because, through that process, God can use the "foolishness of the message preached to save those who believe" (1 Corinthians 1:21).

Do you want God to use you? Would you like to experience transformation? Do you desire to see people saved? Let Christ be lifted up! As Jesus said, "I, if I am lifted up from the earth, will draw all peoples to Myself" (John 12:32).

> Lord, thank You for Your sacrifice. I pray that You would help me sacrifice my own desires to lift You up high that all may see You in me.

Heaven, Life, and the Resurrection

WEEK 26—FRIDAY

Sing Praises to the Lord

Sing to God, you kingdoms of the earth; oh, sing praises to the Lord, to Him who rides on the heaven of heavens, which were of old! Indeed, He sends out His voice, a mighty voice. Ascribe strength to God; His excellence is over Israel, and His strength is in the clouds.

PSALM 68:32-34

David knew the awesome power of God. He also understood the ultimate victory of God, so he invited the nations to worship Him. The nations would benefit from recognizing and surrendering to God's strength and observing His rule over Israel.

David understood the dynamics of praise and the importance of singing to the Lord. Singing has powerful effects on the brain. According to some studies, our bodies release hormones that can relieve stress and anxiety. Research reveals that when a group of people sing together, their heartbeats actually synchronize with each other. What a powerful thought! Charles Spurgeon said, "We have too much sinning against God, but cannot have too much singing to God." There's an important purpose behind God's commands to sing and praise Him. The Bible encourages us to "sing praise" more than fifty times. Whether we are going into battle or facing major obstacles, praising God has the power to change our thoughts, our hearts, and our lives.

> Lord, thank You for giving me plenty to sing about. Help me to not be slack in my praises. Put a new song in my heart and keep me singing all the days of my life!

Jamie Altman, Bethlehem Community Church, Laurel, MS

WEEK 26—WEEKEND

Our Good Shepherd

I am the door. If anyone enters by Me, he will be saved, and will go in and out and find pasture. The thief does not come except to steal, and to kill, and to destroy. I have come that they may have life, and that they may have it more abundantly. "I am the good shepherd. The good shepherd gives His life for the sheep."

JOHN 10:9-11

Most people today don't know much about shepherding, but it was a common occupation in biblical times. The shepherd's job was to supply the sheep with food and water and protect them from predators. The shepherd lived among his flock and was responsible for rescuing those who wandered off and caring for the weak or wounded. It was considered a lowly, dirty, exhausting job. Yet Christ used it to describe Himself.

Jesus humbled Himself, became a man, and lived among sinful, wayward, stubborn human sheep. He laid down His life so all who believe in Him can become part of His flock. He does for us exactly what the shepherds did long ago—He feeds us, protects us, rescues us, strengthens us when we're weak, and cares for the hurting.

As our good shepherd, Christ does not want us merely to have eternal life but also to possess the full experience of life. Following Jesus as our Shepherd leads to blessing, joy, and a growing abundance of eternal life.

> Lord, thank You for the gift of eternal life. I pray that You would help me experience life in all its fullness, found only in You. Keep me close to You and protect me from the evils of this world.

Heaven, Life, and the Resurrection

WEEK 27—MONDAY

Purpose in the Pain

Indeed we count them blessed who endure. You have heard of the perseverance of Job and seen the end intended by the Lord—that the Lord is very compassionate and merciful. But above all, my brethren, do not swear, either by heaven or by earth or with any other oath. But let your "Yes" be "Yes," and your "No," "No," lest you fall into judgment.

JAMES 5:11-12

In a culture often confused by promoters of the prosperity gospel, it's sometimes convenient to buy into the myth that the righteous won't suffer. But Scripture is filled with righteous people who endured great difficulty. James teaches that the blessing comes after we have endured. So what can we learn from the suffering of Job?

First, there is a purpose in your suffering. Job suffered through the loss of his family and fortune and became feeble. While he did not know what God was ultimately teaching him, he knew there was a hand behind the headlines working for God's glory and his good. In the midst of suffering, understand that all things do work together for the good of those who love God (Romans 8:28).

Secondly, there is power in your speech. In difficult times, we are often tempted to say things we do not mean. I've discovered that the lost often pay attention to the reactions of the saved who are in the midst of suffering. What an opportunity for our speech to be seasoned with grace and join Job in the chorus of, "I know that my Redeemer lives" (Job 19:25).

> Father help me never to lose sight that there is always a purpose in the pain, amen.

Chad Campbell, Mount Pisgah Baptist Church, Easley, SC

WEEK 27—TUESDAY

Heaven on My Mind

Then He also said to him who invited Him, "When you give a dinner or a supper, do not ask your friends, your brothers, your relatives, nor rich neighbors, lest they also invite you back, and you be repaid. But when you give a feast, invite the poor, the maimed, the lame, the blind. And you will be blessed, because they cannot repay you; for you shall be repaid at the resurrection of the just."

LUKE 14:12-14

According to a recent study by CareerBuilder, 78 percent of Americans are living paycheck to paycheck. Payday has a way of influencing the thoughts and choices we make each day. This may be the norm in our culture, but Jesus teaches us to lose a temporary mindset and live for heaven's rewards. He offers reminders of what it looks like to live with heaven on our minds.

First, heavenly minded people do not chase temporary benefits. Jesus speaks directly against the natural inclinations of our hearts by saying, "Don't honor people capable of honoring you back." Why? A believer's motive should be to honor God alone. Honoring God with pure intentions means befriending the diseased, favoring the downcast, and nurturing those in darkness for their benefit, not ours.

Heavenly minded people are therefore compelled by timeless blessings. As Jesus speaks to the host, He reminds him of the ultimate repayment. The day when God Almighty restores believers to live in a glorified, immortal, sinless body will be an awesome day indeed! The glorious repayment in eternity far outweighs the most glamorous repayment on earth. Friend, it's worth it to live with heaven in mind.

Father, give me an eternal mindset and heavenly motives, amen.

Heaven, Life, and the Resurrection

WEEK 27—WEDNESDAY

Overcoming Pride

At that time Jesus answered and said, "I thank You, Father, Lord of heaven and earth, that You have hidden these things from the wise and prudent and have revealed them to babes. Even so, Father, for so it seemed good in Your sight. All things have been delivered to Me by My Father, and no one knows the Son except the Father. Nor does anyone know the Father except the Son, and the one to whom the Son wills to reveal Him.

MATTHEW 11:25-27

In this passage, we get a glimpse into the special relationship between God the Son and God the Father. Five times in these three verses the distinctive and intimate name, "Abba, Father" appears. It was this relationship with the Father that drove the prideful Pharisees to condemn Jesus.

One of the greatest obstacles to knowing the Father is pride. We are told that God resists the proud and gives grace to the humble (James 4:6). Pride promotes self, while humility allows God to do the promoting. The scribes and Pharisees were full of pride and missed out on the message that would have led them to repentance and faith.

It's also been said that pride is the only disease that makes everyone sick except the person who has it. In my experience, the prideful are so proud that they believe they are humble. Those who come to Jesus do so with simple childlike faith and with the humility to surrender their lives to Him. As the prophet Micah instructed, let's walk humbly with our Lord (Micah 6:8).

Lord, help me to not promote self but to humbly point others to the Savior, amen.

WEEK 27—THURSDAY

Don't Worry, Be Holy

"Therefore I say to you, do not worry about your life, what you will eat or what you will drink; nor about your body, what you will put on. Is not life more than food and the body more than clothing? Look at the birds of the air, for they neither sow nor reap nor gather into barns; yet your heavenly Father feeds them. Are you not of more value than they? Which of you by worrying can add one cubit to his stature?"

MATTHEW 6:25-27

Our culture offers endless opportunities to engage in the fruitless and faithless task of worry. Dr. Charles Mayo of the Mayo Clinic said, "You can worry yourself to death, but not to life." In the Sermon on the Mount, Jesus makes it clear that worrying is futile. O. S. Hawkins says, "God does not merely frown upon worry, He expressly forbids us to worry." So how do we eliminate the sin of worry?

First, we must set proper priorities. When our priority is earthly possessions or the lack thereof, worry will set it. Second, we must see provision. Jesus points out that birds do not sow, reap, or gather, yet God feeds them. The same God that provides for them cares infinitely more for you and will provide. Finally, we must seek the Prince of Peace. Jesus gives us the prescription for eliminating worry: "Seek first the kingdom of God and His righteousness, and all these things shall be added to you" (Matthew 6:33).

Lord, help me set proper priorities in my life, see provision You have promised, and seek first Your kingdom, amen.

Heaven, Life, and the Resurrection

WEEK 27—FRIDAY

He Shall Reign Forevermore

Then the seventh angel sounded: And there were loud voices in heaven, saying, "The kingdoms of this world have become the kingdoms of our Lord and of His Christ, and He shall reign forever and ever!" And the twenty-four elders who sat before God on their thrones fell on their faces and worshiped God.

REVELATION 11:15-16

Newspapers have a special font for mega-events when regular bold print won't communicate the gravity of the message. It is referred to as "Second Coming Type." It was used when Pearl Harbor was attacked and when JFK was assassinated. It makes the message leap off the page and is reserved only for special events. Friend, there is no coming event more special than when Jesus returns to rule and reign.

First, John points us to the sound of victory signaling that the last days have arrived and Christ's return is imminent. We've only heard about this event most of our lives, but rest assured it will become a reality. It's the day creation has groaned for since Genesis 3.

Second, John hears the song of victory. Some have suggested that the loud voices of verse 15 are heaven's choir. They will sing the chorus, "He shall reign forever and ever." This scene settles any debate about who is in charge. Satan is defeated, and the King of kings has taken His rightful place on the throne.

Regardless of what you face today, even if it seems the enemy is winning, join in the chorus from heaven singing a song of victory: "He shall reign forever and ever."

....

Lord, remind me to today that I can walk in victory, knowing Christ is on the throne, amen.

Chad Campbell, Mount Pisgah Baptist Church, Easley, SC

WEEK 27—WEEKEND

Who Are You Listening To?

"Because he has set his love upon Me, therefore I will deliver him; I will set him on high, because he has known My name. He shall call upon Me, and I will answer him; I will be with him in trouble; I will deliver him and honor him. With long life I will satisfy him, and show him My salvation."

PSALM 91:14-16

The top ten motivational speakers in the United States earn a combined $200 million per year. Americans are listening to their words hoping to find guidance, growth, and gratification. While conferences may sell out for the empty words of mortal men, Christians must listen to the eternal Word of our Creator.

The psalmist directly quotes God, calling our attention to powerful truths about His Word. First, God's Word contains an appeal. The phrase "set his love upon Me" is only possible because of the phrase, "because he has known My name." You cannot love what you do not know. Thankfully, the Word invites us to know God personally. The Bible reveals His Person, inviting us to know His supremacy. The Bible reveals man's problem, informing us of our sin. The Bible reveals His provision, inviting us to know the salvation only found in Christ. Listen to His Word!

God's Word also corresponds with an action. "I will" is written six times in this passage. God's Word has been associated with God's ways from the very beginning. God promises to deliver, answer, honor, and satisfy. Instead of buying into the self-help message of society, let's be a people surrendered to the sufficiency of the Scriptures.

....

Father, tune my heart to listen to Your Word, amen.

Heaven, Life, and the Resurrection

WEEK 28—MONDAY

The House of God

"However, the Most High does not dwell in temples made with hands, as the prophet says: 'Heaven is My throne, and earth is My footstool. What house will you build for Me? says the Lord, or what is the place of My rest? Has My hand not made all these things?'"

ACTS 7:48-50

Stephen was preaching his final sermon and would soon become the first known martyr for Jesus. His sermon drove his listeners over the edge. They stoned him at the direction of Saul, who would later become the apostle Paul. Saul likely couldn't shake this sermon from his mind; it was a powerful moment in the life of the church.

Who was Stephen preaching to and what was he preaching about? In a vacuum, we might assume he was preaching about immorality and sin, and his listeners were enraged because of their sinful lifestyle. But he was preaching to the choir, telling people who were at synagogue every week that they had confined God to a box, or a temple. God does not live in a temple. The universe and our lives are His dwelling place.

We make the same mistake. We put God in our Sunday box and leave Him there. And in the process, we forget He is with us everywhere and always. Be aware today and every day that everywhere you go, God is already there.

Dear Lord, let me live in light of the fact that You are with me all the time. Remove from my mind the idea that I can hide any of my actions, words, and thoughts from You, and let me live in the presence of Your glory.

Joel Southerland, Peavine Baptist Church, Rock Spring, GA

WEEK 28—TUESDAY

Our Heavenly Calling

Holy brethren, partakers of the heavenly calling, consider the Apostle and High Priest of our confession, Christ Jesus, who was faithful to Him who appointed Him, as Moses also was faithful in all His house. For this One has been counted worthy of more glory than Moses, inasmuch as He who built the house has more honor than the house. For every house is built by someone, but He who built all things is God.

HEBREWS 3:1-4

The writer of Hebrews reminds his readers of their divine, heavenly calling; this world is not our home. We are simply ambassadors of heaven in a foreign land. He compares Moses and Jesus but quickly concludes that Jesus is greater than Moses. We would agree, but that does not diminish the contribution of Moses, who served well and fulfilled his heavenly calling. Jesus is the Master Designer and Creator, and it is our privilege to have a part in his plan.

This gives us confidence in at least two ways. First, God has a part for us all to play. No matter what your gifts, abilities, or talents are, God has created you to participate in his master plan. He has built into the design of the kingdom a heavenly calling for you to fulfill. No child of God is worthless. Second, take comfort in the fact that God is the master architect and builder. He is never surprised or delayed. He never experiences setbacks. He knows exactly what is going on with us and how to bring it all together for our good.

Dear Lord, help me accept my heavenly calling and move forward in Your will, knowing You have all things in your control.

Heaven, Life, and the Resurrection

WEEK 28—WEDNESDAY

Drawn

The Jews then complained about Him, because He said, "I am the bread which came down from heaven." And they said, "Is not this Jesus, the son of Joseph, whose father and mother we know? How is it then that He says, 'I have come down from heaven'?" Jesus therefore answered and said to them, "Do not murmur among yourselves. No one can come to Me unless the Father who sent Me draws him; and I will raise him up at the last day."

JOHN 6:41-44

Jesus was extremely popular at times. Large crowds followed Him and shouted praises when He healed or worked miracles. Thousands would stand in His presence and listen. Then there were times when He was unpopular. He could disperse crowds with one sermon. He could upset the religious leaders with one act of forgiveness. He could work the crowd into a frenzy with one comment that asserted His deity.

John 6 is one such passage. The religious leaders were grumbling, complaining, and arguing with Jesus, and Jesus said He was the bread that came down from heaven. The statement about bread upset them; the statement that He "came down from heaven" infuriated them. It equated Him with God. And before this discourse was over, Jesus would lose most of His followers.

That did that not upset Jesus. He knew His true followers would be drawn to His teaching. Those who toughed it out would become men and women who would change the world. For those who are drawn, nothing can separate them from Jesus.

Lord, may I be one who stays true to Jesus, even when times are tough.

Joel Southerland, Peavine Baptist Church, Rock Spring, GA

WEEK 28—THURSDAY

We Have His Presence

Jesus cried out again with a loud voice, and yielded up His spirit. Then, behold, the veil of the temple was torn in two from top to bottom; and the earth quaked, and the rocks were split, and the graves were opened; and many bodies of the saints who had fallen asleep were raised; and coming out of the graves after His resurrection, they went into the holy city and appeared to many.
MATTHEW 27:50-53

Many things significant for the kingdom of God and the Christian life happened on the cross. The sayings of Jesus, the thief being saved, even little movements fulfilled prophecies of the Messiah and Lamb of God.

One of the more overlooked events happened in v. 51. The temple veil was torn in two. The veil was the curtain separating the Holy Place from the holy of holies. Only the high priest could enter that place—with great ceremony one day each year to offer a sacrifice for Israel's sins. No one else had such access to God's presence. Death was the price of disobedience.

The cross changed that. The veil was torn from the top to bottom. The rabbis tell us the veil was thirty feet high, sixty feet wide, and up to four inches thick. It took three hundred priests to manipulate it. It couldn't have been torn by men. It was torn by the hand of God. And it was torn for one reason: so we could have access to God's presence. If God did all that as part of the redemption plan, shouldn't we take advantage of that access?

Lord, You died so I could experience Your presence. Help me abide daily with You.

Heaven, Life, and the Resurrection

WEEK 28—FRIDAY

Let Others Hear

I will praise You, O LORD, among the peoples, and I will sing praises to You among the nations. For Your mercy is great above the heavens, and Your truth reaches to the clouds. Be exalted, O God, above the heavens, and Your glory above all the earth; that Your beloved may be delivered, save with Your right hand, and hear me.

PSALM 108:3-6

This psalm is unusual; it combines two previous psalms (57 and 60). David literally took two other songs and made a third to be used in worship. He intended it as a song of victory—triumphal praise to our God of salvation!

The first sentence of this passage teaches us a lesson. David wasn't singing the Lord's praises just so God's people in God's house could hear him proclaim a God they all knew. He wanted this song to be sung everywhere, especially in the hearing of those who did not know the Lord. He wanted his praise to be a testimony and witness to those far from God.

That's a good word for us. How much do we complain in front of people who don't know Jesus? Complaining doesn't make someone say, "I've got to check out that person's religion." But what if the praise of God was on our lips continually in front of a lost world? What if, in a bad situation and with all the world complaining, we witnessed with thanksgiving and praise for the God who saved us?

Dear Lord, help me be salt and light with my language and conversation, and let praise and thanksgiving be on my lips continually.

Joel Southerland, Peavine Baptist Church, Rock Spring, GA

WEEK 28—WEEKEND

Prayer and Praise

"He shall pray to God, and He will delight in him, He shall see His face with joy, for He restores to man His righteousness. Then he looks at men and says, 'I have sinned, and perverted what was right, and it did not profit me.' He will redeem his soul from going down to the Pit, and his life shall see the light."

JOB 33:26-28

Job is a book of suffering. When the last chapter comes, order has been restored and suffering has been rewarded with blessings and joy. But the first forty-one chapters are hard to read. Job loses everything, and his friends turn on him. Things appear bleak. Today's verses come in the middle of the bleakness.

These are words of a friend trying to comfort Job, but they are not comforting. From time to time, however, the friends did utter truth. Elihu says that when you are in distress, you should pray to God and worship Him so you can see His face with joy and be restored. It's good advice. Prayer and worship do wonders for the vexed soul.

Whatever bleakness you find yourself in today, hear Elihu's words. Spend time in prayer with God. While you are praying, focus on thanksgiving and praise, even though you don't feel like it. Trouble and trials are not an excuse to miss church and corporate or private worship. Job worshiped as soon as trouble hit. It's a good example for us today. It may just lead to joy.

....

Lord, help me stay strong in my trials and spend more time with You in prayer and worship.

Heaven, Life, and the Resurrection

WEEK 29—MONDAY

Strengthened Through Reflection

The Lord stood with me and strengthened me, so that the message might be preached fully through me, and that all the Gentiles might hear. Also I was delivered out of the mouth of the lion. And the Lord will deliver me from every evil work and preserve me for His heavenly kingdom. To Him be glory forever and ever. Amen!

2 TIMOTHY 4:17-18

In Paul's closing exhortations, we catch a glimpse of his personal life inventory. From a Roman prison, Paul noted that while many men had deserted him, the Lord never did. To the contrary, the Lord faithfully strengthened him to persevere in his God-ordained mission. Looking back, Paul could see clearly how God had protected and provided, even in the most harrowing of circumstances. Reflecting on God's faithfulness prompted courage in his heart. He knew that no matter what circumstances he faced, the Lord would never abandon him.

No matter what we face today, we need not face it alone. With Paul, when we reflect on God's past faithfulness, we gain courage for the present and confidence in the future. The Lord is unchanging. The One who delivered you also strengthens you. The One who strengthens you will not abandon you in your difficulties. If God is with you in the present, you can be assured of His victory in the future—a victory you will share in as you press forward in fulfilling His purpose and pleasure in your life.

> Lord, as I look back on Your faithfulness throughout my life, help me be confident that You who began a good work in me will be faithful to complete it. Amen.

Dr. Chris Aiken, Englewood Baptist Church, Rocky Mount, NC

WEEK 29—TUESDAY

Be Strong

Finally, my brethren, be strong in the Lord and in the power of His might. Put on the whole armor of God, that you may be able to stand against the wiles of the devil. For we do not wrestle against flesh and blood, but against principalities, against powers, against the rulers of the darkness of this age, against spiritual hosts of wickedness in the heavenly places. Therefore take up the whole armor of God, that you may be able to withstand in the evil day, and having done all, to stand.

EPHESIANS 6:10-13

No soldier willingly steps into battle without all of his gear. Proper preparation involves knowing who the enemy is and being fully equipped for the mission. As Paul observed the soldiers who guarded him, He drew a connection between their armor and the equipment every Christ-follower needed for battle. Whether belts or boots, breastplates or shields, helmets or swords, every piece of equipment served a purpose.

Still, even the well-equipped soldier could not look to his arsenal as the source of his strength. The Word of God is only as good as the God of the Word. The gospel boots found their stability in the gospel's God. This is why Paul proclaimed that we are to be strong in the Lord and in His power!

No mere implement of war could defeat the devil. A shield of faith might quench fiery darts; the God of our faith crushes Satan. This is good news because victory is assured. Dress for battle, child of God, but rest in the Lord and in the strength of His might.

....

Lord, thank You not only for preparing me for battle but for securing the victory in it. Amen.

Heaven, Life, and the Resurrection

WEEK 29—WEDNESDAY

Promise Fulfilled

"For as the new heavens and the new earth which I will make shall remain before Me," says the LORD, "So shall your descendants and your name remain. And it shall come to pass that from one New Moon to another, and from one Sabbath to another, all flesh shall come to worship before Me," says the LORD.

ISAIAH 66:22-23

Isaiah prophesied to a people who, while chosen by God, were sometimes apathetic in their lifestyles, nominal in their worship, and distracted by the events around them. Still, God's calling on their lives was not based on the people's response but on God's good pleasure. His promises are certain.

In this beautiful passage, the prophet looks forward to a day of realized promises. He clearly sees the powerful work of God in gathering His people to Himself. Those gathered for worship will come not only from Israel but from all nations under heaven. "All flesh" will join together in worship before God.

No sin can frustrate God's promise. God never gets "fed up" with His people. He is ever faithful. In fact, God knew of a saint's future sin at the moment of justification, and He saved him anyway. This is good news for both Jew and Gentile! As we look at God's enduring faithfulness toward Israel, we are even more hopeful in our own salvation. If God will not forsake His promise to them, He will not forsake His purpose for you.

> Father, thank You that my standing before You is settled, not based on my behavior but based on Jesus' shed blood. Amen.

Dr. Chris Aiken, Englewood Baptist Church, Rocky Mount, NC

WEEK 29—THURSDAY

Living in Abundance

When He had taken the five loaves and the two fish, He looked up to heaven, blessed and broke the loaves, and gave them to His disciples to set before them; and the two fish He divided among them all. So they all ate and were filled. And they took up twelve baskets full of fragments and of the fish. Now those who had eaten the loaves were about five thousand men.

MARK 6:41-44

When I began pastoral ministry, I asked a mentor, "Who feeds the pastor?" I was only beginning to learn how God provided for the shepherd's soul. This passage answers perfectly. To meet the needs of thousands, Jesus took what seemed insignificant to His disciples and divided it among throngs of people. Every time Jesus broke the bread and divided the fish, He gave it to His disciples to distribute. The young boy's lunch in the hands of Jesus flowed like an artesian well.

Not only were the people famished; the disciples were also hungry. Yet after they served the crowd, there was sufficient surplus for each disciple to have his own basket of provision.

This is how it often works in our lives. We have little to offer others, but in serving others, we find that God supplies our needs as well as theirs. Had the disciples focused on their own need or resorted to complaining about circumstances, they would have left hungry. But when they committed to serve, relying on Jesus as the source, they experienced Christ's ample supply.

> Lord, thank You for Your abundant supply. Focus my attention on serving others first, and train my heart to trust in Your limitless provision. Amen.

Heaven, Life, and the Resurrection

WEEK 29—FRIDAY

An Eye Toward the Sky

"Now learn this parable from the fig tree: When its branch has already become tender and puts forth leaves, you know that summer is near. So you also, when you see all these things, know that it is near—at the doors! Assuredly, I say to you, this generation will by no means pass away till all these things take place. Heaven and earth will pass away, but My words will by no means pass away."

MATTHEW 24:32-35

During my first overseas assignment with the Army, someone gave me a "short-timers" calendar. As I marked off the completed days of my tour, my excitement and anticipation of my return home grew stronger and more pronounced. Jesus told His disciples that we should have the same type of anticipation about His imminent return. Just as tender branches always predicted the coming of summer, so the prolonging of days anticipates Christ's appearance. Every passing day stirs our hearts in anticipation. The yearning of our hearts cries out with the saints of old, "Even so, come, Lord Jesus!" (Rev. 22:20).

Some may discount the Lord's return as unpredictable since it has delayed so long. Instead of discouragement, we should be overwhelmed with delight. His return is one day closer than yesterday. As the days march on, Jesus exhorts us to resist apathy and grow in anticipation. Prepare. Look. Look again. King Jesus is coming soon! His delay should not shake the foundation of our faith; it should strengthen it.

Lord, teach me to live every moment in increasing anticipation of Your imminent return. Find me faithful as a prepared person, with an eye toward the sky. Amen.

Dr. Chris Aiken, Englewood Baptist Church, Rocky Mount, NC

WEEK 29—WEEKEND

The Great Barometer

Oh, give thanks to the Lord, for He is good! For His mercy endures forever. Oh, give thanks to the God of gods! For His mercy endures forever. Oh, give thanks to the Lord of lords! For His mercy endures forever . . . Oh, give thanks to the God of heaven! For His mercy endures forever.

PSALM 136:1-3, 26

"What do you say?" This familiar refrain peppered my mom's instructions throughout my early childhood. She taught me to be thankful and express gratitude in response to the kindness of others. At some point, I did not need to be reminded to say, "Thank you." It became part of a habitual response. Though good, this is not at the heart of the psalmist's instructions.

We are reminded 26 times in this psalm that God's mercy "endures forever." The word translated "mercy" is powerful, used 245 times in the Old Testament, half of those in Psalms. It speaks of God's faithful, loyal, covenant commitment. No matter your brokenness, God's mercy never fails. No matter your rebellion, His mercy never fails. No matter how long you delay, detour, or disregard obedience to God's directions, His mercy never fails. It neither delays nor diminishes but presses toward us, seeking our repentant return. When we gaze upon His mercy, we are filled to overflowing with awe and appreciation, resulting in perpetual and heartfelt expressions of thanksgiving. Giving thanks is a natural by-product of one's appreciation of God's loyal and steadfast mercy. Our thankfulness, then, is the great barometer of our faith.

....

Lord, stir my heart to recognize all of Your expressions of mercy and receive my thankful response as worship. Amen.

Heaven, Life, and the Resurrection

WEEK 30—MONDAY

Forget Not vs. Familiarity

Bless the LORD, O my soul; and all that is within me, bless His holy name! Bless the LORD, O my soul, and forget not all His benefits: who forgives all your iniquities, who heals all your diseases, who redeems your life from destruction, who crowns you with lovingkindness and tender mercies, who satisfies your mouth with good things, so that your youth is renewed like the eagle's.

PSALM 103:1-5

My wife and I love going to any beach anywhere. Where the scenery is breathtaking, I often notice others seemingly taking it for granted. When I ask what it is like to live in a place like that, they respond, "Meh . . . you get used to it." What kind of answer is that? I would love to see that scenery every day, and I don't think I would ever get used to it. They became so familiar with the beauty around them that it lost its wonder. They were so busy with life that the beauty faded.

When I read Psalm 103, I have to wonder if that's how I am with God. At one point, He was so beautiful in my life that I adored Him. I worshipped Him with everything in me. But then life happened. How do we fight against missing God's beauty that we once so desperately held on to? Do as David did. He preached to himself reminders of God's faithfulness, forgiveness, healing, and redemption. Martin Luther advised preaching the gospel to yourself. It's how we remind ourselves of God's blessings and benefits.

Lord Jesus, may I never forget who You are to me, my Prize; and who I am to You, Your possession! Amen.

Dr. Chad Grayson, Life Community Church, Jamestown, NC

WEEK 30—TUESDAY

Ask Me Anything

Then God said to him: "Because you have asked this thing, and have not asked long life for yourself, nor have asked riches for yourself, nor have asked the life of your enemies, but have asked for yourself understanding to discern justice, behold, I have done according to your words; see, I have given you a wise and understanding heart, so that there has not been anyone like you before you, nor shall any like you arise after you."

1 KINGS 3:11-12

If you could ask God for anything knowing He would give it to you, what would you ask Him for? That's what God offered Solomon at the beginning of his reign. It is interesting what Solomon did *not* ask God for—more money, fame, a blessed life, or food. He asked for an understanding and discerning heart to do God's will and care for His people (vv. 7–9). So God made him the wisest man ever to live and added riches and favor.

I see this as an Old Testament version of Matthew 6:33. Because Solomon prioritized God and His kingdom, God threw in much more as a bonus. That doesn't mean that if you pray this prayer today, you'll get everything you asked for next week. But it does show us something about the character of God that Scripture attests to again and again: If you seek God's kingdom for the sake of His kingdom, He throws in much more joy.

....

Father God, I desire wisdom to do Your will and Your work. I don't want anything for my life outside of Your perfect plan. I'd rather have Jesus than anything! Amen.

Heaven, Life, and the Resurrection

WEEK 30—WEDNESDAY

The Coming Wrath of God

The angel whom I saw standing on the sea and on the land raised up his hand to heaven and swore by Him who lives forever and ever, who created heaven and the things that are in it, the earth and the things that are in it, and the sea and the things that are in it, that there should be delay no longer.

REVELATION 10:5-6

We serve a patient God. When I think about how many times I have messed up and deserved wrath instead of grace, I am amazed I'm still alive. I think of all the people who have heard the gospel and yet chosen not to believe, but God gives them another chance to hear it again. He is long-suffering toward us, not wanting any to perish but for all to come to repentance (2 Peter 3:9). God waits. He gives chance after chance to say yes to His wonderful salvation.

Revelation 10 is a picture of God's mercy in the middle of great tribulation. But there is coming a day when He will not give another chance to say yes. He will not delay His wrath on Satan or unbelievers any longer. The church must take the gospel to the lost and be desperate for God to move . We must be brokenhearted over the millions who will spend eternity separated from Him. Revelation was not written to scare people to death but to shake them to life. Rise up church! Let's rescue the perishing and care for the dying; Jesus is merciful, and Jesus will save!

....

Oh God, break my heart for what breaks Yours! In the name of the One who lives forever, amen.

WEEK 30—THURSDAY

GOAT

Forever, O LORD, Your word is settled in heaven. Your faithfulness endures to all generations; You established the earth, and it abides. They continue this day according to Your ordinances, For all are Your servants. . . . I will never forget Your precepts, for by them You have given me life.

PSALM 119:89–91, 93

Tom Brady is the GOAT! No, Joe Montana is the GOAT! Lebron James or Michael Jordan is the GOAT. Arguments about the Greatest of All Time in a particular sport will continue for years to come—so many opinions, all thought to be backed by the most evidence.

God's Word settles forever the question of who the GOAT of eternity is. The psalmist says God's Word is settled in heaven. In other words, it doesn't matter what opinion we have. When God settles something, it's not up for debate. He's the greatest of all time in creation, faithfulness, love, redemption, authority, everything!

The word "precepts" (v. 93) means rules, guidelines, or teachings. God's Word is teaching and showing us what to do and what not to do. We can risk everything on His Word. Hebrews 4:12 says it is alive. Only something living can give life. Praise God for the living Word of God!

....

> Thank you, Father God, that Your Word is alive! May I never treat it as dry, dull, or dead, but as the dynamite that it is! Amen.

Heaven, Life, and the Resurrection

WEEK 30—FRIDAY

God's Way > My Way

"For My thoughts are not your thoughts, nor are your ways My ways," says the Lord. *"For as the heavens are higher than the earth, so are My ways higher than your ways, and My thoughts than your thoughts. . . . So shall My word be that goes forth from My mouth; it shall not return to Me void, but it shall accomplish what I please, and it shall prosper in the thing for which I sent it."*

ISAIAH 55:8-9, 11

The song "My Way," written in 1967 by Paul Anka, says, "I did it my way"—a statement of "me-ism" and pride. Much of the world and even the church could sing this as an anthem to live by. We are so prone to think our way is best—or to look for a better way.

According to God's Word, the gospel is not the best way or a better way. It is the only way! God's ways and thoughts are higher than ours. We could have never devised a plan for redemption. God said His word will not return to Him empty or void but accomplish what He pleases. Did this happen? Yes, He accomplished all of this in Jesus.

"In the beginning was the Word, and the Word was with God, and the Word was God. . . .

As many as received Him, to them He gave the right to become children of God. . . . And the Word became flesh and dwelt among us, and we beheld His glory . . . full of grace and truth" (John 1:1, 12, 14).

Father, thank You for thinking of me long before I thought of You! Amen.

Dr. Chad Grayson, Life Community Church, Jamestown, NC

WEEK 30—WEEKEND

Jesus Only

Now as they spoke to the people, the priests, the captain of the temple, and the Sadducees came upon them, being greatly disturbed that they taught the people and preached in Jesus the resurrection from the dead. And they laid hands on them, and put them in custody until the next day, for it was already evening. However, many of those who heard the word believed; and the number of the men came to be about five thousand.

ACTS 4:1-4

My youngest son loves to play the games on the back of children's menus. His favorite is the maze. It appears at first that all paths lead to the other finish line. But only one will guide you without hitting any of the roadblocks.

Peter and John were arrested for preaching Jesus' crucifixion and resurrection and performing miracles in His name. They had healed a lame man and explained that this healing demonstrated Jesus' power to save the soul (Acts 3). The religious elites were disturbed—a frequent reaction to believers.

Many believers today are beginning to recognize the hostility toward them. Why? Because we teach the death, burial, and resurrection of Jesus and that He can redeem any sinner, forgive any sin, and restore any brokenness. We teach that He is the only Way to get to God the Father. Those who follow Jesus and speak on His behalf to a hurting, broken, sinful world will face persecution. But be of good cheer—Jesus has overcome the world! (John 16:33).

....

Oh God, thank You for saving me. Thank You for giving me a message to tell the world that You can and will save anyone. Amen

Heaven, Life, and the Resurrection

WEEK 31—MONDAY

God Works from Home

Hear in heaven Your dwelling place, and forgive, and act, and give to everyone according to all his ways, whose heart You know (for You alone know the hearts of all the sons of men), that they may fear You all the days that they live in the land which You gave to our fathers.

1 KINGS 8:39-40

The phrase "working remotely" entered our vocabulary during the global pandemic. My wife and I have two daughters who transitioned to working remotely for months. I read of a major business selling its building and having its employees work remotely permanently. For many of us, our homes became our offices. It was a new concept for most of us, but did you know God works from home?

When King Solomon dedicated the temple, he stood with his arms lifted high and cried out to God to hear his prayer. He appealed to God in His "dwelling place." God works from "home" to hear our prayer and forgive our sin.

Of course, God left home to become a man and live and die for us in our own neighborhood. Now Jesus is alive and back home in heaven. He is interceding for His people right now at God's right hand. He wants us to join Him in His home someday.

God hears the prayers of His people from His throne in heaven. You might say He does His best work from home!

> Oh Lord, I ask You to hear my prayer, forgive my sin, and lead me someday safely home.

Dr. J. Kie Bowman, Hyde Park Baptist Church, Austin, TX

WEEK 31—TUESDAY

He Can Hear You Now

Continue earnestly in prayer, being vigilant in it with thanksgiving; meanwhile praying also for us, that God would open to us a door for the word, to speak the mystery of Christ, for which I am also in chains.

COLOSSIANS 4:2–3

Most of us give little thought to calling a friend or family member across the country, or even around the world. The digital revolution, smartphones, and video chat make great distances seem less restrictive than ever before. But it wasn't always that way.

More than 140 years ago, Alexander Graham Bell placed a telephone call from Salem to Boston. The cities are only about twenty-five miles apart, but the call made history. That day, the inventor also coined a phrase: "long-distance call." Technology has obviously changed and today we can easily call much longer distances. When we do, our voices are transmitted instantly around the corner or around the world.

Have you ever thought about the fact that when you pray, your words are heard in heaven? Jesus taught us to call upon our "Father in heaven" (Matthew 6:9). Your deepest longings are expressed from here, but they are heard from there. Prayer takes you further than any other activity on earth. It instantly carries your words, cares, pain, and hopes into heaven—almost like prayer takes you into heaven before you get there. Prayer takes the servant far, into the presence of the Father who feels near.

....

Oh Lord, You are my Master in heaven. Thank You for hearing me from heaven.

Heaven, Life, and the Resurrection

WEEK 31—WEDNESDAY

Already There

God, who is rich in mercy, because of His great love with which He loved us, even when we were dead in trespasses, made us alive together with Christ (by grace you have been saved), and raised us up together, and made us sit together in the heavenly places in Christ Jesus, that in the ages to come He might show the exceeding riches of His grace in His kindness toward us in Christ Jesus.

EPHESIANS 2:4–7

We never hear grass grow. Still, acousticians say plants emit microsounds. No one has the physiological equipment to perceive everything happening in the natural world. Imagine how much is happening in the spiritual world we simply miss.

Paul assured the Ephesians that Christ made us alive. But, using past tense verbs, he added that we are already raised and seated with Christ. Believers alive today are already raised with Christ and with Him in "heavenly places." It has already occurred.

We have no inherent capacity to understand how we can be both here and there. But neither can we understand how God parted the Red Sea, how a few pieces of bread and fish fed thousands of people, or how Jesus could be nailed to a cross, die, and three days later rise from the dead never to die again. But I believe it! Likewise, by faith, I accept that I'm alive in Christ and am currently seated with Him in heavenly places. I'm going to heaven someday, and I'm already there!

Father, thank You for raising me and seating me with Jesus in heavenly places.

Dr. J. Kie Bowman, Hyde Park Baptist Church, Austin, TX

WEEK 31—THURSDAY

We Need Water!

Jesus answered and said to her, "Whoever drinks of this water will thirst again, but whoever drinks of the water that I shall give him will never thirst. But the water that I shall give him will become in him a fountain of water springing up into everlasting life."

JOHN 4:13-14

I had never been so thirsty in my life. I was ten years old and had been running and playing with a large group of other kids in a grassy open field on a blistering hot summer day. When my dad signaled it was time to go home, I wanted a drink of water, but none was available. The coolers had been emptied and stored away, and in those days we didn't carry bottled water. In the forty-minute ride home, I kept complaining I was "dying of thirst." I was exaggerating, of course. But the thirst was real.

We all need water. Our bodies are approximately 60 percent water, our brains and hearts more than 70 percent. Dehydration can happen fast.

In the longest conversation Jesus ever had with one person in the New Testament, He told a woman beside a well she needed water that could not be held in a bucket. In a brilliant comparison between what the woman needed daily and what Jesus offers for eternity, the Lord created a thirst for water she had never tasted. The water from this life satisfies for the moment, but the water of salvation from Jesus satisfies forever. Jesus offers that water of life. Drink up!

Thank You, Lord for offering me water that springs up to eternal life!

WEEK 31—FRIDAY

Why Less Is More

Then Jesus said to His disciples, "Assuredly, I say to you that it is hard for a rich man to enter the kingdom of heaven. And again I say to you, it is easier for a camel to go through the eye of a needle than for a rich man to enter the kingdom of God."

MATTHEW 19:23-24

Pastors hear a lot of confidential admissions. A longtime pastor of a well-known church recently remarked that the only sin no one had ever confessed to him is greed. Greed is an extremely deceptive sin that weaves itself deeply into our souls.

When Jesus compared a camel squeezing through the eye of a needle to a rich man entering heaven, He knew the image was over-the-top, purposely absurd, and brilliantly memorable. His hyperbole paints a vivid picture, since greed is hard to admit and easy to justify. It's as if Jesus was saying, "If you think greed is acceptable, you must think you can use a fifteen-hundred pound camel as a spool of thread."

The problem of greed is its seductive subtlety. It convinces us to value the wrong things. The accumulation of wealth is highly esteemed in this life but of no value in the next. No one goes to heaven simply because they're poor, but neither does anyone walk with God who refuses to repent of sin. A day of judgment is coming, and accumulated wealth will have no value. All accounts will be settled, and the only thing of value will be our repentance and our faith in Christ.

> Lord, thank You for Your grace. You are worth more to me than everything in this world.

Dr. J. Kie Bowman, Hyde Park Baptist Church, Austin, TX

WEEK 31—WEEKEND

Remember God

O my God, my soul is cast down within me; therefore I will remember You from the land of the Jordan, and from the heights of Hermon, from the Hill Mizar. Deep calls unto deep at the noise of Your waterfalls; all Your waves and billows have gone over me. The LORD will command His lovingkindness in the daytime, and in the night His song shall be with me—a prayer to the God of my life.

PSALM 42:6-8

Discouragement is a kind of temporary spiritual amnesia, often causing us to forget God's faithfulness. In 1983, Russian novelist Aleksandr Solzhenitsyn gave a speech about the history of communism in Russia and its failure as a system of government. He summarized the main reason communism was able to gain such a powerful but devastating stranglehold over what had been, for a thousand years, a predominantly Christian nation. His conclusion was simple and direct. He believed people had forgotten God. Forgetting God is not just political suicide; it destroys our personal lives as well.

Fortunately, faith has a long memory. Memory and faith actually go together. When the psalmist was discouraged, for instance, he forced himself to remember God. His mind drifted back to a time spent in God's presence at the foot of snow-covered Mount Hermon, at the headwaters of the Jordan River. By reminding himself of God's faithfulness in the past, his faith and hope were restored.

When you feel discouraged, remind yourself of God's faithfulness in the past. By jogging yourself out of "spiritual amnesia," your faith will be renewed.

> Lord, today I will remember Your faithfulness in the past and I ask You to restore my hope.

Heaven, Life, and the Resurrection

WEEK 32—MONDAY

New Start

"And now, Israel, what does the Lord your God require of you, but to fear the Lord your God, to walk in all His ways and to love Him, to serve the Lord your God with all your heart and with all your soul, and to keep the commandments of the Lord and His statutes which I command you today for your good?"

DEUTERONOMY 10:12-13

The children of Israel were completing forty years of wandering in the wilderness. They had made a plethora of mistakes and were on the edge of the promised land, and Moses was giving them final words of challenge. It was time for a new start!

Moses combined attitude and action in five directives for this new start. The attitude was to "fear the Lord"—to have a reverential fear that motivates worship and obedience. This proper fear leads a person to a godly walk that has three components. First, you respond to God's love for you by expressing your love to Him. Second, you serve the Lord without reservation or qualification. Third, you keep His commands and decrees. And, he said, this will all be for your own good.

Do you need a new start—a do-over? God is gracious, and His Word gives a straightforward account of how to respond to His divine grace. It even throws in a guarantee that it will be for your benefit! Embrace these five things and make a new start today.

....

> Lord, today I want a new start in my walk with You. Thank You for Your grace, and guide me by Your Word. Amen.

Dr. Danny Wood, Shades Mountain Baptist Church, Birmingham, AL

WEEK 32—TUESDAY

Life Is Sacred

The LORD God formed man of the dust of the ground, and breathed into his nostrils the breath of life; and man became a living being. The LORD God planted a garden eastward in Eden, and there He put the man whom He had formed. And out of the ground the LORD God made every tree grow that is pleasant to the sight and good for food. The tree of life was also in the midst of the garden, and the tree of the knowledge of good and evil.

GENESIS 2:7-9

Life is sacred. Genesis 1:27 tells us that God made human beings in His own image, setting us apart from the animals. Today's passage provides more details and further establishes the differences. The keys are the verbs "formed" and "breathed."

God did not speak man into existence but formed him as a potter would mold clay. It was personal and intentional. He breathed into the nostrils of the man—"Breathed" being a warmly personal word implying the face-to-face intimacy of a kiss. Humanity's life therefore comes from the breath of the Creator Himself.

Your life is sacred. You have been personally created by God for a purpose. Your life has meaning and value because you were formed by God in His own image and "the breath of the Almighty gives [you] life" (Job 33:4). Value your life and those around you today because life is sacred.

....

Thank You, Lord, for the gift of life. I praise You that I have been wonderfully created in Your image, and I commit this day to bring You honor and glory. Amen.

Heaven, Life, and the Resurrection

WEEK 32—WEDNESDAY

Mindful of the Things of God

He began to teach them that the Son of Man must suffer many things, and be rejected by the elders and chief priests and scribes, and be killed, and after three days rise again. He spoke this word openly. Then Peter took Him aside and began to rebuke Him. But when He had turned around and looked at His disciples, He rebuked Peter, saying, "Get behind Me, Satan! For you are not mindful of the things of God, but the things of men."

MARK 8:31-33

How often do you argue with God over your circumstances? How often do you pull Jesus to the side and rebuke Him because the way He is doing things is just not right?

Jesus was traveling with his disciples and asked them who people were saying He was. Peter nailed the right answer by saying Jesus was the Christ. With that established, Jesus began to speak openly and plainly about His coming suffering, death, and resurrection. And for this, Peter took Jesus aside and rebuked Him.

Peter heard the "suffer" and "killed" but apparently missed the "rise again." Jesus accused Peter of thinking like the world and not being mindful of the things of God. The Bible says that God's ways are higher than our ways and that He is working all things together for good (Isaiah 55:9; Romans 8:28). In the midst of difficult circumstances, be mindful of the things of God, remembering the victory of the cross and the power of the resurrection.

Lord today I confidently place my life and circumstances into Your hands. I trust You with all my heart and lean not on my own understanding. Amen.

Dr. Danny Wood, Shades Mountain Baptist Church, Birmingham, AL

WEEK 32—THURSDAY

Safe Keeping

"For I have come down from heaven, not to do My own will, but the will of Him who sent Me. This is the will of the Father who sent Me, that of all He has given Me I should lose nothing, but should raise it up at the last day. And this is the will of Him who sent Me, that everyone who sees the Son and believes in Him may have everlasting life; and I will raise him up at the last day."

JOHN 6:38-40

Safe-deposit boxes are used to keep valuables, important documents, and sentimental keepsakes protected. But what about your most precious possession, your soul? Is it safe?

Jesus says He will not lose those who are given to Him by the Father, who accept Him as Savior,. He does not turn you away when you come, nor does He subsequently disown you. The "keeping" ministry of Jesus will include securing His own people at the last judgment. To receive and embrace Jesus Christ is to have the confidence of being raised up at the last day.

Your responsibility is perfectly clear: simply believe in the Son of God and commit your life to Him, and He will keep you until the consummation of the resurrection life "at the last day." God has joined together the possession of eternal life now and the hope of resurrection at the last day for those who have come to Christ in faith. You cannot get any safer than that!

> Thank You, Lord for saving my soul and for the assurance that You will safely keep me into eternity. Amen.

WEEK 32—FRIDAY

Kingdom-Minded Praying

Then God said to Solomon: "Because this was in your heart, and you have not asked riches or wealth or honor or the life of your enemies, nor have you asked long life—but have asked wisdom and knowledge for yourself, that you may judge My people over whom I have made you king—wisdom and knowledge are granted to you; and I will give you riches and wealth and honor, such as none of the kings have had who were before you, nor shall any after you have the like."

2 CHRONICLES 1:11-12

Solomon became king of the people once led by Moses, Joshua, Samuel, and David. Those were big sandals to fill. The task seemed overwhelming. So when God appeared to him in a dream and asked him what he wanted—without conditions, a blank check—Solomon prayed for wisdom to lead God's people. He did not ask to be wise so he could become a famous wise man; he asked so God's people would be wisely governed. He wanted God to give him the ability to do what God had called him to do so God would be glorified.

God was pleased with Solomon's kingdom-minded prayer, attitude, and request. He not only granted the request but made promises beyond what Solomon imagined.

God is available to hear your prayers today. Pray as Solomon did. Remember to praise and honor God for who He is and what He has done. Admit your limitations and utter dependence on Him, and promise to serve Him well in whatever He calls you to do.

> Lord, give me what I need today to serve and honor You and advance Your kingdom. Amen.

Dr. Danny Wood, Shades Mountain Baptist Church, Birmingham, AL

WEEK 32—WEEKEND

Resurrected Bodies

The first man was of the earth, made of dust; the second Man is the Lord from heaven. As was the man of dust, so also are those who are made of dust; and as is the heavenly Man, so also are those who are heavenly. And as we have borne the image of the man of dust, we shall also bear the image of the heavenly Man.

1 CORINTHIANS 15:47-49

No one wants to grow up to be a ghost. How attractive would heaven be if you floated around as a disembodied spirit for eternity? God created us to have physical bodies and has planned for us to have bodies for eternity.

The "first man" was Adam, and "those who are made of dust" are all humans in sharing an earthly origin and living in a perishable and mortal body. The "second man" is Jesus Christ, and "those who are heavenly" are those who have received Him as Savior. All believers will "bear the image of Christ" in eternity, clothing themselves with His imperishable and immortal image. We will spend our lives in bodies that reflect His state after His resurrection.

The nature of Jesus' resurrected life shows that we will maintain our unique identity and personality. Relationships will continue. We will be able to eat, walk, talk, and have all five senses stretched to their glorious limits. And we will be wonderfully and totally led by the Holy Spirit. Oh, the glorious riches of heaven!

Lord, as I walk through the challenges of today, remind me of the wonderful promises of heaven. Amen.

WEEK 33—MONDAY

The Mystery of God's Wisdom

To make all see what is the fellowship of the mystery, which from the beginning of the ages has been hidden in God who created all things through Jesus Christ; to the intent that now the manifold wisdom of God might be made known by the church to the principalities and powers in the heavenly places.

EPHESIANS 3:9–10

Do you enjoy a good mystery? In the New Testament, a mystery is something previously known only to God but revealed in the gospel. The Lord revealed to Paul that His redemptive plan for salvation was through Jesus Christ and not through keeping laws. Having been a devout Pharisee, this was undoubtedly a hard conclusion for him to reach. But God showed him that the gospel was open to everyone, Jew and Gentile alike.

This wonderful mystery is described as "the manifold wisdom of God." "Manifold" in Greek can describe a beautiful, colorful, embroidered pattern in an expensive garment or a hillside of wildflowers in the spring. This was how the Holy Spirit led Paul to describe what the baptized, blood-bought body and bride of Christ would be like with both Jewish and Gentile believers in it. Every local church under Christ is a personal, physical manifestation of God's wisdom and a witness to Christ's power in bringing different people together in unity of faith and love. No wonder Paul was unashamed to declare the gospel. May we be just as determined to do the same for people today.

> Lord, help me see my church family as a picture of Your wisdom and the power of the gospel displayed for others to see. Amen.

Dr. Bryan E. Smith, First Roanoke Baptist Church, Roanoke, VA

WEEK 33—TUESDAY

Camping on the Way to Heaven

If indeed, having been clothed, we shall not be found naked. For we who are in this tent groan, being burdened, not because we want to be unclothed, but further clothed, that mortality may be swallowed up by life. Now He who has prepared us for this very thing is God, who also has given us the Spirit as a guarantee.

2 CORINTHIANS 5:3-5

Have you ever spent the night camping in a tent? A good friend of mine used to work for the US Forest Service and spent many nights in a tent to fight wildfires. He said there are numerous challenges to contend with: heavy rains, cold temperatures, hot nights, strong winds, and swarms of mosquitos. Years ago, my son and I went camping on a hunting trip. We didn't have a rain fly cover, and early the next morning with below-freezing temperatures, we bumped the ceiling of our tent and covered, ourselves with a cold shower!

Like an old camping tent, our physical bodies become increasingly uncomfortable. God created us as spiritual creatures but placed us in a physical world, thus the need for our "earth suits." Eventually these bodies will hold us down more than they will hold us up. The older I become, the more I realize God created me to live in anticipation of living again. What death separates, Christ has promised in the power of His resurrection to put back together perfectly and eternally. He's even guaranteed His promise with the indwelling, abiding presence of the Holy Spirit.

Lord, thank You that because You saved me, I am living now to live again. Amen.

Heaven, Life, and the Resurrection

WEEK 33—WEDNESDAY

The Best Bread of All

Then Jesus said to them, "Most assuredly, I say to you, Moses did not give you the bread from heaven, but My Father gives you the true bread from heaven. For the bread of God is He who comes down from heaven and gives life to the world." Then they said to Him, "Lord, give us this bread always."

JOHN 6:32-34

I'm a big bread fan. I would rather give up eating dessert than bread. So naturally I love eating at restaurants where you walk in the door and see a wall full of every kind of bread and bagel imaginable. But no matter how much delicious bread people eat, they will always be hungry again.

Jesus reminded the people that the manna Moses gave to their forefathers after their exodus from Egypt was temporary and limited to this world. This bread didn't come from Moses but from God. Jesus said He was a different kind of bread, the "true bread from heaven." The manna of Moses' day could only give life to the body, but Jesus as the true bread can give life that nourishes body, soul, and spirit.

Sin always kills and destroys because it cuts us off from the One who made us. Jesus came into the world to give abundant and everlasting life to all who would believe in Him. But as manna had to be gathered and eaten to benefit the Israelites, so must a person receive Jesus Christ by faith in order to experience the blessing of heaven's true bread of life forever.

....

Lord, show me someone with whom I can share the Bread of Life today. Amen.

Dr. Bryan E. Smith, First Roanoke Baptist Church, Roanoke, VA

WEEK 33—THURSDAY

The Giver of Life

For the Father loves the Son and shows Him all things that He Himself does; and He will show Him greater works than these, that you may marvel. For as the Father raises the dead and gives life to them, even so the Son gives life to whom He will. For the Father judges no one but has committed all judgment to the Son.
JOHN 5:20-22

Have you ever known someone who "over promised" but "under-delivered"? It's a common problem. Sometimes promises are made with sincere intentions of keeping them, and sometimes they seem to be a ploy to gain a personal advantage.

When Jesus ministered to the multitudes, His disciples marveled at His authority over demons, sickness, the lame, nature, and even death itself. Jesus said He did these things because they came from His heavenly Father. He claimed equality with God the Father in both His works and His judgment. "Like father, like son" was never truer than with the divine relationship of God the Father and God the Son. That's why dishonoring and rejecting Jesus the Son also dishonors and rejects God the Father.

Jesus demonstrates His oneness with the Father every time He gives new life to someone who believes in Him. This is a spiritual resurrection of a lost person, who was spiritually dead until raised to walk in newness of spiritual life. If you hear Jesus' voice as He knocks on your heart's door, welcome Him in and experience what it means to be truly alive.

....

    Lord, I ask You right now to forgive my sins, come into my heart and save me. Amen.

Heaven, Life, and the Resurrection

WEEK 33—FRIDAY

Learning to Fear

"Also it shall be, when he sits on the throne of his kingdom, that he shall write for himself a copy of this law in a book, from the one before the priests, the Levites. And it shall be with him, and he shall read it all the days of his life, that he may learn to fear the LORD his God and be careful to observe all the words of this law and these statutes."

DEUTERONOMY 17:18-19

Fear is something every person knows all too well. Modern psychology has identified all sorts of fears, from a fear of heights to a fear of one's own relatives. During the COVID pandemic, people feared the dreaded virus. It was a difficult and frightening time for many, especially for those who were most at risk.

The Bible describes a different kind of fear that comes from reading God's Word. It's a fear that is godly, helpful, needed, and available to anyone willing to learn it. God said that a king's education should include learning to fear the Lord by reading, copying, and following His Law as taught in Deuteronomy. When we commit to reading God's Word and obeying it, we will learn to fear Him. When we have respect, reverence, and awe for God, we are learning to fear Him. When we seek to keep Christ as the centerpiece of our hearts while basing our decisions on His authority, we are learning to fear Him.

Lord, teach me to fear You as I read Your Word and obey it. Amen.

Dr. Bryan E. Smith, First Roanoke Baptist Church, Roanoke, VA

WEEK 33—WEEKEND

God's Word of Hope

Remember the word to Your servant, upon which You have caused me to hope. This is my comfort in my affliction, for Your word has given me life. . . . Your statutes have been my songs in the house of my pilgrimage. I remember Your name in the night, O LORD, and I keep Your law. This has become mine, because I kept Your precepts.

PSALM 119:49-50, 54-56

What gives us hope in this life? The truth that God will comfort us despite our afflictions and disappointments. The psalmist said God's Word gave him life and helped him sing in the midst of his difficulties while leading him to remember God during the night.

When my mom was struggling with failing health, she told me she would sometimes be awakened in the early-morning hours with a flood of anxious thoughts. She responded by reciting Scripture and Christian hymns and songs. Then, while she lay in her bed, she would call on God's name and raise her hand in prayer. Many times it felt as though God was holding her hand as she drifted off to sleep.

When we value God's Word enough to hide it in our hearts, God's hope will be our comfort in difficult and disappointing days. It's not a matter of using Him for a comfortable life but wanting to know and follow Him because we love Him more than we love His gifts. Call on God's name in your long nights. A Christian's hope springs eternal because it's found in the eternal God who will not let him go.

Lord, thank You for the hope I have in You today and forever. Amen.

Heaven, Life, and the Resurrection

WEEK 34—MONDAY

Choose Life

I call heaven and earth as witnesses today against you, that I have set before you life and death, blessing and cursing; therefore choose life, that both you and your descendants may live; that you may love the Lord your God, that you may obey His voice, and that you may cling to Him, for He is your life and the length of your days; and that you may dwell in the land which the Lord swore to your fathers, to Abraham, Isaac, and Jacob, to give them."

DEUTERONOMY 30:19-20

An obedient life cooperates with the Holy Spirit in the process of being set apart to God and set apart from sin. Scripture calls this sanctification. Though God is the author and finisher of His good work in us, He has also called us to cooperate with the work of His Spirit. So we have to make choices. When we choose obedience to God, we choose life and blessing. When we choose disobedience and sin, we make a choice that is inconsistent with God's life in us.

The purpose of God for our lives is to be conformed to the image of Jesus. As we obey and yield to God's Spirit, we are shaped more into the image of perfect humanity—the image of the Lord. And since He is our very life, to choose obedience to Him is to choose life, blessing, and the redemption God has designed for us.

Father, You alone give life and are life. Apart from You, we merely exist and do not truly live. We surrender this day to Your life in us, and we welcome the work of Your Spirit in conforming us to be more like Jesus.

Jerry Gillis, The Chapel at Crosspoint, Getzville, NY

WEEK 34—TUESDAY

Life in the Kingdom

"Assuredly, I say to you, among those born of women there has not risen one greater than John the Baptist; but he who is least in the kingdom of heaven is greater than he. And from the days of John the Baptist until now the kingdom of heaven suffers violence, and the violent take it by force. . . . He who has ears to hear, let him hear!"

MATTHEW 11:11-12, 15

John the Baptist was a great man, the Elijah figure who would prepare the way for the Messiah (v. 14). He was a bridge between the prior age and the dawning of a new one, yet those of us who have been born from above through faith in Jesus belong to the age of the kingdom of heaven. What a privilege!

The response to John's preaching and then to Jesus' message was overwhelming—like that of sheep stuffed in a pen and then finally released (see Micah 2:12-13). It was like a violent advance toward freedom for those who received it. But the opposite was also true; there was strong opposition to the kingdom by forces of evil. Running toward freedom in the kingdom of heaven will always be worth it, even when the forces of evil do everything in their power to stand against the freedom of your new life in Jesus.

> Father, give us passion for living in the ways of Your kingdom, and let us seek it first—above all else—even when we face the attacks of the enemy. The privilege of walking in the freedom of the kingdom is always worth whatever it takes, so please strengthen us to do so.

Heaven, Life, and the Resurrection

WEEK 34—WEDNESDAY

The Greatness of Obedience

"For assuredly, I say to you, till heaven and earth pass away, one jot or one tittle will by no means pass from the law till all is fulfilled. Whoever therefore breaks one of the least of these commandments, and teaches men so, shall be called least in the kingdom of heaven; but whoever does and teaches them, he shall be called great in the kingdom of heaven."

MATTHEW 5:18–19

Only God has the right to determine the greatest and the least in the kingdom of heaven. Greatness in the kingdom is found in obedience to the King. The King of the kingdom of heaven is good, true, just, and worthy of our allegiance and obedience. As Jesus told His disciples, "Anyone who loves me will obey my teaching" (John 14:23, NIV). As the Son obeyed His Father in all things, so should we obey Jesus in all things. Jesus is the demonstration of true humanity—of true greatness, which was found in His trust and obedience to His Father. Ours should be no less. Every word breathed out by God is for our instruction, correction, encouragement, and shaping into the image of Jesus. And in looking more like Jesus, we begin to see what true greatness actually consists of.

> Father, strengthen my heart to embrace a greatness that is different from the way earthly kingdoms define it—power, wealth, attainment, and prominence. Shape my heart, mind, and actions into the image of Jesus and give me a hunger and thirst for Your Word. Help my life reflect willing and joyful obedience to Your Word so I can be used to show the world how trustworthy Your words are.

Jerry Gillis, The Chapel at Crosspoint, Getzville, NY

WEEK 34—THURSDAY

Beyond Description

Your mercy, O Lord, is in the heavens; Your faithfulness reaches to the clouds. Your righteousness is like the great mountains; Your judgments are a great deep; O Lord, You preserve man and beast. How precious is Your lovingkindness, O God! Therefore the children of men put their trust under the shadow of Your wings.

PSALM 36:5-7

Trying to describe God's nature and character moves us beyond words to word pictures. The Hebrew people often used analogies to describe God's majesty, and the psalmist here writes with beautiful imagery to express the inexpressible: the extraordinary nature and character of God. Mercy that reaches the heavens. Faithfulness that reaches the clouds. Righteousness like great mountains, and judgments like the deepest sea. We reach for images when the beauty and splendor of what is being described is hard to comprehend.

It is comforting that while God can be known, He is also bigger, better, and more beautiful than anything we can say. And it is awe-inspiring to think that a God this big—this good and beautiful—has offered His love to an undeserving world. God's salvation for us, which demonstrates His mercy, faithfulness, righteousness, wisdom, and love, feels beyond description. But it can be summarized in a word: Jesus.

> When my words fail, Lord, and my mind cannot fully or appropriately conceive of Your infinite wisdom, love, and worth, please let my heart leap with praise, joy, and thanks for all that You are. What You have done for the world and for me is beyond the words I could share, but I pray that my life will demonstrate Your grace and kindness to me.

Heaven, Life, and the Resurrection

WEEK 34—FRIDAY

Shepherd and King

Yea, though I walk through the valley of the shadow of death, I will fear no evil; for You are with me; Your rod and Your staff, they comfort me. You prepare a table before me in the presence of my enemies; You anoint my head with oil; my cup runs over. Surely goodness and mercy shall follow me all the days of my life; and I will dwell in the house of the Lord forever.

PSALM 23:4-6

King David knew life as a shepherd and a king, so when he reflected on God he used these pictures to describe Him. As the Great Shepherd, God guides our hearts to safety and comfort in Him, even when we are faced with death or evil. As the Great King, He vindicates His people, provides for them, and graciously gives them His shelter. God shows His people the tender care of a shepherd and the sovereign power of a king. And for King Jesus, who would come in the royal line of David, we see the same. Jesus leads His people—His church—with the tender care of a shepherd and the authority of a king. In Jesus, we will always be welcomed, be led in truth, be provided for, and be loved. Trust that today, by faith in Jesus, you will be well-led and well-fed.

....

> Father, I praise You for the grace You have shown the world in Jesus, our Great Shepherd, who was also the sheep sacrificed for us. No matter what I face today or in the days to come, my confidence in You as the One who leads me and loves me to life will always be my comfort.

Jerry Gillis, The Chapel at Crosspoint, Getzville, NY

WEEK 34—WEEKEND

The God Who Remembers

"O Israel, you will not be forgotten by Me! I have blotted out, like a thick cloud, your transgressions, and like a cloud, your sins. Return to Me, for I have redeemed you." Sing, O heavens, for the LORD has done it! Shout, you lower parts of the earth; break forth into singing, you mountains, O forest, and every tree in it! For the LORD has redeemed Jacob, and glorified Himself in Israel.

ISAIAH 44:21-23

After all of Israel's transgressions, God had not forgotten His people. The Lord made a promise to a people He had chosen, and He never failed to remember them, even when they felt as if He had forgotten them. His words remind us that God initiated the relationship with His people, made a covenant with them, and would remember and fulfill His promise.

Thankfully, that is still true today because this is who God is. While we were sinners, God initiated His love toward us through the gift of His Son, Jesus. As we exhibit faith that the death and resurrection of Jesus for our sins grants us forgivness and life eternal, we can rest assured that none of us who are in Christ can ever be forgotten by God. The only response to that news is grateful worship.

....

Thank You, Father, that You are the God who remembers me but forgets my sins because of the grace shown to me in Your Son, Jesus. I worship You and thank You for initiating love toward me, and I praise You for Your beautiful kindness. May my life be a reflection of my gratitude.

Heaven, Life, and the Resurrection

WEEK 35—MONDAY

The Winning Walk

Therefore we also, since we are surrounded by so great a cloud of witnesses, let us lay aside every weight, and the sin which so easily ensnares us, and let us run with endurance the race that is set before us, looking unto Jesus, the author and finisher of our faith, who for the joy that was set before Him endured the cross, despising the shame, and has sat down at the right hand of the throne of God.

HEBREWS 12:1-2

The Christian life is challenging. Do not give up. Scripture reminds us that many have walked the faith walk before us. Their lives and testimonies cheer us on. The writer of Hebrews gives us three insights that produce the Winning Walk.

First, lay aside anything that captures your attention away from Jesus. It could be something good that becomes a weight that distracts you from victory in the believer's walk. It could be sin that so easily slips into your life and ensnares you. Like a disciplined athlete, strip those things away so you can run the race of faith. (Action Step: Lay Aside)

Second, have a strategic focus. Athletes who run to win keep their eyes on the finish line. They see themselves standing with the trophy held high. For the believer, the focus is always Jesus. He is the champion who perfects our faith. (Action Step: Look Upward)

Finally, claim your purpose—to be the best reflection of Jesus in your world. Jesus said we are the light of the world that can't be hidden, so let your good deeds "shine" (Matt. 5:14-16). (Action Step: Look Inward)

Dear Jesus, may I discipline my life to run the race well. Amen.

WEEK 35—TUESDAY

The Powerful Word

"For as the rain comes down, and the snow from heaven, and do not return there, but water the earth, and make it bring forth and bud, that it may give seed to the sower and bread to the eater, So shall My word be that goes forth from My mouth; it shall not return to Me void, but it shall accomplish what I please, and it shall prosper in the thing for which I sent it."

ISAIAH 55:10-11

Bill Stafford was a renowned evangelist whom God used to charge up our "spiritual batteries" whenever he came to our church. Believers can become depleted and in need of revival. Bill would hold the Word of God high and shout, "This is my source, my force, and my course." The church would shout back, "Amen"! I was dialed into the message. My Source: Jesus is my life, as the Word reveals. My Force: Jesus empowers me to live the Christian life, as found in Scripture. My Course: The Word refreshes and sets the direction of my life.

The Word of God is powerful. Isaiah paints a wonderful word picture of rain and snow and their purpose. They fall to nourish and make the earth fruitful. Just as moisture brings forth life and growth on vegetation, so does the Word of God nourish us in our spiritual journeys. It's like the rain and the snow. We take it into our lives, and it never fails. It replenishes and refreshes our weary souls.

....

God, help me every day to rely on Your powerful Word. May it refresh my soul and make me more like You. Amen.

WEEK 35—WEDNESDAY

The Action of Reconciliation

Let us search out and examine our ways, and turn back to the LORD; let us lift our hearts and hands to God in heaven. We have transgressed and rebelled; You have not pardoned.

LAMENTATIONS 3:40-42

We are created for relationship with Holy God. Allow that to sink in. Humanity is the crown jewel of God's creation; that is a majestic and beautiful thought. We are different from all other living creatures made by God. He created us in His image to walk with Him in intimacy and fellowship.

We were made with the capacity to love God and fellowship with Him, but sin places a barrier between us and Holy God. Since the garden of Eden, this has been a problem for people and nations. When that relationship with God is strained or broken because of sin, God's Word tells us what to do. We must allow His Spirit to search and examine our ways in order for us to recognize the sin that has strained our intimacy with Him and hindered our fellowship. The Holy Spirit reveals how far we have wandered from Him.

Recognition is just the first step. Then we must confess or agree with God that sin is our problem. Tell Him you are sorry for sin and its impact on your relationship with Him. The writer of these verses models for us repentance and confession. "We have sinned and rebelled; Lord, forgive us." Doing this brings reconciliation. Intimacy and fellowship are restored.

....

Lord, search me and see if there is any offensive way in me. Forgive me and lead me into right fellowship with You. Amen!

Dr. Frank Cox, North Metro Baptist Church, Lawrenceville, GA

WEEK 35—THURSDAY

Hope in the Resurrection

So also is the resurrection of the dead. The body is sown in corruption, it is raised in incorruption. It is sown in dishonor, it is raised in glory. It is sown in weakness, it is raised in power. It is sown a natural body, it is raised a spiritual body. There is a natural body, and there is a spiritual body. And so it is written, "The first man Adam became a living being." The last Adam became a life-giving spirit.

1 CORINTHIANS 15:42–45

The COVID virus that spread throughout the world in 2020 proved to be no respecter of persons regardless of age, health, or ethnicity. It was deadly. But when believers think of death, we have hope. Events such as a pandemic remind us that these bodies are sown in corruption. Our current body is natural, controlled by the mind, emotions, and will. God designed it that way for this life only. This old earth suit will be laid to rest, but because our hope is in Jesus, one day we will be raised in power. God has designed our resurrected body for eternity.

The reality of eternity and the resurrected body is glorious. John was told that "God will wipe away every tear from their eyes; there shall be no more death, nor sorrow, nor crying. There shall be no more pain, for the former things have passed away" (Revelation 21:4). For believers in Jesus, our future is one of tremendous hope in the power of the resurrection.

> Our Lord and Creator, may our hope be in You alone. While we have been sown in a natural body, we praise You we will be raised in a spiritual body. Amen.

Heaven, Life, and the Resurrection

WEEK 35—FRIDAY

True Kingdom Investment

"Do not lay up for yourselves treasures on earth, where moth and rust destroy and where thieves break in and steal; but lay up for yourselves treasures in heaven, where neither moth nor rust destroys and where thieves do not break in and steal. For where your treasure is, there your heart will be also."

MATTHEW 6:19-21

Can you remember the first penny you earned? Neither can I. I do recall my parents teaching me that money is never to be my master. Instead, I am to invest in heaven. At first it was confusing, but the older I grew, the more I realized it was never my money. It always belongs to God, my Provider. Everything that comes to me comes from Him. I can remember my dad asking, "Do you trust in money more than you trust in God to provide"? He wanted me to always see God as my source.

God's purpose is for us to always be a blessing with His money that He entrusts to us. Bobby Choate, a LifeGroup teacher at our church, says, "If you are giving money away for God because God told you to, the spout will never dry up!" God gives it, and my responsibility is to keep it flowing for kingdom purposes.

Our relationship to money is a great indicator to our life commitment. A life bent toward Jesus will invest in people and ministry. Only in heaven will we be able to see the true dividends. It is called Kingdom Investment.

Lord, may my heart be committed to You and may I be a conduit to invest Your resources for the kingdom. Amen!

Dr. Frank Cox, North Metro Baptist Church, Lawrenceville, GA

WEEK 35—WEEKEND

The Secret to a Blessed Life

"See, I have set before you today life and good, death and evil, in that I command you today to love the Lord your God, to walk in His ways, and to keep His commandments, His statutes, and His judgments, that you may live and multiply; and the Lord your God will bless you in the land which you go to possess."

DEUTERONOMY 30:15-16

At the end of a great, long sermon, Moses gave Israel the secret to a successful life as the people of God. And as a fiery preacher, he called for a decision.

Followers of God through Jesus Christ must realize that this sermon could be preached in a New Testament setting today. We all want a good, prosperous life. This message tells us that it comes through a simple command of God. Israel experienced failure and had to wonder if they could do better. We too will fail at times, and we will wonder the same.

God's prescription for a good, prosperous, enriched, blessed, and spiritual life is simple: to love God and obey His commands, or teachings. God is clear about our ability to obey, and we must. As we walk in His ways, we discover a tremendous promise. We will live in His power as He blesses us.

This is the call of discipleship. Jesus always summons us to obedience. Sin always builds a barrier between the disciple and his Lord. Obedience always breeds blessings. Jesus calls for a decision just as Moses did: "Trust and obey for there is no other way to be happy in Jesus, than to trust and obey."

Lord, I want Your best. Help me to walk in obedience to Your Word. Amen.

Heaven, Life, and the Resurrection

WEEK 36—MONDAY

People Are Watching

For they themselves declare concerning us what manner of entry we had to you, and how you turned to God from idols to serve the living and true God, and to wait for His Son from heaven, whom He raised from the dead, even Jesus who delivers us from the wrath to come.

1 THESSALONIANS 1:9-10

Paul wrote, "Imitate me, just as I also imitate Christ" (1 Corinthians 11:1). Today's passage shows how Paul's imitation of Christ moved the Thessalonians toward faith in Him. Likewise, their example moved the saints in Macedonia and Achaia toward faith (1 Thessalonians 1:6–8).

Like the Thessalonians, people watch you too. Your faith walk impacts the people around you, whether they are family, friends, coworkers, or a store clerk. Does your testimony shine bright, or has it grown dim in the midst of life's struggles? Jesus said we are the "light of the world" and should not hide our light under a basket. He instructed us to let our light shine so our works would be seen and bring glory to God (Matthew 5:14–16). If our light is not shining, what must we change for it to shine?

First, we must admit that we need a course correction. Next, we must be willing to make the necessary changes. Finally, we must submit to the Lord as He continues to shape us into His likeness daily (Philippians 1:6). Begin by praying this prayer:

....

Jesus, I want to be a witness for Your glory. Forgive me as I have settled for less than Your best for me. Help my light to shine bright so others can see You in me.

Tim DeTellis, New Missions, Orlando, FL

WEEK 36—TUESDAY

The Excellence of God

For such a High Priest was fitting for us, who is holy, harmless, undefiled, separate from sinners, and has become higher than the heavens; who does not need daily, as those high priests, to offer up sacrifices, first for His own sins and then for the people's, for this He did once for all when He offered up Himself.

HEBREWS 7:26-27

One of the most devastating compromises in life is, "That's good enough." The quest for excellence is often missing and seems unimportant to many today. This compromise draws us into a web of deceit that "good enough" is all we can accomplish and nothing more. Not so with God. Everywhere we turn, we see His creation and are confronted by His goodness, perfection, righteousness, love, and excellence. God gave His excellence, Jesus, as a sacrifice for our sins, rather than something that would just be "good enough."

Do you fall into the trap of "that's good enough?" Have you ever stopped short of excellence only to learn later that if you had persevered, you would have overcome? Jesus was able to see God's promise through the cross and persevered to bring you God's excellence by His sacrifice (Hebrews 12:2). "Good enough" would have been utterly insufficient.

You can choose excellence as well and persevere by the power and grace of the Holy Spirit. Jesus' call is for you to overcome your situation and be victorious (Revelation 21:7). Today, set your aim to persevere and to overcome!

Lord, I want to be a person who pursues Your excellence in all I do. Show me each day how to demonstrate Your excellence. Strengthen me when I grow weary so Your power will help me overcome.

Heaven, Life, and the Resurrection

WEEK 36—WEDNESDAY

Power Through Unity

"Assuredly, I say to you, whatever you bind on earth will be bound in heaven, and whatever you loose on earth will be loosed in heaven. Again I say to you that if two of you agree on earth concerning anything that they ask, it will be done for them by My Father in heaven. For where two or three are gathered together in My name, I am there in the midst of them."

MATTHEW 18:18-20

The greatest model of agreement and unity is the Godhead—Father, Son, and Holy Spirit. By this, we see that God values unity. Jesus prayed that we would be one as He and the Father are one. He knew this would show the world that God had sent Him and cause people to believe (John 17:21).

There was unity when people gathered in prayer in "one accord" on the Day of Pentecost. A sound like a mighty wind came suddenly, and the Holy Spirit filled everyone present (Acts 2:1–4). This unity unleashed God's power to work through men and women to carry His Word to the nations.

Today's passage implies that our prayers are strongest when prayed with other believers who agree. To fully experience this power of unity, we must find ways to pray in agreement with other Christians. This puts us in harmony with Jesus and activates His promise to be present when "two or three are gathered" in His name (Matthew 18:20). When we do, God's power will flow through us to reach the world with His love and mercy.

Father, help me discover ways to unite with other Christians in prayer, then help us to work together to see Your kingdom come on earth.

Tim DeTellis, New Missions, Orlando, FL

WEEK 36—THURSDAY

The Value of Words

For the word of the Lord *is right, and all His work is done in truth. He loves righteousness and justice; the earth is full of the goodness of the* Lord. *By the word of the* Lord *the heavens were made, and all the host of them by the breath of His mouth.*

PSALM 33:4-6

Have you noticed that the value of words has diminished over time? Whether in ads, radio shows, or online forums, words seem to be worth less than before. Or maybe the promises behind the words have lost value. Whatever the case, do you find yourself ignoring what is said because you doubt its veracity?

Today's passage notes that God's word is right and true and filled with His creative power. "God is not a man, that He should lie" (Numbers 23:19). These bookends hold the message that God loves righteousness and justice, and the earth is filled with His goodness. Shouldn't we therefore apprehend this truth in order to make sense of our lives today?

Like Elijah, we must learn that to hear the Lord, we have to listen for His "still small voice" (1 Kings 19:11–12). God's Word is true and vital for navigating today's world. We must be able to "hear" Him in order to incorporate His Word into our daily walk. Likewise, God's love, mercy, and faithfulness are reinforced by regularly reading His Word in the Bible.

> Father, Your Word is truth. I want to hear Your voice in my heart and fully embrace Your plan for my life. Help me discover ways to silence the noise around me.

Heaven, Life, and the Resurrection

WEEK 36—FRIDAY

Keep Your Vows

And [Hannah] was in bitterness of soul, and prayed to the Lord and wept in anguish. Then she made a vow and said, "O Lord of hosts, if You will indeed look on the affliction of Your maidservant and remember me, and not forget Your maidservant, but will give Your maidservant a male child, then I will give him to the Lord all the days of his life, and no razor shall come upon his head."

1 SAMUEL 1:10-11

When Hannah made her vow to the Lord, she was unable to bear children. She knew God was her only hope to have a son, so she asked Him for one. The vow she made was simple: if You give me a son, I will give him back to You. Though the vow was simple, carrying it out was not. But she did keep it. When Samuel was of age, she turned him over to the high priest to be raised in the presence of God.

Hannah knew something about making a solemn promise that many people ignore. She knew she was obligated to keep her word and not delay in completing it. She also knew that the Lord would hold her accountable (Deuteronomy 23:21).

Have you ever made a vow to God and then failed to carry it out? If you are like most, you probably have. God may have brought it to mind, but take heart—He is gracious and merciful, slow to anger and abundant in lovingkindness (Jonah 4:2).

....

Lord, forgive me for breaking the vows I have made to You and to others. Help me avoid making rash promises and honor those I have already made.

Tim DeTellis, New Missions, Orlando, FL

WEEK 36—WEEKEND

God's Promise to You

He shall regard the prayer of the destitute, and shall not despise their prayer. This will be written for the generation to come, that a people yet to be created may praise the Lord. *For He looked down from the height of His sanctuary; from heaven the* Lord *viewed the earth.*

PSALM 102:17-19

Yesterday's devotion highlighted how a destitute woman, Hannah, cried out to the Lord for relief. We saw how God answered her prayer and how she faithfully fulfilled her vow. Today's passage reveals God's amazing promise to generation upon generation. He regards the prayers of the destitute and does not despise them. He looks upon the earth from heaven, sees our condition, and responds with loving compassion and mercy.

Are you destitute today? Do you need compassion and mercy from the God of heaven and earth? Call out to Him. Ask Him for what you need. He hears you and will supply all of your needs (Philippians 4:19). His love for you is immeasurable and without end, so powerful that He sent His only Son, Jesus, to bear all your sins so you can live in close companionship and fellowship with Him (John 3:16).

Nothing is too heavy for God. You may think you are beyond help, but God is faithful and will forgive your sins, no matter what they are! Today you can unload that heavy burden that has pressed you down far too long. Just pray this short prayer and give your burdens to the Lord:

> Father, I believe Jesus died for my sins. Thank You for Your love and forgiveness. Now help me to forgive myself and others, even as You have forgiven.

Heaven, Life, and the Resurrection

WEEK 37—MONDAY

Jesus, Our High Priest

Now this is the main point of the things we are saying: We have such a High Priest, who is seated at the right hand of the throne of the Majesty in the heavens, a Minister of the sanctuary and of the true tabernacle which the Lord erected, and not man.

HEBREWS 8:1-2

The writer of Hebrews is unknown, but his central message is clear: Jesus is superior. The sacrificial system recorded in Leviticus depended on the high priest to make atonement for the people year after year. His work was never done. Hebrews shows us that all the rituals, regulations, and even the high priest's role are perfectly fulfilled in the person of Jesus Christ. He is our High Priest.

As High Priest, *Christ has all authority.* He forgives our sins, hears our prayers, and is seated in a position of authority "at the right hand of the throne." Being seated is a picture of rest. Old Testament priests could never sit down, but Christ finished His work. Even from the cross, He cried out, "It is finished." We can rest in the work of our High Priest.

As High Priest, *Christ ministers to us.* His work of redemption is finished, but His ministry to us never ceases. He gives grace, supplies peace, leads our steps, and reminds us of His love each time we bow before His throne in prayer. It's not a throne of judgment but of grace. It's the future gathering place where all the redeemed will worship Him.

....

Jesus, we crown You with praise. You are worthy of all praise. You are our High Priest. We rejoice in You. We rest in You. Amen.

Jeff Crook, Christ Place Church, Flowery Branch, GA

WEEK 37—TUESDAY

Jesus Knows

And he said, "All these things I have kept from my youth." So when Jesus heard these things, He said to him, "You still lack one thing. Sell all that you have and distribute to the poor, and you will have treasure in heaven; and come, follow Me."

LUKE 18:21-22

If you are familiar with the Gospels, you'll remember this encounter Jesus had with the rich young ruler. The young man came to the right person: Jesus. He came at the right time: while still young. He asked the right question: about eternal life. He knew in his heart something was missing. He had the vitality of youth and the perks of success, yet he was still empty. And Jesus, like a skilled physician, gave a clear diagnosis: "You still lack one thing."

The context of this passage exposes the deceitfulness of wealth. Sin always deceives, whether it is sinful love of money or sinful lust for things. Sin is quite appetizing but also quite addictive. The young man was controlled by money. That was his "one thing." Sadly, the account ends with the young man walking away. If he had done the one thing Jesus told him to do, his entire future would have changed.

Are you aware that Jesus knows what you need? Are you willing to do exactly what He instructs you to do? Did you catch the last two words Christ told the young man? "Follow Me." This is the one thing that cannot be lacking in our lives. Are you following Jesus?

....

> God, show me what is lacking in my life. I want to follow You with my whole heart. Amen.

Heaven, Life, and the Resurrection

WEEK 37—WEDNESDAY

Can't Fake It

"Not everyone who says to Me, 'Lord, Lord,' shall enter the kingdom of heaven, but he who does the will of My Father in heaven. Many will say to Me in that day, 'Lord, Lord, have we not prophesied in Your name, cast out demons in Your name, and done many wonders in Your name?' And then I will declare to them, 'I never knew you; depart from Me, you who practice lawlessness!'"

MATTHEW 7:21-23

The Bible tells us that Jesus has eyes of flaming fire; nothing gets by His penetrating sight. He sees the heart and knows our motives. His words to some—"I do not know you"—are stinging words, but true and needed. They prompt sobering questions: "Am I for real, or am I faking it?" "How do I know if I really know Christ personally?"

"He who does the will of My Father" points us to the answers. Are you looking back to an experience you had with Christ? Doing the will of God is not a one-and-done event. Jesus also said many would say, "Look what I did for the Lord." But a relationship with Jesus is not a checklist of things we do for Him. An authentic relationship with Jesus Christ is a daily walk. It's not a perfect walk; there will be trip-ups and falls along the journey. But faltering is not the same as faking. When we falter, it's a reminder how we are utterly dependent on Jesus.

....

Lord, thank You that we can genuinely know You. Every day, I choose You. You are my Lord and Savior. Keep me in Your truth, and empower me to live it out. Amen.

Jeff Crook, Christ Place Church, Flowery Branch, GA

WEEK 37—THURSDAY

Don't Forget to Eat Today

I will never forget Your precepts, for by them You have given me life. I am Yours, save me; for I have sought Your precepts. The wicked wait for me to destroy me, but I will consider Your testimonies. I have seen the consummation of all perfection, but Your commandment is exceedingly broad.

PSALM 119:93-96

Psalm 119 is the longest chapter in the Bible, and all 176 verses are about the greatness of God's Word. Charles Spurgeon loved this psalm and said: "We might do well to commit it to memory." Even memorizing today's passage would be worthwhile.

The psalmist wrote that he would never forget God's precepts because they give life. "Precepts" is a synonym for the Word of God. Imagine his passion as he essentially says, "I will not neglect Your Word, Lord! I will not let a day pass without feeding on Your Word. It's my daily nourishment, just like food to my body."

Can you imagine having to be reminded to eat daily? The Bible tells us, "Man shall not live by bread alone, but by every word that proceeds from the mouth of God" (Matthew 4:4). How silly to think we can miss daily nourishment from the Word. When we forget the precepts, we become unhealthy and stumble into all kinds of things that aren't good for us. Don't lose your taste for Scripture. Feed daily on the satisfying precepts of God's Word.

....

God, help me not to forget this truth: The Bible will keep me from sin, or sin will keep me from the Bible. Help me hide Your Word in my heart so I will not sin against You. Amen.

Heaven, Life, and the Resurrection

WEEK 37—FRIDAY

God Is Great

You, Yourself, are to be feared; and who may stand in Your presence when once You are angry? You caused judgment to be heard from heaven; the earth feared and was still, when God arose to judgment, to deliver all the oppressed of the earth.

PSALM 76:7-9

"Great" is part of our everyday vocabulary. We tell people to have a "great" day, generously tip the server for "great" service, and say it's "great" when we get good news. Do we overuse the word? If everything is great, is anything really great?

In Psalm 76, the psalmist proclaims that God is great. We can never overuse the word when we speak of God. His faithfulness is great. His grace is greater than our failure. What are some ways we can express His greatness?

We should: Proclaim God's greatness, being specific about it, each time we pray; Express God's greatness in our worship. This means worship should never be dull or dreaded – a point always worth some self-examination; Testify of God's greatness by living a life of gratitude. An ingrate doesn't see "great," but a grateful heart knows the greatness of God; Speak of God's greatness when we share the gospel with others.

The Bible says, "Great is the Lord, and greatly to be praised; and His greatness is unsearchable" (Psalm 145:3). If God's greatness is unsearchable, the greatness we attribute to God should be unstoppable.

My Lord and my God, I proclaim Your greatness with every breath. You are great and greatly to be praised! Amen.

Jeff Crook, Christ Place Church, Flowery Branch, GA

WEEK 37—WEEKEND

A Clear Conscience

I have hope in God, which they themselves also accept, that there will be a resurrection of the dead, both of the just and the unjust. This being so, I myself always strive to have a conscience without offense toward God and men.

ACTS 24:15-16

The poem "Myself" by Edgar Guest is a sober reflection:
> I have to live with myself and so
> I want to be fit for myself to know.
> I want to be able as days go by,
> always to look myself straight in the eye;
> I don't want to stand with the setting sun
> and hate myself for the things I have done."

Paul was serious about having a good conscience, one that is void of offense toward God and people, in which no one can point a finger at with accusations of wrongs that have not been made right. James Madison wrote, "Conscience is the most sacred of all property." Consider the true riches of a clear conscience:

Freedom. We are free from fear of being found out. A clean conscience means we have nothing to hide because we are living in the light.

Authority. Our lives preach a message, either good or bad. A clear conscience brings confidence and authority to our life message. Duplicity brings a death blow to it.

....

> Lord, You have set me apart to be holy. And when I am wholly Yours, my heart's desire is to keep a clear conscience. May nothing come between my soul and You, my Savior.

Heaven, Life, and the Resurrection

WEEK 38—MONDAY

A Promise for God's People

"If My people who are called by My name will humble themselves, and pray and seek My face, and turn from their wicked ways, then I will hear from heaven, and will forgive their sin and heal their land."

2 CHRONICLES 7:14

The context of this popular verse must drive not only our understanding of its meaning but also our application of its truth. Originally given to Israel during its return from exile, these words were a reminder of what God had done during Solomon's reign as well as a reassurance of what He would do as they rebuilt the nation. "My people" refers to Jews who received both the Abrahamic and Davidic covenants and applies to current believers in Jesus, not a nation in general.

In other words, God can revive His people as they humble themselves, pray, and seek His face while simultaneously tearing down the country in which they live. Israel's land was tied to their identity as a people and their covenant with God; we should not falsely equate our "land" with our nation. More accurately, God will heal our churches from apathy and compromise. Granted, no nation will suffer because its Christians seek the Lord with humility and repentance, and such could be the doorway to a genuine revival. This is not, however, the focus or agenda here. Instead, we should examine our lives with full assurance that God will hear, forgive, and heal what is broken by sin when we cry out to him in faith.

Lord, help me humble myself before You. Forgive my sins and show me Your face. Help me live in light of Your blessings. Amen.

Dr. Adam B. Dooley, Englewood Baptist Church, Jackson, TN

WEEK 38—TUESDAY

Learning to Listen When God Speaks

"But please, Job, hear my speech, and listen to all my words. Now, I open my mouth; my tongue speaks in my mouth. My words come from my upright heart; my lips utter pure knowledge. The Spirit of God has made me, and the breath of the Almighty gives me life."

JOB 33:1-4

After his three friends accosted him, a fourth companion named Elihu stepped into Job's misery to offer some counsel of his own. These verses are his attempt to establish the right to speak. Elihu was angry with Job for justifying himself and calling God into question (32:2) but was also agitated by the three friends who condemned Job (32:3). While his words were more compassionate, Elihu fell into the same arrogant generalization as he "comforted" a hurting friend (36:4). Yet God revealed important truth through his efforts.

We learn from this advisor that no single person can fully explain God's perspective or agenda when we suffer. Elihu exercised more restraint and respect in speaking to Job (32:4-7), and his motive seemed pure; he acknowledged he was a man just like his suffering friend (33:4-6). His goal was not to discourage Job (33:7). He rightly explained that God speaks to us in various ways, particularly when we are hurting. He misinterpreted some of Job's words, but he at least acknowledged that no one has a monopoly on God's will or ways. During seasons of difficulty, we should listen carefully for God's voice through the circumstances we face and the people who surround us.

> Lord, speak truth into my life through whatever means You see fit. Mold me during my trials, and teach me when I face heartache. Help me recognize Your voice. Amen.

Heaven, Life, and the Resurrection

WEEK 38—WEDNESDAY

Lifting Your Gaze

I will lift up my eyes to the hills—from whence comes my help? My help comes from the LORD, who made heaven and earth. He will not allow your foot to be moved; He who keeps you will not slumber.

PSALM 121:1-3

The Pilgrim Psalms were sung by Jews journeying to Jerusalem to worship the Lord at the temple during feasts. Their effort to enter God's presence becomes a beautiful analogy of our journey to the heavenly Jerusalem, where we will forever be in the presence of God (Revelation 21:2-4). With their eyes on the hills of Jerusalem, these joyful travelers acknowledged that the Maker of all creation protected them as they moved closer to their goal.

Likewise, with our eyes fixed on eternity, we experience the daily provision and security found in the Lord. Though the perils of life vary, we know God will steady our steps as He protects us from evil and watches over our souls (121:7). Are you facing adversity? The Lord is your help. Do you fear the slippery slope of temptation? He will not allow your foot to be moved. Do you worry that God is apathetic or unmoved by your burdens? He will not sleep or slumber. Because the Lord made heaven and earth, we know He reigns supreme over all that happens therein. These assurances lift our gaze to a place we've never been, even as we pilgrim through a world that feels less and less like home.

Lord, increase my faith today and fill my heart with joy. Protect me from evil and guide my steps. Help me rest knowing that You are involved in every detail of my life. Amen.

Dr. Adam B. Dooley, Englewood Baptist Church, Jackson, TN

WEEK 38—THURSDAY

We Shall Behold Him

"In those days, after that tribulation, the sun will be darkened, and the moon will not give its light; the stars of heaven will fall, and the powers in the heavens will be shaken. Then they will see the Son of Man coming in the clouds with great power and glory. And then He will send His angels, and gather together His elect from the four winds, from the farthest part of earth to the farthest part of heaven."

MARK 13:24-27

Controversies surrounding end-times prophecies should not prevent us from heeding their warnings. Jesus' goal was not to make us experts on things to come but to make us more faithful in the here and now. As earth prepares for God's final judgment, the sun and moon will darken, stars will fall from heaven, and cosmic powers will be shaken (Revelation 6:12–14). We will finally see the Lord in full power and glory, and He will gather His people from across the earth (7:9–10).

Though no one knows when these events will occur (Mark 13:32), the wait will be worth it! Our faith will become sight when we finally meet the Lord. Every saint from every generation will stand before the Lamb of God crying out, "Salvation belongs to our God who sits on the throne, and to the Lamb" (Rev. 7:9–10). So until He comes, remain alert (Mark 13:33), resist ungodliness (Titus 2:12–13), share the gospel with others (Acts 1), purify your heart even as He is pure (1 John 3:3), and comfort one another (1 Thessalonians 4:13–18).

Father, keep my heart anchored to heaven. Help me walk in purity and holiness. Give me an opportunity to tell someone about You today. Amen.

Heaven, Life, and the Resurrection

WEEK 38—FRIDAY

A Holy Warrior

All the host of heaven shall be dissolved, and the heavens shall be rolled up like a scroll; all their host shall fall down as the leaf falls from the vine, and as fruit falling from a fig tree. "For My sword shall be bathed in heaven; indeed it shall come down on Edom, and on the people of My curse, for judgment."

ISAIAH 34:4-5

Isaiah perfectly weaves the themes of God's holy wrath and cleansing grace together. After pronouncing judgment on the nations of the world (chs. 13–24), He reveals numerous laments and reasurances (chs. 28–33). In these verses, he singles out Edom as a picture of the earth's reprobate nations. The "host of heaven" refers to God's enemies in both heavenly and natural realms ("armies" in 34:2). The Lord will utterly destroy them like a leaf that falls from a vine or fruit that is severed from a fig tree (34:2–4).

Like a rolled-up scroll, God will end the age of insurrection in which His fame is mocked by the wicked. Because His sword of wrath is "bathed in heaven," He will likely first destroy the minions of hell, who initiate so much of the earth's resistance to the heavenly kingdom. The message is clear; God will not be mocked. Through this glorious picture of God's strength, Isaiah compels us to marvel at His holiness as we humble ourselves before Him.

> Father, I acknowledge Your holiness today. Help me live in ways that honor You. Protect me from compromise. Forgive me for celebrating the coming judgment of others without also realizing my vulnerability to the same. Amen.

Dr. Adam B. Dooley, Englewood Baptist Church, Jackson, TN

WEEK 38—WEEKEND

A Story Worth Telling

"Now it happened, as I journeyed and came near Damascus at about noon, suddenly a great light from heaven shone around me. And I fell to the ground and heard a voice saying to me, 'Saul, Saul, why are you persecuting Me?' So I answered, 'Who are You, Lord?' And He said to me, 'I am Jesus of Nazareth, whom you are persecuting.'"

ACTS 22:6-8

So dramatic was Paul's Damascus road experience (Acts 9:1–19) that he shared it with others on many occasions (22:6–16; 26:1–32). Here his goal was to persuade Jews that his conversion was a legitimate expression of Judaism—that acknowledging Jesus as the fulfillment of Old Testament Scripture is rooted in faithfulness to the Jewish faith, not a deviation from it. The Law was to help Israel look forward to Christ even as the New Testament helps us look back at Him.

Not even the noonday sun could rival the glory of Jesus' presence. The clear identification of Jesus of Nazareth further affirms the resurrection. We also see the solidarity of our Savior with His people: "Why are you persecuting Me?" By killing Christians, Saul oppressed the Lord Himself though they had not physically met.

Paul's story, like every good testimony, marks a clear encounter with Christ, the conviction of sin, and the commitment to bow before Jesus as Savior and Lord. Do you remember the day you met the Lord? When did you last share your conversion experience? Who could benefit from learning how God changed your life?

.....

Lord, thank You for changing my life and giving me a story to tell.
Open a door even today for me to share my testimony of faith. Amen.

Heaven, Life, and the Resurrection

WEEK 39—MONDAY

The Untapped Reservoir

For this reason I bow my knees to the Father of our Lord Jesus Christ, from whom the whole family in heaven and earth is named, that He would grant you, according to the riches of His glory, to be strengthened with might through His Spirit in the inner man, that Christ may dwell in your hearts through faith; that you, being rooted and grounded in love.

EPHESIANS 3:14-17

Imagine being able to sit with Paul and ask him about the most important prayer he would pray for you. It would be spectacular! We already have that prayer; he wrote it to Christians in Ephesus, and it is not a simple prayer. It is a prayer not only for blessing but for the most amazing blessing possible. Paul asked God the Father to give you the greatest possible strength any person could possess—not physical strength but a strength in your spirit by the power and presence of the Holy Spirit. He wrote of this strength when he declared, "I can do all things through Christ who strengthens me" (Philippians 4:13).

The great tragedy is that so many Christians depend on their own strength and fail. The promises of God seem distant. Faith is impossible. Love is missing. When that happens, doubt and fear control. All the while, there is an untapped reservoir of strength in the inner man, waiting to be released. Now is the time to discover that strength and live a life that would have been impossible before.

Holy Spirit, make me aware of Your presence and teach me how to release that strength.

Dr. David Edwards, DaveEdwardsSpeaks.com, Oklahoma City, OK

WEEK 39—TUESDAY

The Invading Work of the Resurrection

Now if Christ is preached that He has been raised from the dead, how do some among you say that there is no resurrection of the dead? But if there is no resurrection of the dead, then Christ is not risen. And if Christ is not risen, then our preaching is empty and your faith is also empty.

1 CORINTHIANS 15:12-14

Hundreds of thousands of books have been written to explain each detail of Christian thought and culture. Paul cuts through it all to pinpoint the single event around which everything in the Christian faith revolves: the resurrection. Through His resurrection, Jesus overcame sin and offers forgiveness and salvation to the world. His resurrection means He has the power to make His life real in us. It diagnoses the condition of our souls: we were all dead because of sin. Christianity is about retrieving our life from the jaws of death, and Jesus' great victory not only gives us life but changes and rearranges our life before God. By receiving the salvation offered through the resurrection of Jesus, we become true sons and daughters of God.

Bringing our spirits back to life is the most important component of Christianity. Think of the ramifications of our faith without resurrection. As Paul insisted, our faith is empty if Christ is not risen. We can be thankful that the tomb is empty and our hearts are alive. Jesus changes everything.

....

Lord Jesus, I yield to the work of Your resurrected life. Invade all of me.

WEEK 39—WEDNESDAY

Jesus Still Works

Jesus answered and said to him, "Because I said to you, 'I saw you under the fig tree,' do you believe? You will see greater things than these." And He said to him, "Most assuredly, I say to you, hereafter you shall see heaven open, and the angels of God ascending and descending upon the Son of Man."

JOHN 1:50-51

Jesus called Nathanael to be a disciple by giving him a glimpse into the supernatural things he would experience. Nathanael was blown away and answered, "You are the Son of God!" (John 1:49). That was only the beginning. In the three years Nathanael followed Jesus, he saw amazing things—people raised from the dead, blind eyes opened, lepers healed, five thousand fed with two small fish and a few pieces of bread. Ultimately, Nathanael experienced the greatest miracle, the resurrection of the Lord Jesus.

Miracles were not reserved for the twelve who followed Jesus as disciples. They became the way of life for the early church and the hallmark of the church throughout the centuries. The wonderful news is that miracles are still taking place across the world and are available to each Christian.

Do not think of miracles as relics of the ancient past. Expect them in your life. The miracles Nathanael experienced are still ours today. Jesus still heals, blesses, opens doors, and restores families. You will have no need that the miraculous power of the Lord Jesus cannot meet.

....

Lord, move miraculously in my life just as You have in countless thousands of others. The miracles You promised Nathanael can be mine. Help me accept them, expect them, and live in them.

Dr. David Edwards, DaveEdwardsSpeaks.com, Oklahoma City, OK

WEEK 39—THURSDAY

Nothing Is Too Small for God

Then He commanded the multitudes to sit down on the grass. And He took the five loaves and the two fish, and looking up to heaven, He blessed and broke and gave the loaves to the disciples; and the disciples gave to the multitudes.

MATTHEW 14:19

This was the miracle experienced by more people than any other. Many drank when He turned water into wine at a wedding. Entire cities were present as He healed the sick and cast out demons. But each person in this multitude received. They ate the fish and the bread.

This miracle tells us that Jesus works to meet people's needs no matter how mundane. It is easy to expect the Lord to perform great miracles, and He does. A person healed from a deadly disease, a family saved from drowning in a massive flood, a lost child rescued—the list of how the Lord intervened with a miracle could go on and on. But the only problem the multitude faced that day was the possibility of missing a meal.

Nothing is too small. No need is too insignificant. No hurt is too trivial to be beyond the possibility of a genuine miraculous intervention. Whatever you are facing, regardless of the size of the challenge, you have every right as a Christian to call upon your heavenly Father in the name of the Lord Jesus and ask for a miracle. And you can do so with great confidence that the miracle you need will come!

....

Lord, I bring You all the large and small things I'm facing. I ask You to multiply the crumbs into abundance.

Heaven, Life, and the Resurrection

WEEK 39—FRIDAY

Open Doors and Opportunities

May the Lord give you increase more and more, you and your children. May you be blessed by the Lord, who made heaven and earth. The heaven, even the heavens, are the Lord's; but the earth He has given to the children of men.

PSALM 115:14–16

The world can be a lonely, harsh place where it seems impossible to get ahead or find lasting success. It's easy to be overwhelmed with constant economic changes and lack of opportunities. But in the midst of challenges, God gives specific promises for us to learn and believe. The heart of them is that the Lord is our help in whom we can trust.

As you let God help and follow His direction, remarkable things take place. He intervenes, and you begin to experience more and more. You will move into open doors that lead to greater opportunities. A young Moabite widow named Ruth is a prime example (Ruth 1–4). In her loss and poverty, she chose to follow God, opening her to ideas and possibilities she had never known. In faith, she took chances that could have been risky and experienced unimaginable blessings of wealth, security, and purpose. The young, impoverished widow became the great grandmother of David, Israel's greatest king.

God's promises are not just for a few lucky ones. They are for you. Regardless of how desperate you may be, the same promises that have worked for millions of others will work for you. Discover them and follow them. They will lead you to genuine blessings.

....

Lord Jesus, I don't know how You're going to meet my needs, but I know You can and will.

WEEK 39—WEEKEND

Stay Focused. Stay Faithful.

The heavens are Yours, the earth also is Yours; the world and all its fullness, You have founded them. The north and the south, You have created them; Tabor and Hermon rejoice in Your name. You have a mighty arm; strong is Your hand, and high is Your right hand. Righteousness and justice are the foundation of Your throne; mercy and truth go before Your face.

PSALM 89:11-14

The challenge to believe in a real God who made the heavens and earth can be difficult. We are surrounded by voices that insist the cosmos is the product of chance and the idea of a creator is superstitious. The psalmist's contention that the heavens and earth belong to God seems impossible to many.

The tragedy is that many Christians have been so intimidated by the doubters that they give way to doubt, which slowly destroys faith in a powerful heavenly Father. When trouble comes, the faith needed to call upon the mighty arm of the Lord is missing, and the Christian falls into defeat.

Keep your faith strong! Stay focused and faithful. Reject the voices that deny God. Do not be embarrassed or intimidated about what you believe. You know God. You have heard His voice, experienced His presence, and seen His power. Your faith in the person and position of God allows you to believe in His power to do great things in your life. It releases the mighty arm of the Lord, His strong right hand.

Lord Jesus, strength and power are Your roots. I rest in all the ways I have seen You work. All I have and all I know, I owe to You.

Heaven, Life, and the Resurrection

WEEK 40—MONDAY

Life and Favor

Remember, I pray, that You have made me like clay. And will You turn me into dust again? Did You not pour me out like milk, and curdle me like cheese, clothe me with skin and flesh, and knit me together with bones and sinews? You have granted me life and favor, and Your care has preserved my spirit.

JOB 10:9-12

In Job's pain, he questioned if the God who made him was only going to destroy him, wouldn't it have been better if he had died at birth? We often cannot understand why God would give us a life full of suffering if we are only going to die. God could have saved Himself and us a lot of trouble!

Job did not understand what God was doing, but Satan and suffering were being defeated. There was purpose in his pain. At the end, he said, "My ears had heard of you but now my eyes have seen you" (Job 42:5). God blessed the latter part of his life more than the first, and he lived to see his descendants to the fourth generation (Job 42:12, 16).

God loves us and cares for us from the womb to the tomb. Whatever your pain, God always has the last word. He tells us not to fear. The best is yet to come. Heaven will make it all worthwhile, and we will look back and understand what Paul meant when he said, "I consider that our present sufferings are not worth comparing with the glory that will be revealed in us" (Romans 8:18, NIV).

Father, thank You that there is purpose in my pain. I trust You.

WEEK 40—TUESDAY

Heaven and Earth

"Assuredly, I say to you, whatever you bind on earth will be bound in heaven, and whatever you loose on earth will be loosed in heaven. Again I say to you that if two of you agree on earth concerning anything that they ask, it will be done for them by My Father in heaven. For where two or three are gathered together in My name, I am there in the midst of them."

MATTHEW 18:18-20

This promise is repeated from Matthew 16:19, and if Jesus repeats something, we know it's important. When the church prays in agreement, heaven backs up the church, and Jesus validates the requests. When the church makes earthly requests for heavenly intervention, what is bound in heaven is bound on earth, and what is loosed in heaven is loosed on earth.

Bind means to restrain, and loose means to set free. Resurrection power is at our disposal to restrain the enemy and power of sin and free the saints and loose anything that has made us captive. Just as a government stands behind its embassy in a foreign land, our God in heaven stands behind us as we live in what C. S. Lewis called "enemy occupied territory." Our citizenship is in heaven, but we have the power of our homeland here and now.

Let us value Christian community and agree together in prayer, praying as Jesus did, "Your will be done on earth as it is in heaven" (Matthew 6:10). Prayer is not a religious ritual; it directly communicates with our God so heaven's power may be released in our situation.

Father, thank You for the privilege of prayer! Help me remember Your power as I pray.

Heaven, Life, and the Resurrection

WEEK 40—WEDNESDAY

Increase and Decrease

He must increase, but I must decrease. He who comes from above is above all; he who is of the earth is earthly and speaks of the earth. He who comes from heaven is above all. And what He has seen and heard, that He testifies; and no one receives His testimony. He who has received His testimony has certified that God is true.

JOHN 3:30–33

John's disciples faced a predicament. He had been baptizing; now Jesus was baptizing too, and people were flocking to Him (v. 26). John's response is a model for us.

John didn't get distracted from his mission or let insecurities or pride get in the way. He didn't get offended or criticize his disciples for lack of understanding. He knew that comparison kills contentment. He humbled himself and pointed to Jesus. He was an earthly man with limited knowledge, but Jesus was sent from heaven and is above all. Jesus alone is worthy of praise. His glory alone has eternal value. John even shared the gospel: "Whoever believes in the Son has eternal life, but whoever rejects the Son will not see life, for God's wrath remains on them" (v. 36, NIV).

How do you respond in a competitve, divisive, jealous, judgmental culture? Are you fighting for your own glory and recognition or fighting for His? Are you trying to prove yourself or Him? "All people are like grass, and all their faithfulness is like the flowers of the field. . . . The grass withers and the flowers fall, but the word of our God endures forever" (Isaiah 40:6–8, NIV).

Father, help me be humble and always point others to You.

Dr. Grant Ethridge, Liberty Live Church, Hampton, VA

WEEK 40—THURSDAY

Day and Night

*Behold, bless the L*ORD*, all you servants of the L*ORD*, who by night stand in the house of the L*ORD*! Lift up your hands in the sanctuary, and bless the L*ORD*. The L*ORD *who made heaven and earth bless you from Zion!*

PSALM 134:1-3

What a privilege it is to bless the Lord! Bless means to adore, kneel before, praise, salute, and thank. We serve a God who is alive and allows us to come before Him not only with our requests but also our praise.

God inhabits praise, and His blessing shows up wherever He does. Giving thanks to God and praising Him helps us remember how good He has been to us and keeps our focus on Him. We can be thankful for all He has done and, first and foremost, for who He is. His name is above every name. He is the Most High. He is the faithful, loving Creator of heaven and earth.

Worship always begins with God. It focuses on His name and His nature. Start your day looking forward in faith, and end it by looking back on His faithfulness. The psalms teach us to thank God for His lovingkindness and faithfulness. His lovingkindness is better than life. His love endures forever.

Thanksgiving and praise are not only instruments of worship but weapons of war. The fall of our adversaries is all God's doing, His work on our behalf. The battle is the Lord's. Because of the cross and resurrection, we have victory. The joy of Lord is our strength.

Father, I lift my hands in surrender and give You the highest praise!

WEEK 40—FRIDAY

Temporary and Eternal

Lift up your eyes to the heavens, and look on the earth beneath. For the heavens will vanish away like smoke, the earth will grow old like a garment, and those who dwell in it will die in like manner; but My salvation will be forever, and My righteousness will not be abolished.

ISAIAH 51:6

Life on earth is fickle. One day you may have a job, a relationship, health, or security, and the next day you don't. Much of what we live for today can be gone tomorrow. We don't know what a day may bring, and sometimes that can be depressing. Maybe you give many hours to your job, strain to please unpleasant people, or obsess over physical fitness. Whatever it is, today's verse reminds us that all things on earth are temporary. Only the Lord and His kingdom will last forever.

Solomon concluded that everything in this life is meaningless, like chasing after the wind. He thought it was a blessing to find enjoyment, but at the end of the day, this is "the conclusion of the whole matter: Fear God and keep His commandments. . . . For God will bring every work into judgment, including every secret thing, whether good or evil" (Ecclesiastes 12:13–14).

Don't be discouraged over what will pass away. Even when the earth and skies are no more, God's dwelling place will stand. Nothing will compare to the joy of being with Him in heaven! May we adjust our focus and live in pursuit of what will last forever.

....

> Father, thank You for my salvation and the hope of heaven. Help me live now with eternity in mind.

Dr. Grant Ethridge, Liberty Live Church, Hampton, VA

WEEK 40—WEEKEND

Gospel and Glory

We give thanks to the God and Father of our Lord Jesus Christ, praying always for you, since we heard of your faith in Christ Jesus and of your love for all the saints; because of the hope which is laid up for you in heaven, of which you heard before in the word of the truth of the gospel.

COLOSSIANS 1:3-5

Do you ever feel as if living out your calling successfully is impossible? The assignment is always greater than our ability. Yet God's assignment to us is a gift. He's not looking for our ability but our availability. I once heard Ron Dunn say that weakness is the stage on which God displays His power.

In today's passage, Paul commends Colossian believers. They were living the Christian life successfully, fulfilling their calling because of their hope laid up in heaven (v. 5). It wasn't by the Colossians' strength or giftedness but by God's strength and promises of what's to come.

Paul said he was an apostle "by the will of God" (v. 1) and was able to labor by "all the energy Christ so powerfully works" in him (v. 29, NIV). He reminded the Colossians that it was the Father who had qualified them (v. 12), and that in Him, all things hold together (v. 17).

When you are tired and weary, remember the hope of heaven. Remember who called you and began the good work in you. He will be faithful to complete it (Philippians 1:6)!

....

Father, thank You for equipping me to do what You have called me to do.

Heaven, Life, and the Resurrection

WEEK 41—MONDAY

Wonderfully Saved Through Jesus' Sacrifice

Therefore it was necessary that the copies of the things in the heavens should be purified with these, but the heavenly things themselves with better sacrifices than these. For Christ has not entered the holy places made with hands, which are copies of the true, but into heaven itself, now to appear in the presence of God for us.

HEBREWS 9:23-24

The old covenant required the earthly high priest to go into the holy of holies and make a sacrifice of atonement every year. The new covenant would replace this sacrificial system with Jesus Himself. God was so satisfied with what Jesus did that He highly exalted Him and gave Him a name that is above every other name.

We must remember that God does not accept us as we are. Jesus accepts us and then presents us to God through Himself. When we enter God's presence, God sees Jesus instead of us. He sees Jesus' righteousness instead of our unrighteousness. He sees Jesus' sacrifice instead of our sin.

Christ did not go into the earthly holy of holies. He went into the presence of God, the real, heavenly holy of holies. He did that for us, and when He went in, He took us with Him! Jesus' sacrifice was better than the sacrifices of old covenant priests because it had to be done only once, and He took us into the holy of holies with Him. For this reason, we celebrate Christ! He is the foundation of our salvation. Everything rests upon Him.

Jesus, thank You for saving my soul by Your ultimate sacrifice to the Father!

Dr. Steve Folmar, Covenant Church, Houma, LA

WEEK 41—TUESDAY

Walk Holy Before God

"Am I a God near at hand," says the LORD, *"and not a God afar off? Can anyone hide himself in secret places, so I shall not see him?" says the* LORD; *"Do I not fill heaven and earth?" says the* LORD.

JEREMIAH 23:23-24

The people of Israel were being led astray by false prophets. These prophets had not received a word from God, nor had He sent them. Because of their false teachings the people of God were living in sin. These prophets were offering a false hope. They were teaching that one could continue to live in sin and still have peace.

God was about to pour out His anger. He reminded Israel that nothing is out of His reach, and nothing is beyond His understanding or His all-seeing eye. Holy God requires holiness from His prophets and His people. He will not tolerate evil connected to His name. It is important to remember that our God is holy and expects His people to live holy lives.

The Christian must understand that our loving, forgiving God is also a God of wrath. It might help us if we were more concerned about the holy wrath of God. There is no place where we can hide our sin from our heavenly Father, though the blood of Jesus will cover it and remove it. We must be reminded that He is all-seeing.

....

> Father, forgive us for not taking our sin more seriously. We know that You know every good and every bad choice we make. Help us to walk in Your holiness.

Heaven, Life, and the Resurrection

WEEK 41—WEDNESDAY

Our God Settles All Accounts

"But God draws the mighty away with His power; He rises up, but no man is sure of life. He gives them security, and they rely on it; yet His eyes are on their ways. They are exalted for a little while, then they are gone. They are brought low; they are taken out of the way like all others; they dry out like the heads of grain."

JOB 24:22-24

Job endured unspeakable pain and tragedy. In his pain, he prayed that God might place a curse on the wicked by allowing them to have success. He wanted them to enjoy success for a time, but then for the Lord to establish His control over them so they would not be able to enjoy their power and success but become disillusioned. Nothing would satisfy them; their lives would have no meaning. Just when the wicked thought they had arrived, God would rush in and rob them of their zest for life. The higher they rose, the further they would fall.

Most of us have prayed this prayer or had these thoughts at one time or another. It is hard for us to understand why the wicked of this world flourish while godly people suffer. Job was reminding his friends that God is on His throne and the wicked will meet their proper fate in His time.

Father, we trust You. Please help us remember that You are the judge, and when You settle accounts, the godly will be justified and the evil will be punished.

WEEK 41—THURSDAY

God's People Are to Be Generous

"Bring all the tithes into the storehouse, that there may be food in My house, and try Me now in this," says the Lord of hosts, "If I will not open for you the windows of heaven and pour out for you such blessing that there will not be room enough to receive it."

MALACHI 3:10

Our God is a God of His word. He made a covenant with Israel and intended to keep His promise. In spite of Israel's rebellious history, God still held out the offer of repentance. He demanded that Israel respond by ceasing their selfish, rebellious actions.

God called the Israelites "sons of Jacob" (v. 6), running from Him just as Jacob did. They didn't realize they had drifted from the Lord—a very dangerous situation. So He gave them an example of one way they had wandered off the righteous path. They had been robbing God of tithes and offerings (v. 8). He placed a challenge before them: to test Him in this area and watch Him respond.

God blesses generosity. He expects His people to exhibit their appreciation of the many blessings He has bestowed upon them by sharing those blessings. One way to do that is to bring your tithe into the storehouse. God's church uses that money to minister in many ways. He even makes a promise—that if we test Him in this, we will be amazed at the blessings given to us for our obedience.

> Father, help us trust You by giving out of the abundance You have blessed us with. In our obedience, let us see the reality of Your promise. Help us bless You by blessing others.

Heaven, Life, and the Resurrection

WEEK 41—FRIDAY

Sing A Hymn of Praise!

Then I looked, and I heard the voice of many angels around the throne, the living creatures, and the elders; and the number of them was ten thousand times ten thousand, and thousands of thousands, saying with a loud voice: "Worthy is the Lamb who was slain to receive power and riches and wisdom, and strength and honor and glory and blessing!"

REVELATION 5:11-12

In a burst of praise, all the angels, elders, and every creature in the universe joins together to worship the Redeemer. The song declares what Jesus deserves because of His sacrificial death on the cross.

While Jesus was on earth, people did not give Him the honor He deserved. On earth, He was born in weakness and died in weakness. They mocked His kingship and attire. Yet He was the recipient of all the power of heaven. He was the poorest of the poor, yet He owned all the riches of heaven. Men laughed at Him and called Him a fool, yet He was the picture of wisdom. He was hungry on earth, yet He is the bread of life. He was thirsty, yet He is the living water.

Today in glory, Jesus possesses all strength. He has received all honor and glory. We are reminded that He is worthy of all our praise. And our hymns of praise will go on for all eternity.

....

May our hearts and souls praise You, Jesus. May You be adored by Your children. Receive our praise, for You are worthy!

Dr. Steve Folmar, Covenant Church, Houma, LA

WEEK 41—WEEKEND

A Trick Question

For in the resurrection they neither marry nor are given in marriage, but are like angels of God in heaven. But concerning the resurrection of the dead, have you not read what was spoken to you by God, saying, 'I am the God of Abraham, the God of Isaac, and the God of Jacob'? God is not the God of the dead, but of the living."

MATTHEW 22:30-32

According to Mosaic law, if a man died with no male heirs, his brother would take his wife and have children with her in his brother's name. The Sadducees did not believe in the resurrection, so they attempted to trip Jesus up with a trick question. What if a woman had seven husbands? Then whose wife would she be in the resurrection?

Jesus answered by telling them that we will be like angels in the resurrection. He did not say we will *be* angels but that we will be *like* angels and will have no need for sex and marriage. Since there is no death in heaven, therefore there is no need to repopulate. Jesus showed that He is the God of the resurrection by speaking of Abraham, Jacob, and Isaac in the present tense. "I am," not "I was" the God of Abraham.

It can be dangerous to speculate about our future life. We must rest on the authority of the Word of God, for only there can we find the truth that answers our questions about the future.

....

Heavenly Father, help us trust You with our future. You have all knowledge and wisdom, and we do not. Help us accept Your perfect will for our lives.

Heaven, Life, and the Resurrection

WEEK 42—MONDAY

Here Today, There Tomorrow!

Do not overwork to be rich; because of your own understanding, cease! Will you set your eyes on that which is not? For riches certainly make themselves wings; they fly away like an eagle toward heaven.

PROVERBS 23:4-5

Even though we are just passing through, we spend a lot of time and thought pursuing money instead of investing our time and thought in kingdom things. Our focus needs to be intentional. It controls our direction, and our direction indicates our desires. This is why Jesus said your treasure is where your heart is (Matthew 6:21). We should be more concerned with our spiritual account than with our financial account because God's economy is not like ours. The difference we make in people's lives—through serving, prayer, winning souls, and more—is deposited in His kingdom economy.

Only in heaven will we know the importance of our prayers in lives, families, and ministries. Only there will we see the fruit of our evangelism. Making a difference for the kingdom should be every believer's goal and desire. The devil comes to kill, steal, and destroy, and if you allow him to steal your focus, he will deplete your spiritual account. You have one life with numbered days. Focus on storing up riches in heaven. Do your actions reflect that Jesus is first in your life? How are you spending your days? You cannot take your financial account with you, but your spiritual account is an eternal investment.

> Lord, help me this day to set my sights on kingdom things—the things that matter to You. Lord, take control of my focus and help me concentrate on eternal investments. Amen.

Brian Fossett, Fossett Evangelistic Ministries, Dalton, GA

WEEK 42—TUESDAY

His Masterpiece

In a great house there are not only vessels of gold and silver, but also of wood and clay, some for honor and some for dishonor. Therefore if anyone cleanses himself from the latter, he will be a vessel for honor, sanctified and useful for the Master, prepared for every good work. Flee also youthful lusts; but pursue righteousness, faith, love, peace with those who call on the Lord out of a pure heart.

2 TIMOTHY 2:20-22

Most churches are composed of believers with different levels of spiritual maturity. Some are spiritual giants; others seem content to be average. The difference is desire. We have to make up our minds to know and pursue God more than any other thing.

I heard a preacher say, "Watch out for gold, glory, and girls because they will take you down." The Bible says to put away youthful lusts because they distract us from becoming strong, honorable vessels for God's use. To be prepared for every good work, we must become more like Jesus by spending time with Him in prayer and His Word. Whatever brings dishonor to God in our lives must go. The way we live should put a smile on Jesus's face.

Are you making Jesus smile? Are you calling on the Lord with a pure heart? Lay down whatever keeps you from pursuing righteousness, faith, love, and peace. To be God's masterpiece, allow Him to shape, mold, and fashion you into a vessel that pleases Him. Then he can use you as He sees fit.

Lord, help me become more like You. I lay down every impurity. I desire to please You, not people. Use me and make me Your masterpiece. Amen.

WEEK 42—WEDNESDAY

How's Your Spiritual Appetite?

Jesus answered them and said, "Most assuredly, I say to you, you seek Me, not because you saw the signs, but because you ate of the loaves and were filled. Do not labor for the food which perishes, but for the food which endures to everlasting life, which the Son of Man will give you, because God the Father has set His seal on Him."

JOHN 6:26-27

So much of what we do revolves around food. It nourishes us, sustains us, and helps us grow. What we put in our bodies determines our physical health and appearance. It even determines how we act. Keeping my large family fed helps them not develop grumpy attitudes. We are happiest when we are filled.

Athletes understand the importance of maintaining a healthy diet. It affects their performance. They know junk food will impede training, practice, and performance. The same applies to our spirits. Feeding your spirit carnal things of the world will impede your kingdom effectiveness. Spiritual strength comes from a daily diet of Jesus through His Word.

Our spiritual diet matters. If we fill ourselves with things of this world, our flesh will be strong, and we will become arrogant and selfish. If we choose a healthy spiritual diet of prayer and God's Word, we will become strong, selfless, and kind. We will be more like Jesus.

Lord, help me be more like You. Give me an appetite for kingdom things. Nourish me with Your Word. Amen.

Brian Fossett, Fossett Evangelistic Ministries, Dalton, GA

WEEK 42—THURSDAY

Jesus, the Godman

This is He who came by water and blood—Jesus Christ; not only by water, but by water and blood. And it is the Spirit who bears witness, because the Spirit is truth. For there are three that bear witness in heaven: the Father, the Word, and the Holy Spirit; and these three are one. And there are three that bear witness on earth: the Spirit, the water, and the blood; and these three agree as one.

1 JOHN 5:6-8

The Trinity can be difficult to understand. I tell people I believe in God (the Father and Creator), Jesus (the Son and Redeemer), and Holy Spirit (the Comforter and Guide). God had a plan for our salvation, Jesus was that plan, and the Holy Spirit draws us to Jesus to reveal that plan.

We are all sinners in need of a Savior. We all choose how we live and die, whether with God or without Him. Jesus loved us so much that He left the splendor of heaven, came to earth, lived a sinless life, and went to the cross for our sins. He rose again on the third day, victorious over death, hell, and the grave. He is the living God, "the way, the truth, and the life" (John 14:6). There is no other way but by Him. Do you believe God has a plan for you and that Jesus is that plan? Have you asked Him to come into your life?

....

> Lord, I am a sinner. I stand in need of a Savior. I believe Jesus is that Savior. Come into my heart and forgive me of my sin. Thank You for hearing my prayer and saving me. Amen.

WEEK 42—FRIDAY

First Things First

"But seek the kingdom of God, and all these things shall be added to you. "Do not fear, little flock, for it is your Father's good pleasure to give you the kingdom. Sell what you have and give alms; provide yourselves money bags which do not grow old, a treasure in the heavens that does not fail, where no thief approaches nor moth destroys. For where your treasure is, there your heart will be also."

LUKE 12:31-34

We've heard it many times: "You can't take it with you." Yet many people live as if they are going to take it all with them. The Bible says you cannot serve God and mammon, or wealth (Luke 16:13). The Bible also says the love of money—not money itself—is the root of all evil (1 Timothy 6:10).

Seeking the kingdom of God means establishing the fact that you are a part of the kingdom. The most important thing in life is being born again and having a relationship with God through His son, Jesus. This is why we were made—to love and worship God, not money, titles, degrees, or wealth. We all have a God-sized void in our hearts, and we can never fill it with alcohol, drugs, sex, or anything else. It can only be filled with a right relationship with Jesus. You can never out-give God and all good things come from God.

Lord, help me always seek You first. Help me love You more than any other thing. Lord, lead me, guide me, and protect me as I seek Your kingdom. Amen.

Brian Fossett, Fossett Evangelistic Ministries, Dalton, GA

WEEK 42—WEEKEND

Awakening

*Mercy and truth have met together; righteousness and peace have kissed. Truth shall spring out of the earth, and righteousness shall look down from heaven. Yes, the L*ORD *will give what is good; and our land will yield its increase. Righteousness will go before Him, and shall make His footsteps our pathway.*
PSALM 85:10-13

People often say we need a great awakening—a revival. An awakening takes place when we repent and turn from our wicked ways and realize God's goodness and tender mercies. We are revived when we understand the incredible love Jesus showed for us all by giving His all on the cross. Being revived as an individual believer ushers in corporate revival in churches, and a great awakening happens when our churches are revived. It only takes a spark to keep a fire going, and we need to be that spark. When a true revival takes place, people are changed, lives are revived, and souls are saved. God illuminates our path so we can follow Him, and when we choose to make His footsteps our pathway, we can never go wrong.

....

> Lord, revive my spirit. Let me be a spark for revival. Restore our land and send a great awakening. Thank You, Jesus. Amen.

Heaven, Life, and the Resurrection

WEEK 43—MONDAY

Do You Believe This?

Martha said to Him, "I know that he will rise again in the resurrection at the last day." Jesus said to her, "I am the resurrection and the life. He who believes in Me, though he may die, he shall live. And whoever lives and believes in Me shall never die. Do you believe this?" She said to Him, "Yes, Lord, I believe that You are the Christ, the Son of God, who is to come into the world."

JOHN 11:24-27

Jesus made seven "I am" statements in the gospel record, none more powerful than this one: "I am the resurrection and the life." We know that Lazarus, the brother of Mary and Martha, had been dead for four days and that Mary and Martha were both disappointed that Jesus had not come in time to heal him. Martha's words in v. 21—"If You had been here"—hint at this disappointment. She believed that Lazarus would not have died and now hoped that Jesus would raise him from the dead.

Jesus taught Martha and us that the resurrection was not so much an event but a Person, and Jesus is that person! When we put our faith in Him, we pass from death into life and will never die. The great question is, "Do you believe this?" By Jesus' word, death is swallowed up in life, hope is renewed, faith is restored, joy replaces sorrow, and graves release their captives. Jesus is the resurrection! Death may win plenty of battles, but death has lost the war!

....

Jesus, I believe You are the resurrection and the life! Help me remember today in whom I have placed my faith.

Roy G. Mack, Grace Fellowship Church, Niles, OH

WEEK 43—TUESDAY

The Last Enemy

The last enemy that will be destroyed is death. For "He has put all things under His feet." But when He says "all things are put under Him," it is evident that He who put all things under Him is excepted. Now when all things are made subject to Him, then the Son Himself will also be subject to Him who put all things under Him, that God may be all in all.

1 CORINTHIANS 15:26-28

Humanity has one great common enemy. Death tears apart husbands and wives, loved ones, and friends. It is no respecter of persons; it cares not about how young or old someone is or how much they are loved. It casts its looming shadow across all humanity and embitters our existence. No matter how much beauty is found in someone's life, we eventually have to say, "Please bury my dead out of my sight." We are compelled to look away. When someone dies, we are always shocked by the news, even though we know that everyone eventually dies.

But Jesus has already put death under His feet. He has conquered death and the grave. We must all face death, but we face it with the knowledge that it no longer has all its horrors. It is already defeated. As has been said, "We are all born with the meter running and don't know how much time we have." Let's make the most of the life we have been given.

....

Father, help me live today not in fear of death but in faith in Your finished work—Your life, death, burial, and resurrection—which overcame death and put it under Your feet.

Heaven, Life, and the Resurrection

WEEK 43—WEDNESDAY

The Upside-Down Kingdom

Then He came to Capernaum. And when He was in the house He asked them, "What was it you disputed among yourselves on the road?" But they kept silent, for on the road they had disputed among themselves who would be the greatest. And He sat down, called the twelve, and said to them, "If anyone desires to be first, he shall be last of all and servant of all."

MARK 9:33-35

Our world's system is all about who is first. We are consumed with comparisons. We compare social media posts, houses, furnishings, vehicles, compensation, vacations, our children, and their success or lack thereof. There seems to be a race to be first, be best, and have the most.

Success in this world's system means being served, not serving others. Jesus taught that His kingdom is an upside-down kingdom. Things are not as they seem. In the 1970s, many movies were made that came to be known as "disaster movies." I remember a tidal wave flipping a cruise ship over in *The Poseidon Adventure*. At a key moment, a leader of the people trying to survive was trying to convince them that the way up and out of the ship was actually down because the ship was upside down. The people were confused, and many rejected that advice. So it is with Jesus' teaching today; the way up is first down. If you want to be first, be last and serve everyone.

Heavenly Father, help me understand Your kingdom. To gain, may I learn to give; help me lose my life to find Yours. Amen.

Roy G. Mack, Grace Fellowship Church, Niles, OH

WEEK 43—THURSDAY

Evacuation

After these things I looked, and behold, a door standing open in heaven. And the first voice which I heard was like a trumpet speaking with me, saying, "Come up here, and I will show you things which must take place after this." Immediately I was in the Spirit; and behold, a throne set in heaven, and One sat on the throne.

REVELATION 4:1-2

Some Bible scholars believe this verse refers to an event we call the "rapture" of the church. A trumpet will sound, an archangel will shout, and the body of Jesus Christ—His church, His bride—will be presented to Him. However this is interpreted, everyone in the world is traveling down the same road together: fear of economic downturns, viruses, quarantines, vaccines, military conflicts, political polarizations, racial divisions, and social injustices of our times sweep us all onto one broad road. But we are headed to a fork in the road, a marker in time, a moment that only God the Father knows. At that moment, multitudes of people will continue down a broad road that is heading to tribulation and judgment, but those of us who know Christ as Savior are headed for an evacuation. In a moment, in the twinkling of an eye, heaven's door will open, we will hear a shout and a trumpet blast, and we will be called to heaven to be with Him.

> Heavenly Father, help me live today with my eyes on heaven's door, with my ears listening for the trumpet, my mind on Your promises, and my heart ready to see Your glory. Amen.

WEEK 43—FRIDAY

Have Mercy

Preserve my life, for I am holy; You are my God; save Your servant who trusts in You! Be merciful to me, O Lord, for I cry to You all day long. Rejoice the soul of Your servant, for to You, O Lord, I lift up my soul. For You, Lord, are good, and ready to forgive, and abundant in mercy to all those who call upon You.

PSALM 86:2-5

This beautiful psalm is not ascribed to any particular event in David's life, which leads us to believe it may be a prayer he prayed often—one we could also use regularly in our own lives. David reminds himself that God is his God, and he trusts Him. He calls on God to be merciful to him. He reminds himself to rejoice in the Lord to whom he lifts up his own soul. He remembers that he serves a good God who is ready to forgive and full of mercy.

If you believe these things are true in your life, you have much to offer a hurting world today, particularly mercy. We live in a cruel and hurting world that questions the goodness of God. It does not know about a God who is ready to forgive and show mercy to those who would call upon Him. But mercy sets the context for much of Jesus' teachings. He shows mercy to the lame, the leper, the blind, a woman caught in adultery, a crooked tax collector, and many more. We need to remember to show mercy because we have been shown mercy.

Lord, remind me of Your mercy and forgiveness as I have mercy on others today.

Roy G. Mack, Grace Fellowship Church, Niles, OH

WEEK 43—WEEKEND

The Daily Bread Test

Then the Lord said to Moses, "Behold, I will rain bread from heaven for you. And the people shall go out and gather a certain quota every day, that I may test them, whether they will walk in My law or not. And it shall be on the sixth day that they shall prepare what they bring in, and it shall be twice as much as they gather daily."

EXODUS 16:4-5

We think of being tested as facing some difficult task. But in this instance, how difficult could the test be when God was simply going to provide food from heaven every day for the Hebrew people to collect. This was not a difficult challenge but an act of a loving provision. The test was whether they were willing to trust God in His provision.

The purpose for that test was the same as it is for us today: to expose and to train. Jesus said we do not live by bread alone (Matthew 4:4, Deuteronomy 8:3). We are also to pray for daily bread (Matthew 6:11). We are to trust His Word and rest in Him, "to Sabbath." But how often do our actions expose mistrust of God to provide for all our needs? How often does hoarding His provisions expose us as people who think more of the gifts than of the Giver? And how often does our constant gathering, without ever taking time to Sabbath, expose us as people who are not resting in God? God gives us our bread that we in turn would learn to live by His Word.

Father, thank You for this invitation to examine myself and ask, "Do I really trust You?"

Heaven, Life, and the Resurrection

WEEK 44—MONDAY

Your Little Corner of the World

"Therefore whoever confesses Me before men, him I will also confess before My Father who is in heaven. But whoever denies Me before men, him I will also deny before My Father who is in heaven."

MATTHEW 10:32-33

Do the people in your little corner of the world know where you stand with Jesus? In Matthew 10, Jesus shared His plan with His disciples. He talked about the power they would have for accomplishing the task, described the assignment they had been given, and then reminded them of His sovereignty. Nothing they faced would catch Him off guard.

This is true for us as well. Jesus' words in this passage are both clear and convicting. You were saved to be sent. If you possess a relationship with Christ, He expects you to profess Him right where you are.

In the community of faith, there is no such thing as an undercover follower of Jesus. Determine to make Him known this week. Go out in His power, committed to represent Him well. Will you face challenges in this task? Of course. But He is with you. Decide now that those in your little corner of the world will know what Jesus means to you.

Heavenly Father, You are worthy of being praised and proclaimed. As I enter into this week, I ask for boldness and clarity as I commit to professing Jesus right where I am. Amen.

Paul Purvis, Mission Hill Church, Temple Terrace, FL

WEEK 44—TUESDAY

Everything You Need

What is the exceeding greatness of His power toward us who believe, according to the working of His mighty power which He worked in Christ when He raised Him from the dead and seated Him at His right hand in the heavenly places, far above all principality and power and might and dominion, and every name that is named, not only in this age but also in that which is to come.

EPHESIANS 1:19-21

If you are a follower of Jesus, you already have access to everything you need for your life journey (2 Peter 1.3). Are you giving everything you have to bring glory to all that He is?

In Paul's letter to the Ephesians, he began by explaining our position "in Christ." Here he prayed that the Christ-followers in this church would understand all that God had given to them to become all He wanted them to be.

When you truly understand who Christ is and begin to discover what He empowers you to be, it revolutionizes your life. The same power Jesus used to conquer the grave is available to you. That's why Paul gives us this amazing reminder: "Now to him who is able to do far more abundantly than all that we ask or think, according to the power at work within us, to him be glory in the church and in Christ Jesus throughout all generations, forever and ever" (Ephesians 3:20–21, ESV).

Decide right now to let God's power accomplish its full work in your life today.

> Holy God, may the same power used to raise Christ from the grave be evident in my life today for Your glory. In Jesus' name, amen.

Heaven, Life, and the Resurrection

WEEK 44—WEDNESDAY

There Is None Like You!

He said: "Lord God of Israel, there is no God in heaven or on earth like You, who keep Your covenant and mercy with Your servants who walk before You with all their hearts."

2 CHRONICLES 6:14

In this prayer of Solomon, we see the importance of understanding who God is and what He is capable of. The king praised God's character and power. As he prayed, he declared God's greatness. He knew God was capable of answering the prayers of His people, whatever they were. In fact, God's response to this prayer is one of the most familiar verses in all the Bible: "If My people who are called by My name will humble themselves, and pray and seek My face, and turn from their wicked ways, then I will hear from heaven, and will forgive their sin and heal their land" (2 Chronicles 7:14).

Here we learn a powerful principle of prayer. When you approach God with all that you are, He makes available all that He has. Praise unlocks the bounties of heaven.

What attributes of God mean the most to you today? Spend some time this week worshipping God for who He is. Worship Him with all your heart. Trust Him to respond as only He can.

....

Dear God, I praise You today for who You are. I worship You in Your majesty. There is none like You! Amen.

Paul Purvis, Mission Hill Church, Temple Terrace, FL

WEEK 44—THURSDAY

Beyond Denial

Jesus said to him, "It is as you said. Nevertheless, I say to you, hereafter you will see the Son of Man sitting at the right hand of the Power, and coming on the clouds of heaven."

MATTHEW 26:64

Every day, you have opportunities to testify to who Jesus is and what He means to you. In the moments leading up to His crucifixion, Peter, one of His closest friends and followers, could not imagine that he would deny Christ. Yet just as Jesus prophesied, he did—three times. Nevertheless, even as Peter watched from a guilty distance, Jesus did not hesitate to proclaim who He was. Our strength to testify for Jesus must come from the example of Jesus Himself.

At the core of the Christian faith is this simple question: Do I agree with Jesus about who He says He is? Before and after His proclamation, Peter denied Him. You may have denied Him at some point too, and you may deny Him again. That does not change who He is. Our denial does not diminish His divinity.

As you seek to be a witness for Christ, make sure you are looking to Christ. Find your strength to testify "in Him." Recognize your weakness, but commit on this day to acknowledge who Jesus is and what He means to you. Determine to live in such a way that those in your little corner of the world have no doubt that you stand with Him.

Dear Jesus, please forgive me for the times I have denied You before others. Give me strength today to proclaim who You are with boldness and clarity!

Heaven, Life, and the Resurrection

WEEK 44—FRIDAY

The Privilege of Praise

I will praise You, O LORD, among the peoples, and I will sing praises to You among the nations. For Your mercy is great above the heavens, and Your truth reaches to the clouds. Be exalted, O God, above the heavens, and Your glory above all the earth; that Your beloved may be delivered, save with Your right hand, and hear me.

PSALM 108:3-6

When you encounter God, you will always be drawn to praise Him. Moses did so as he stood on holy ground, Isaiah did as he responded with unclean lips, and David does in this psalm. Like each of these Biblical heroes, we do the same when we experience God's mercy and truth.

What are you known for in your little corner of the world? Are you known "among the peoples" as a person of praise? If you are always looking to God and praising Him for who He is, you will spend less time looking at this world and worrying about its problems.

In a world filled with negativity, choose to be known for something positive. Do whatever it takes to praise God regardless of the circumstance. Whether things are going poorly or well, give Him praise. God desires and deserves your worship. Jesus told us that even the rocks would give Him praise if we don't (Luke 19:40). Don't surrender that privilege. Give Him glory in your little corner of the world. Take time right now to praise God for who He is!

Mighty God, my life and my lips offer You praise today. No rock is going to take my place. Praise Your Holy name!

Paul Purvis, Mission Hill Church, Temple Terrace, FL

WEEK 44—WEEKEND

An Attitude of Gratitude

Oh, give thanks to the God of gods! For His mercy endures forever. Oh, give thanks to the Lord of lords! For His mercy endures forever: To Him who alone does great wonders, for His mercy endures forever; to Him who by wisdom made the heavens, for His mercy endures forever.

PSALM 136:2-5

God has brought you to the end of another week. You could not have done this without Him. Do you have an attitude of gratitude? Have you recognized the week's blessings? In a world filled with ungrateful people, Christ followers should always be quick to express our thanks. God has given us a gift for which we should be deeply grateful: His grace (2 Corinthians 9:15).

Think about God's grace as you meditate on these words from John Newton:

> *Amazing grace!*
> *How sweet the sound,*
> *That saved a wretch like me!*
> *I once was lost, but now am found,*
> *Was blind, but now I see.*

Thank God for His grace in your salvation. Thank Him for His grace in your sanctification. Thank Him for the grace that will bring about your glorification. When you really understand who He is and what He's done for you in Jesus, you will spend your whole life in gratitude. Give thanks to the God of gods today!

....

Everlasting Father, I praise You! Thank You, Jesus, for Your grace in my life. Give me an attitude of gratitude as I seek to live for Your glory. Amen.

Heaven, Life, and the Resurrection

WEEK 45—MONDAY

The View Beyond Jordan

"O Lord God, You have begun to show Your servant Your greatness and Your mighty hand, for what god is there in heaven or on earth who can do anything like Your works and Your mighty deeds? I pray, let me cross over and see the good land beyond the Jordan, those pleasant mountains, and Lebanon."

DEUTERONOMY 3:24-25

Moses gazed beyond the Jordan and longed to go with his people into the future God had prepared. But he would not go. His time was over, and he handed the reins of leadership to Joshua, who led the people into the promised land. But Moses saw it.

We too get glimpses of glory. Eternity will come to us in God's time, but along the way we are encouraged to see where we are going. We know what our future holds. We will often face times of disappointment, sadness, and despair. Some prayers are not yet answered. Some sicknesses are not yet healed. Some miracles do not come. We stand at gravesides, weep over losses, and grieve, yet we do not grieve as others do because we are people of hope. Why? Because we get glimpses of what awaits.

The resurrection of Jesus is all the proof we need that there is more to come. As He rose, we too will rise. In the end, we will cross over. A good land will be ours. He will make all things new one day.

> Father, thank You for giving me glimpses into eternity to encourage me today. Strengthen me in the truth that one day I will cross over and be with You.

Dr. William Rice, Calvary Baptist Church, Clearwater, FL

WEEK 45—TUESDAY

A New Kingdom

And seeing the multitudes, He went up on a mountain, and when He was seated His disciples came to Him. Then He opened His mouth and taught them, saying: "Blessed are the poor in spirit, for theirs is the kingdom of heaven. Blessed are those who mourn, for they shall be comforted. Blessed are the meek, for they shall inherit the earth."

MATTHEW 5:1-5

Jesus began his most famous sermon with a series of statements known as the Beatitudes—the "blessed are" statements in Matthew 5:3–11, in which He describes a new way of life. It's almost as if Jesus is saying that everything we ever thought about real happiness was upside down.

Blessed are the "poor in spirit . . . those who mourn . . . the meek." Is this what the blessed life really looks like? We value self-confidence and bravado, not someone who is humble and contrite (poor in spirit). We don't want to mourn. We want to feel happy. We don't value meekness. We value strength and confidence.

Yet Jesus invites us into a new way to live. It begins with humbling ourselves, grieving over our sin, and submitting our will to His. Our natural inclination is to grasp what we want out of life, to live for our pleasures and seek more possessions. We want to be exalted. But Jesus knows better. He knows that to live, you must first die, and to be great, you must be willing to serve. You may think you know the road to happiness, but the truly blessed life begins with trusting Jesus.

Father, help me trust You and follow Your path to blessing today.

Heaven, Life, and the Resurrection

WEEK 45—WEDNESDAY

A Savior Comes

"For there is born to you this day in the city of David a Savior, who is Christ the Lord. And this will be the sign to you: You will find a Babe wrapped in swaddling cloths, lying in a manger." And suddenly there was with the angel a multitude of the heavenly host praising God and saying: "Glory to God in the highest, and on earth peace, goodwill toward men!"

LUKE 2:11-14

Good news! A Savior is born. The angelic announcement has been repeated often at Christmas seasons. Yet for many, the story seems less than enthralling. Why is the birth of this child such good news? It is only good news when we realize how badly we need a Savior.

Jesus came to save the lost. If the problem had been ignorance, a teacher would do. If it had been government, a leader would do. If it had been religion, a prophet would do. If it had been war, a soldier would do. All of those are problems, of course, but there is a greater problem at the root of every other problem. We are sinners. All of us have come short of God's glory. We didn't just need help. We needed a Savior.

I once heard of a cult that claimed they existed to make bad men good and good men better. The message of Jesus is much better than that! He makes dead men live. There are other leaders, other prophets, and other great men. But there is only one who can save us from our sin. There is only one Savior. His name is Jesus.

Father, thank You for sending a Savior to rescue me.

Dr. William Rice, Calvary Baptist Church, Clearwater, FL

WEEK 45—THURSDAY

Coming Again

Now when He had spoken these things, while they watched, He was taken up, and a cloud received Him out of their sight. And while they looked steadfastly toward heaven as He went up, behold, two men stood by them in white apparel, who also said, "Men of Galilee, why do you stand gazing up into heaven? This same Jesus, who was taken up from you into heaven, will so come in like manner as you saw Him go into heaven."

ACTS 1:9-11

Christians live in promises that are past, present, and future. We can look back and know we have been forgiven. We can live in confidence today that Jesus is alive and His Spirit indwells us. Yet we also look ahead. There are promises yet to be fulfilled, and this is the greatest. Jesus is coming again.

As Jesus ascended into heaven, bringing an end to His earthly ministry as God incarnate, the angels reiterated a promise He had already made: He will one day return. The angels also declared that He would come again in the same manner that He was taken into heaven.

Jesus ascended triumphantly. He had risen from the dead and fulfilled His Father's plan. He will return triumphantly to redeem His church and judge the world. He ascended suddenly. It happened in a moment, in the twinkling of an eye. In the same manner, Jesus will one day return. Some will be ready, but others will not. Are you ready for Jesus to return?

> Father, I long for the day when Jesus returns. May Your kingdom come on earth as it is in heaven. Even so, come Lord, Jesus.

Heaven, Life, and the Resurrection

WEEK 45—FRIDAY

Promises Made, Promises Kept

I have obeyed the voice of the Lord my God, and have done according to all that You have commanded me. Look down from Your holy habitation, from heaven, and bless Your people Israel and the land which You have given us, just as You swore to our fathers, 'a land flowing with milk and honey'.

DEUTERONOMY 26:14-15

God keeps His promises. Long before Moses could look into the promised land and see the glorious vision unfolding for Israel, God had made a promise to Abraham that one day he would become a great nation and inherit this promised land. The promise endured through Isaac, Jacob, and Joseph, through the years of slavery in Egypt, through the disappointment of wandering in the wilderness. At last, near the end of his life, Moses could see that the promise of God was going to come at last.

God keeps His promises. He did then, and He does now. What has He promised us? He will finish what He started. He will see us through. He will remain with us to the very end. And when the time comes, He will carry us over to the other side. He has prepared a place for us, and it is greater than anything we could imagine. It is a land of promise, a place of blessings beyond compare.

Sometimes God's promises are long in coming. You may grow weary or discouraged, but you can always rest in this assurance. God will keep His promise. He always does.

....

Father, thank You for all Your great promises. Help me always trust You and live in the assurance that Your promises will come to pass.

Dr. William Rice, Calvary Baptist Church, Clearwater, FL

WEEK 45—WEEKEND

A Greater View

"O LORD of hosts, God of Israel, the One who dwells between the cherubim, You are God, You alone, of all the kingdoms of the earth. You have made heaven and earth. Incline Your ear, O LORD, and hear; open Your eyes, O LORD, and see; and hear all the words of Sennacherib, which he has sent to reproach the living God."

ISAIAH 37:16-17

When earth is in chaos, worship is the reminder that heaven is still calm. God is in charge. When King Hezekiah of Judah faced a major crisis, he did what we must learn to do. He prayed.

Sennacherib, the Assyrian king, had surrounded Jerusalem and was threatening its annihilation. Its people could not overcome such an army, but in their crisis, Hezekiah prayed to the God of heaven. His prayer is an affirmation of God's greatness. God is the Creator of all. He sits enthroned in heaven. His power and authority are above all human authorities, and He rules over the kingdoms of men.

It doesn't always seem that way. We wonder why heaven is silent, why God doesn't act, why there is suffering and heartbreak. We don't always have answers, but we can always pray and worship. We can affirm what we know to be true regardless of the circumstances. There will still be questions. "In the world," Jesus said, "you will have tribulation" (John 16:33) But there is power in prayer and worship. They give us a different point of view. They remind us that God is in charge and He can be trusted.

....

Father, we trust You and believe that Your guidance is key to a prosperous life. Thank You for being a trustworthy God.

Heaven, Life, and the Resurrection

WEEK 46—MONDAY

Overwhelmed?

No man shall be able to stand before you all the days of your life; as I was with Moses, so I will be with you. I will not leave you nor forsake you. Be strong and of good courage, for to this people you shall divide as an inheritance the land which I swore to their fathers to give them.

JOSHUA 1:5-6

Have you ever been overwhelmed by something God wanted you to do? Imagine how Joshua must have felt. He was chosen by God to follow Moses, one of the most gifted leaders and godliest men of all time. Moses single-handedly brought Egypt, the most powerful nation in the world, to its knees. God spoke to Moses face-to-face as one speaks to a friend. Now Joshua was called to take his place and lead God's people into the promised land.

I'm sure Joshua woke up at night covered in sweat as he thought about the daunting task before him. Yet God told him to be strong and courageous. Then God said, "Do not be afraid" (v. 9). How can we be strong and not afraid when our task seems overwhelming? We remember God's promises. He promised His presence: "I will be with you. I will not leave you nor forsake you." He promised His protection: "No man shall be able to stand before you." When God calls us to do something, we need not fear because the One who calls us is the One who walks with us. And He is the almighty God.

Father, give me the courage to do whatever it is You call me to do for Your glory. Amen.

Rocky Purvis, Northside Baptist Church, Lexington, SC

WEEK 46—TUESDAY

Prophesy

Therefore, being a prophet, and knowing that God had sworn with an oath to him that of the fruit of his body, according to the flesh, He would raise up the Christ to sit on his throne, he, foreseeing this, spoke concerning the resurrection of the Christ, that His soul was not left in Hades, nor did His flesh see corruption. This Jesus God has raised up, of which we are all witnesses.

ACTS 2:30-32

I've heard a lot of prophecies about things that were going to happen, and most of them didn't come to pass. The truth is there are a lot of false prophets in our world today—people who give messages supposedly from God but that are from their own imaginations. In the Bible, a prophet of God was always right. If not, he would be put to death.

We are told in the Bible that David was not only a king but also a prophet. And most of the prophecies that he gave were about the future King, the Messiah, who would sit on his throne and rule forever. One of those is in Psalm 16, quoted in Acts 2:25-28—a prophecy that Jesus will overcome death. Over a thousand years before Jesus was born, David spoke of His resurrection. That's one reason I trust the Bible. It's filled with prophecies that have proven true. And that's one reason I have hope for the future. There are more prophecies to be fulfilled! Don't lose hope. Trust in His promises.

> Father, help me trust Your Word and hold true to Your promises today. Amen.

WEEK 46—WEDNESDAY

I Am

"But I am the Lord your God, who divided the sea whose waves roared—the Lord of hosts is His name. And I have put My words in your mouth; I have covered you with the shadow of My hand, that I may plant the heavens, lay the foundations of the earth, and say to Zion, 'You are My people.'"

ISAIAH 51:15–16

What do you do when your world is falling apart—when everything you've put your hope in crashes down around you? Do you give up and call it quits or turn your back on the one you've put your hope in? Or do you lean in and hold on tighter to the One who promises never to leave or forsake you?

The people of Israel were going through difficult times, and times were going to get worse. They would be conquered and exiled—possessions taken, families separated, people carried off in chains or put to death. But in the midst of their pain, God gave them a reminder of who He is and who they were. He is the great "I am," the One who parted the sea and commands heaven's armies, the One who created the heavens and earth. He is almighty God. And then He reminds them who they are—His people, whom he holds in the palm of His hand.

If God is holding you in the palm of His hand, you have nothing to fear. So trust Him. Even when your world is falling apart.

....

Father, today I trust in You. I am secure in Your hand. Amen.

Rocky Purvis, Northside Baptist Church, Lexington, SC

WEEK 46—THURSDAY

Surrender

"For I have not spoken on My own authority; but the Father who sent Me gave Me a command, what I should say and what I should speak. And I know that His command is everlasting life. Therefore, whatever I speak, just as the Father has told Me, so I speak."

JOHN 12:49-50

The Trinity is impossible to fully comprehend—the Father, Son, and Holy Spirit, together one God throughout eternity and yet three Persons. The Father isn't more God than the Son, and the Holy Spirit isn't less God than the Father. They are one, each of them fully God. Yet when Jesus came to die for our sins on the cross, He fully surrendered His will and even His words to the Father.

Think about that. Jesus relinquished His rights as God to speak or act unless the Father directed. Why? Could it be that He was giving us an example of what it looks like to surrender completely, to give ourselves wholly to the One who created us, loves us, and really does have a plan for our lives? I believe that when we surrender our words and our way to the One who created us, we will discover that life is not only better; it is easier—not because our circumstances are always easier but because we are walking with the One who controls the current of history and not against Him.

Have you fully surrendered? If not, why not? His way is not just a better way. It's the best way!

....

Father, today I surrender my life fully to You—my words, my will, and my walk. Amen.

Heaven, Life, and the Resurrection

WEEK 46—FRIDAY

Walk in Obedience

*But the mercy of the L*ORD *is from everlasting to everlasting on those who fear Him, and His righteousness to children's children, to such as keep His covenant, and to those who remember His commandments to do them. The L*ORD *has established His throne in heaven, and His kingdom rules over all.*

PSALM 103:17-19

This is one of my favorite psalms. It begins and ends with, "Let all that I am praise the Lord" (NLT). *All* that I am—not just my lips but my eyes, ears, mind, hands, feet, heart. Let me be so consumed with God's goodness that every fiber of my being is praising Him. Throughout this psalm, David gives us reason after reason to praise the Lord. He forgives all my sins. He heals all my diseases. He redeems me from death. He fills my life with good things.

Then in verse 17 we discover that His goodness isn't just poured out on us but on our children and our children's children too! I love that. God has blessed me with four children and ten grandchildren thus far, and His mercy will be extended to them as I walk in obedience to Him. I so want my children and grandchildren to know God's mercy firsthand. And when I walk in obedience to Him, it opens the way for them to see His goodness in my life and experience it for themselves. That's motivation enough for me to remember His commands and do them. What about you?

Father, today I pray I will walk in obedience so those who come after me will see and experience Your mercy. Amen.

Rocky Purvis, Northside Baptist Church, Lexington, SC

WEEK 46—WEEKEND

Crying Out

I will cry out to God Most High, to God who performs all things for me. He shall send from heaven and save me; He reproaches the one who would swallow me up. God shall send forth His mercy and His truth.

PSALM 57:2-3

Who do you cry out to when you're in need? A trusted counselor? A loving spouse or parent? A concerned friend? Whenever David found himself in need, he cried out to God. The name used here is God Most High, *Elohim Elyon*. In other words, nothing and no one can compare to our God. He is head and shoulders above all other gods. No other god can get in the arena with our God. No other god can step onto the stage with Him. He is the unrivaled, all-powerful, all-wise, all-sufficient Creator of the heavens and the earth. All things have their origin in Him. Without Him, there would be nothing. And we get to cry out to Him when we are in need.

Think about that. There is nothing you will ever face, no enemy who will ever come against you, that He is not able to overcome. He is God Most High, and He loves you and longs to take care of you. So when you are in distress, when you have a need, cry out to God and He will send help. What is your need today? Let Him know.

....

Father, I desperately need _____. Amen.

Heaven, Life, and the Resurrection

WEEK 47—MONDAY

A Journey of Joy

"I say to you that likewise there will be more joy in heaven over one sinner who repents than over ninety-nine just persons who need no repentance."

LUKE 15:7

A person who becomes a follower of Jesus Christ embarks on a lifelong adventure of making a difference in the world. Jesus is our model for living a focused life filled with the joy He gives. One of our greatest joys along this journey comes when we share the message of the gospel and lead others to trust Christ as Savior. Sharing the gospel and inviting others to follow Him must be the focal point of our journey with the Lord.

In Luke 15, Jesus shares three parables centered on the joy that comes from finding what has been lost. In the first, He was being criticized for being in the presence of sinners—outcasts of far less status than the scribes and Pharisees who were complaining. Instead of rebuking them, Jesus spoke to them in a method they all could identify with. He reminded them of the joy that comes from the recovery of just one lost sheep who had wandered away from the fold.

Can you recall an experience when you witnessed the repentance of someone who was lost and received the glorious gift of eternal salvation? Or when you witnessed the repentance of someone who had drifted from their commitment to Christ and His church? If so, you can testify of the joy that comes when sinners repent and get right with the Lord.

Dear Lord, help me to never get over the joy of leading others to know You. Amen.

Brent Thompson, Heflin Baptist Church, Heflin, AL

WEEK 47—TUESDAY

The Blessing of Persecution

"Blessed are those who are persecuted for righteousness' sake, for theirs is the kingdom of heaven. Blessed are you when they revile and persecute you, and say all kinds of evil against you falsely for My sake. Rejoice and be exceedingly glad, for great is your reward in heaven, for so they persecuted the prophets who were before you."

MATTHEW 5:10-12

I have yet to meet anyone who enjoys being persecuted. Even the thought of it causes us to become anxious and withdrawn. But followers of Jesus cannot escape or avoid persecution. In today's text from the Sermon on the Mount, Jesus challenges us to look beyond the temporary effects of persecution and to cast our eyes toward eternal rewards. We can be certain that others who seek to detour and derail us from living a life surrendered to Christ will seek to discourage us with "all kinds of evil." Yet in the midst of it all, Jesus reminds us to find joy in our pain as we faithfully follow Him.

Have you ever had anyone speak evil against you falsely? Have you felt the sting of the words and actions of others attempting to cause you to forsake your calling and commitment to the Lord? If so, Jesus said you are in good company. The prophets, the disciples, and even our Lord Himself were persecuted before us. They persevered, and so can we.

....

> Dear Lord, help me remember when I am persecuted by the words and actions of others that I can still find joy in Your presence. Help me stay focused on Your perfect will for my life. I want to live every day for Your glory. Amen.

Heaven, Life, and the Resurrection

WEEK 47—WEDNESDAY

Seeking After the Heart of God

The Lord looks down from heaven upon the children of men, to see if there are any who understand, who seek God. They have all turned aside, they have together become corrupt; there is none who does good, no, not one.

PSALM 14:2-3

Do you ever stop and consider what the world's activity looks like from heaven's point of view? When I'm on an airplane, the world looks different from the air than it does on the ground. Our perspective is affected by our point of view. In our text today, David paints a dismal portrait of human activity as it pertains to seeking God. As the Lord surveys the world, David declares that people have "turned aside" and "become corrupt." The sinful condition of the world is exactly why Jesus came to earth. He came to redeem us from our fallen, sinful condition.

David pursued the heart of God. Yet even in his pursuit, he strayed and failed God miserably. He paid a horrible price for his disobedience and was drawn back to the Lord through heartfelt repentance.

How about you? Are you truly seeking after God's heart? Have you failed in the past and see no need to seek Him in the present? The pathway to seeking Him begins with repentance. David poured his heart out to God in Psalm 51 and experienced the joy of restoration. God can do the same for you.

....

Dear Lord, may I faithfully seek Your heart today. Take charge of my mind and cleanse my heart. Help me be different from the world so others can see You in me, amen.

Brent Thompson, Heflin Baptist Church, Heflin, AL

WEEK 47—THURSDAY

What a Meeting in the Air

For the Lord Himself will descend from heaven with a shout, with the voice of an archangel, and with the trumpet of God. And the dead in Christ will rise first. Then we who are alive and remain shall be caught up together with them in the clouds to meet the Lord in the air. And thus we shall always be with the Lord. Therefore comfort one another with these words.

1 THESSALONIANS 4:16-18

We live in a world filled with darkness, negativity, and pain. We have all experienced this reality in variety of ways—living under the threat of illness, experiencing social unrest, living with pandemic restrictions, dealing with conflict in a polarizing world. All of these things have had a significant effect on everyone, including the body of Christ. Yet our difficulties in a changing society create opportunities to learn new and innovative ways of sharing the gospel and staying connected with our church family.

In today's text, Paul teaches us to keep our eyes on the promise of Christ's coming and not just the pain of the present. Soon and very soon, we will meet the Lord in the air, never to be separated from Him or His people. During the COVID pandemic, I was asked if I had any idea when social distancing would end. I responded by saying I didn't know exactly when, but I did know where. Praise God, there will be no social distancing at that meeting in the air!

Dear Lord, help me live each day with expectation of meeting You in the air. Thank You for loving me. Amen.

Heaven, Life, and the Resurrection

WEEK 47—FRIDAY

Faithful to the Finish

Revive me, O Lord, according to Your word. Accept, I pray, the freewill offerings of my mouth, O Lord, and teach me Your judgments. My life is continually in my hand, yet I do not forget Your law. . . . Your testimonies I have taken as a heritage forever, for they are the rejoicing of my heart. I have inclined my heart to perform Your statutes forever, to the very end.

PSALM 119:107-109, 111-112

Throughout this psalm, the psalmist repeats his need for revival as he struggles with the many difficulties of this life. He recognizes his tendency to stray and calls on God to help him overcome the challenges in his path. Many times, I have found myself in the same situation. I too have struggled to maintain the focus needed to avoid life's pitfalls. All of God's children need times of refreshing and revival to remain faithful to the finish.

The key to revival is found in verse 112: "I have inclined my heart to perform Your statutes forever, to the very end." The psalmist literally set his heart toward the Lord so he could fellowship with Him and receive direction for his future. He was determined to finish strong and not stumble into a pit before completing his course. Where is your heart pointed today? Is it inclined toward the Father or pointed in some other direction? Real revival comes when our hearts are focused on Him.

Dear Lord, incline my heart toward You today. I cannot finish strong on my own. I need You every hour. Amen.

Brent Thompson, Heflin Baptist Church, Heflin, AL

WEEK 47—WEEKEND

A Divine Interruption

The next day, as they went on their journey and drew near the city, Peter went up on the housetop to pray, about the sixth hour. Then he became very hungry and wanted to eat; but while they made ready, he fell into a trance and saw heaven opened and an object like a great sheet bound at the four corners, descending to him and let down to the earth.

ACTS 10:9-11

It is amazing how many interruptions we encounter daily. Advancements in technology have been exponential over the last thirty years. Many have brought much convenience to our lives, for which we are all grateful. But some have made it increasingly difficult to experience times of solitude, meditate on God's Word, and communicate with our Lord. Our world is filled with static that muffles God's voice as He speaks to our hearts.

Peter had his prayer time interrupted with hunger pains. Even though his hunger came as a distraction, the Lord used it to teach him something new. He would use this event in Peter's life to move him toward the man He'd created him to be. Peter's mindset and ministry would be forever changed during this encounter with the Lord.

As you prepare to worship with the body of Christ this weekend, take time to prepare your heart and mind to encounter the Lord. Listen for God to speak through the songs and sermon in corporate worship. Each time you meet Him in worship, you will go away changed.

> Dear Lord, prepare my heart to meet with You this weekend. I am grateful for all You do and who You are. Amen.

Heaven, Life, and the Resurrection

WEEK 48—MONDAY

Abundant Life Today!
Eternal Life Tomorrow!

What then if you should see the Son of Man ascend where He was before? It is the Spirit who gives life; the flesh profits nothing. The words that I speak to you are spirit, and they are life.

JOHN 6:62-63

Why did Jesus come? This is one of the most important questions a person can ask. Jesus answered it in John 10:10—"I have come that they may have life, and that they may have it more abundantly." Jesus came to not only give eternal life in the future, but to give life, meaning, and purpose right now. Many people who think they are living are only existing. Many live to appease the desires of the flesh. But the flesh only brings temporal gratification and profits nothing. Abundant and joyful life comes through Christ. Eternal life comes through Him!

When we place our trust in Christ, through the power of the Holy Spirit, He gives life. His Word—both the written and spoken word of God—brings life. Indeed, Christ's words are true, "Whoever wishes to save life will lose it, but whoever loses his life for My sake will find it" (Matthew 16:25). To embrace Jesus is to embrace life.

Do you have life? Are you experiencing real, joyful, abundant life today? Do you have the hope of eternal life in heaven tomorrow? Abundant, joyful, eternal life comes through Christ. Today, choose Jesus. Choose life!

> Father, thank You for the abundant life I have today and the eternal life I have in Christ! Amen.

Dr. Kelly Bullard, First Baptist Church Summerfield, Summerfield, NC

WEEK 48—TUESDAY

The Privilege of Prayer

Whatever prayer, whatever supplication is made by anyone, or by all Your people Israel, when each one knows his own burden and his own grief, and spreads out his hands to this temple: then hear from heaven Your dwelling place, and forgive, and give to everyone according to all his ways, whose heart You know (for You alone know the hearts of the sons of men).

2 CHRONICLES 6:29-30

One of God's greatest blessings is being a dad. He has blessed my wife and me with two wonderful sons. My youngest is three and often extends his arms and hands upward saying, "Hold me, Daddy! Hold me!" His words and posture are a reminder of how we come to our heavenly Father. When we pray, we come with hands and arms spread open wide. Sometimes we spread our arms in praise, saying, "Father, You are so good!" Other times we spread them in petition, saying, "Hold me, Father! Hold me!"

Prayer really is a privilege. When we pray, we have the wonderful opportunity to enter into God's presence, bringing Him both our praises and petitions. Solomon reminds us God will hear from His dwelling place in heaven and answer according to His ways and faithfulness. When we pray, we can trust in Him.

Today, do not forsake the privilege of prayer. Take the time to offer your praise to God for who He is and what He has done. Do not hesitate to offer your petitions—He knows your heart and desires before you ask!

Father, thank You for the privilege of prayer. May Your will be done in my life as it is in heaven. Amen.

WEEK 48—WEDNESDAY

Walking in Humility

"Do not call anyone on earth your father; for One is your Father, He who is in heaven. And do not be called teachers; for One is your Teacher, the Christ. But he who is greatest among you shall be your servant. And whoever exalts himself will be humbled, and he who humbles himself will be exalted."

MATTHEW 23:9-12

One of the best-selling books in history is Charles Sheldon's *In His Steps*. This classic work was first published in 1896 and has sold over fifty million copies. Sheldon asks the question, "What would Jesus do?" When we consider the life of Christ, we recognize a life marked by humility. To walk "in His steps" is nothing short of walking in humility.

As Jesus spoke to His disciples, He warned them not to take pride in their positions, titles, or achievements. These were the sins of the Pharisees. Instead He encouraged them to live a life marked by humility and service.

The New Testament is filled with teachings on the virtue of humility (Romans 12:3; Ephesians 4:2; Philippians 2:3; Colossians 3:12; James 4:10; 1 Peter 5:5). The repeated encouragement reminds us that there is no room for pride in the heart of a child of God. Our boasting must be only in the cross of Christ (Galatians 6:14). We can never say, "Look at me and what I have done." Our testimony must always be, "Look at Christ and what He has done!" We all stand in need of His love, grace, and mercy.

Heavenly Father, give us grace to walk in humility this day and grant us opportunities to serve others in Your name. Amen.

Dr. Kelly Bullard, First Baptist Church Summerfield, Summerfield, NC

WEEK 48—THURSDAY

From Fear to Faith

I will praise You, O Lord, among the peoples; I will sing to You among the nations. For Your mercy reaches unto the heavens, and Your truth unto the clouds. Be exalted, O God, above the heavens; let Your glory be above all the earth.

PSALM 57:9-11

Psalm 57 is a deeply personal psalm of lament. As David wrote these words, he was fearful for his life and hiding in a cave from Saul and his army. This psalm begins with his petition for protection but ends with his praise for God's faithfulness and glory. His words remind us it is possible, in the midst of fear, to praise God for His faithfulness.

But how do we move from a place of fear to a place of faith? In verses 1–6, David offers a petition for protection. He feels the closeness of his oppressors and his impending doom. But the musical notation "Selah," a pause, is at the end of verse 6. The pause led David to ponder God's faithfulness in his life, which led him from fear to faith and from petition to praise!

Fear is never of God. Paul reminded Timothy, "God has not given us a spirit of fear, but of power and of love and of a sound mind" (2 Timothy 1:7). As you face your fears, rise above your circumstances to see the God who loves you and has wonderful plans for your life. When you glimpse His glory, you too can praise Him even in the valley.

> Father, help me rise above my fears today and proclaim Your faithfulness. Let me praise You even in my valleys. Amen.

WEEK 48—FRIDAY

The Way Up Is Down

Therefore God also has highly exalted Him and given Him the name which is above every name, that at the name of Jesus every knee should bow, of those in heaven, and of those on earth, and of those under the earth, and that every tongue should confess that Jesus Christ is Lord, to the glory of God the Father.

PHILIPPIANS 2:9-11

Life is full of paradoxes: "You have to spend money to make money"; "this is the beginning of the end"; "it was a bittersweet moment." Consider Socrates' famous statement, "I know one thing: that I know nothing." These appear to be contradictory, yet they are true.

The message of Paul's hymn in Philippians 2:5-11 is deeply meaningful, richly theological, and profoundly encouraging. We find in it the humiliation of Christ (vv. 5-8) and His exaltation (vv. 9-11). His example and the testimony of Scripture seems paradoxical but true—the way up is down. In His incarnation, Christ humbled Himself. In his ascension, God exalted Him.

In His exaltation, Christ stands as King, with every human knee bowing before Him and every tongue confessing that He is Lord. He gives new and eternal life to those who humble themselves, repent, and turn to Him. Those who exalt themselves will be humbled, and those who humble themselves will be exalted (Matthew 23:12).

Have you truly humbled yourself in repentance and faith? Do you know for certain you have eternal life? Why not make that personal confession today: Christ is my Lord!

Lord Jesus, even now I humble myself in recognizing my need of You. I believe, repent, and confess You as my Lord. In Jesus' name, amen.

Dr. Kelly Bullard, First Baptist Church Summerfield, Summerfield, NC

WEEK 48—WEEKEND

A Covenant Relationship

"I will betroth you to Me forever; yes, I will betroth you to Me in righteousness and justice, in lovingkindness and mercy; I will betroth you to Me in faithfulness, and you shall know the Lord. "It shall come to pass in that day that I will answer," says the Lord; "I will answer the heavens, and they shall answer the earth."

HOSEA 2:19-21

Life is full of memorable moments like the joy of a wedding celebration. Most center around one special moment—the entrance of the bride. The groom and minister enter, taking their places at the altar. The wedding party processes down the aisle to assigned locations. Finally, the "Wedding March" begins. The doors open, the congregation stands, and the bride makes her entrance. The hoopla never centers around the groom; there is no "Here Comes the Groom!" In the moment, all eyes are on the bride.

In today's passage, God the Bridegroom declares His betrothal to His bride, Israel. But the focus here is the Bridegroom, not the bride. All eyes are on the Lord, not Israel. Israel's covenant of redemption is not determined by her faithfulness but by God's righteousness, justice, lovingkindness, and mercy.

The glorious message of the gospel echoes that of God to His people Israel. We, the church, are His bride, brought into a covenant relationship with God through the blood of Christ. We are heirs of His righteousness, justified by His blood, crowned with His lovingkindness, and recipients of His mercy!

....

God, thank You for Your love and mercy expressed through Christ.
May my life reflect Your goodness and faithfulness. Amen.

Heaven, Life, and the Resurrection

WEEK 49—MONDAY

The Lord Is in Control

For I know that the Lord is great, and our Lord is above all gods. Whatever the Lord pleases He does, in heaven and in earth, in the seas and in all deep places. He causes the vapors to ascend from the ends of the earth; He makes lightning for the rain; He brings the wind out of His treasuries.

PSALM 135:5-7

Reflection is the gracious tool that leads to worship and praise. As the children of God in Christ, we get to reflect who the Lord is and what He does within His creation.

Human governments and inventions come and go, but Christ remains the same in each generation. He is the all-powerful Creator at work in the lives of His people today, tomorrow, and forever. The Lord is in perfect control in this season of your life. He is in control of the seasons of victory and defeat. All seasons are under His loving guidance, and He is at work in all seasons in the lives of His people.

Reflect upon the Lord and trust in the Holy Spirit to lead you to worship and praise! You can be confident that He has you in His all-knowing hands this morning, afternoon, and evening.

> Father, open my eyes and ears to the fact that You are in total control of this season of my life. I can worship and praise You not because I'm in a season of victory or defeat but because You are Lord of all seasons.

Steven Cox, Peace Baptist Church, Whiteville, NC

WEEK 49—TUESDAY

Hear His Voice

When He had been baptized, Jesus came up immediately from the water; and behold, the heavens were opened to Him, and He saw the Spirit of God descending like a dove and alighting upon Him. And suddenly a voice came from heaven, saying, "This is My beloved Son, in whom I am well pleased."

MATTHEW 3:16-17

Christ dealt with the complexity of life and ministry all the time. He held meetings, addressed failures and successes of others, enjoyed celebrations, endured false accusations from religious leaders, and spent time with loved ones. What helped Him stay focused on His task of seeking and saving the lost? He had constant communion with the Father. He was available to hear the Father's voice.

Constant communion with the Father is the greatest need for His children in this life. The complexity of life can rob you of hearing His voice. The temptation is to get so busy being active that you are not active in the Word of God. Even from the beginning of Mark's Gospel, we see this communion at work. Jesus called disciples, demonstrated power over the demonic world, gathered followers, and told a fever to flee. He was busy, but He prioritized communion with the Father (Mark 1:35).

Flee from busyness that keeps you from spending time in God's Word. You'll be glad you did. The Father is still speaking!

....

Father, may Your voice be the priority in my life and ministry.

Heaven, Life, and the Resurrection

WEEK 49—WEDNESDAY

Be Selfless

But when the apostles Barnabas and Paul heard this, they tore their clothes and ran in among the multitude, crying out and saying, "Men, why are you doing these things? We also are men with the same nature as you, and preach to you that you should turn from these useless things to the living God, who made the heaven, the earth, the sea, and all things that are in them.

ACTS 14:14-15

I've had the great privilege of discipling five young men for six years. I've watched them grow taller than me and advance in grade levels each year. There have been many tears, disagreements, hamburgers, youth trips, basketball games at the park, and much more. I learned quick that these youth, whom I love and cherish deeply, needed the Almighty more than they needed me. The temptation is for leaders to gain followers for themselves and forget to point people to the living God.

Barnabas and Paul made a great impact for the kingdom, but both knew it had to be a selfless impact. The Lord blesses ministry He knows will be selfless. When you have a selfless ministry, you'll be able to point people to Christ more than to you.

These young men thought is was cool that a youth pastor could score points and cross them over on the ball court. But we are called to use our gifts, ministires, personalities, backgrounds, intellects, occupations, and much more to point people to the living God. Only Jesus can save!

Holy Spirit, use me to point people to Christ!

Steven Cox, Peace Baptist Church, Whiteville, NC

WEEK 49—THURSDAY

His World

Yours, O LORD, is the greatness, the power and the glory, the victory and the majesty; for all that is in heaven and in earth is Yours; Yours is the kingdom, O LORD, and You are exalted as head over all. Both riches and honor come from You, and You reign over all. In Your hand is power and might; in Your hand it is to make great and to give strength to all.

1 CHRONICLES 29:11-12

Are you consumed with the reality that God is owner of all creation? Money, cars, clothes, technology, buildings, and everything else would not be here without our Lord speaking this world into existence.

When we start to have a right view of the Lord's ownership of all creation, servanthood and stewardship follow. When the weekend approaches, we typically think of relaxing. But what if the Lord is calling you to use your time and resources this weekend to point people to His greatness? What senior adult needs a phone call of encouragement? What youth needs to get out of a violent home and be around your loving family? We point people to God's greatness when we live attractive lives—lives that give strength and encouragement to those around us. And we are called to use our resources to make a difference. Everything on this planet really belongs to our loving Lord. Be the difference-maker who points people to the One who can truly make a difference.

Father, this is Your world. Use me to make a difference for Christ's sake!

WEEK 49—FRIDAY

Victory in Christ

Seeing then that we have a great High Priest who has passed through the heavens, Jesus the Son of God, let us hold fast our confession. For we do not have a High Priest who cannot sympathize with our weaknesses, but was in all points tempted as we are, yet without sin. Let us therefore come boldly to the throne of grace, that we may obtain mercy and find grace to help in time of need.

HEBREWS 4:14-16

A broken home, violence, drugs, false views of sexuality, and much more characterized my childhood. When Jesus saved me in 2012, I started to learn that I could have victory over my sins in the power of the Father, Son, and Holy Spirit.

The book of Hebrews is about victory in Jesus Christ. He is the Creator, superior to all created things, and the final sacrifice for human sins. He gives the church daily victory over sin. We no longer have to make excuses!

When I started my journey with Christ, I learned that I could quit blaming my childhood for my daily sins. Christ came to redeem and transform me. He breaks generational curses and patterns. He renews our minds with His perfect Word. He empowers us with the Holy Spirit of promise. We are the redeemed who experience grace and forgiveness daily in Christ. We no longer have to make excuses for living in sin. We have access in Him to pray to our Father to keep us close to His desires for us.

....

Father, help me quit making excuses for my sins, and help me live for You!

Steven Cox, Peace Baptist Church, Whiteville, NC

WEEK 49—WEEKEND

Keep Praising

Because Your lovingkindness is better than life, my lips shall praise You. Thus I will bless You while I live; I will lift up my hands in Your name. My soul shall be satisfied as with marrow and fatness, and my mouth shall praise You with joyful lips.

PSALM 63:3-5

The tough seasons of life reveal who or what we worship. We've all experienced difficult years when we had to constantly get our hearts in tune with the Lord and stay in an attitude of worship. When life is so uncertain, how do we do that? We acknowlege the eternal love of God. We worship Him because He proves His love to us in Christ. Yes, the world is full of uncertainity, but Jesus' life, ministry, sufferings, burial, and resurrection prove the love of God that is now and forever true.

Even when life is full of pain and suffering, it can also be full of praise and worship. We don't ignore the pain, but we must praise and worship in and through it. The love of God is the motivator of praise, not of pain. This kind of praise will confuse worldly people and systems but can also be a means of winning souls to God's love. Could our present sufferings be the platform the Lord uses to draw many to Christ? Keep worshipping and praising Him in the storms of life. Today is the day of salvation!

Father, use my current sufferings to lead people to Your love in Christ. Help me praise You in the storms of life.

WEEK 50—MONDAY

Every Spiritual Blessing

Blessed be the God and Father of our Lord Jesus Christ, who has blessed us with every spiritual blessing in the heavenly places in Christ, just as He chose us in Him before the foundation of the world, that we should be holy and without blame before Him in love.

EPHESIANS 1:3-4

God graciously blesses all of His children. All in Christ are abundantly blessed with every spiritual blessing in the heavenly places. None in Christ are destined to be seated in the nosebleed section of glory. None will be served leftovers or scraps of food that fall from the table at the marriage supper of the Lamb. None hold a standby ticket, waiting to enter the kingdom of God upon someone else's forfeit or cancellation.

All in Christ have been given everything required to be who they were created to be and do what He calls them to do. Jesus came that "they may have life, and that they may have it more abundantly" (John 10:10) "And of His fullness we have all received, grace for grace" (John 1:16). "Every good gift and every perfect gift is from above, and comes down from the Father of lights, with whom there is no variation or shadow of turning" (James 1:17). "For the Lord God is a sun and shield; the Lord will give grace and glory; no good thing will He withhold from those who walk uprightly" (Psalm 84:11).

> Lord, thank You for blessing me with "every spiritual blessing in the heavenly places in Christ." Help me always live in light of that reality.

Mark Lashey, LifeHouse Church, Townsend, DE

WEEK 50—TUESDAY

For My Name's Sake

Then He said to them, "Nation will rise against nation, and kingdom against kingdom. And there will be great earthquakes in various places, and famines and pestilences; and there will be fearful sights and great signs from heaven. But before all these things, they will lay their hands on you and persecute you, delivering you up to the synagogues and prisons. You will be brought before kings and rulers for My name's sake."

LUKE 21:10-12

Jesus did not warn His disciples of the difficulties they would face so they could consider whether or not they would continue to follow Him. He warned them to prepare them. He wanted them to be prepared and to endure the obstacles and opposition they would face for His name's sake. In addition, He promised to be with them always, even to the end of the age (Matthew 28:20).

The Apostle Paul, having acknowledged some of the hardships he had already faced for Christ's sake, rejoiced that through Christ, he could endure anything (Philippians 4:13) He went to "the ends of the earth" to tell others about Jesus and the salvation available in His name. Eventually Paul was imprisoned and faced execution for Jesus' sake, but he had no regrets. He wrote, "I have fought the good fight, I have finished the race, I have kept the faith. Finally, there is laid up for me the crown of righteousness, which the Lord, the righteous Judge, will give to me on that Day, and not to me only but also to all who have loved His appearing" (2 Timothy 4:7-8).

> Lord Jesus, give me the faith to do whatever, whenever, wherever for Your name's sake. I thank You for always being with me.

Heaven, Life, and the Resurrection

WEEK 50—WEDNESDAY

Looking for Mercy

Unto You I lift up my eyes, O You who dwell in the heavens. Behold, as the eyes of servants look to the hand of their masters, as the eyes of a maid to the hand of her mistress, so our eyes look to the Lord our God, until He has mercy on us.

PSALM 123:1–2

God has revealed Himself as merciful. His mercies "are new every morning" (Lamentations 3:22–23). Not only does He desire to show mercy, He is also able to show mercy. He is mighty to save and strong to redeem.

As sinners, we all deserve condemnation. "All have sinned," and "the wages of sin is death" (Romans 3:23; 6:23). Yet those who have believed in Jesus are shown mercy by grace through faith in Him. We need not worry at all about condemnation for in Him, there is no condemnation (Romans 8:1). In Christ we can come to God who is "rich in mercy" (Ephesians 2:4). We can approach Him with bold and confident expectation "in time of need" (Hebrews 4:16).

Even more than servants who "look to the hand of their masters," those in Christ can "look to the Lord our God." In Christ, we are invited to gaze as beloved children on the face of our heavenly Father and, from His hand, receive abundant mercy.

Lord, You are merciful. Thank You for making a way through Jesus Christ for me to come boldly before You at any time. I am so thankful for all the ways You show me mercy. You are a good Father.

Mark Lashey, LifeHouse Church, Townsend, DE

WEEK 50—THURSDAY

At the End of the Time

And at the end of the time I, Nebuchadnezzar, lifted my eyes to heaven, and my understanding returned to me; and I blessed the Most High and praised and honored Him who lives forever: For His dominion is an everlasting dominion, and His kingdom is from generation to generation. All the inhabitants of the earth are reputed as nothing; He does according to His will in the army of heaven and among the inhabitants of the earth. No one can restrain His hand or say to Him, "What have You done?"

DANIEL 4:34-35

God allows and even ordains humbling circumstances for those He loves. King Nebuchadnezzar was brought low that he might come to know the Most High. He likely would not have traded the experiences that gave him a clearer picture of God. God used humbling experiences to reveal Himself as the One "who lives forever." Nebuchadnezzar did "at the end of the time" what he had not done before. He worshiped the everlasting God whose "kingdom is from generation to generation."

Similarly, Paul acknowledged his "thorn in the flesh" as having kept him humble (2 Corinthians 12). Though the thorn brought him low, God gave him more than sufficient grace to endure it. Paul actually began to rejoice in the weakness it caused him because he experienced God's power in a way he would not have otherwise. He acknowledged that though he had initially prayed for relief, he would gladly boast in his infirmities, that Christ's power would rest on him (v. 9).

Lord, I thank You for the ways You reveal Yourself to me, even when they are difficult.

Heaven, Life, and the Resurrection

WEEK 50—FRIDAY

Set Free

I have made the earth, and created man on it. I—My hands—stretched out the heavens, and all their host I have commanded. I have raised him up in righteousness, and I will direct all his ways; He shall build My city and let My exiles go free, not for price nor reward," says the LORD of hosts.

ISAIAH 45:12-13

When God's people were slaves and exiles in Babylon, God reminded them of His power and authority through words Isaiah had prophesied long before. God is sovereign over all He has created, and He promised His people that they would be set free and that Jerusalem, then in ruins, would be rebuilt. At the time, they saw no clear path for that promise becoming a reality. But God was at work. Years later, He raised up Cyrus, the pagan king of Persia, to accomplish what He promised.

Throughout the Old Testament, God also promised He would send One who would set men free from the bondage of sin. While that too seemed impossible, it is an encouraging reminder that the One who "made the earth and created man on it" made the promise. To fulfill that promise, God sent Jesus to die and then be "raised up in righteousness." He "direct[ed] all his ways," specifically to the cross, where His blood was shed to "[take] away the sin of the world" (John 1:29). Only by grace through faith in Jesus, "not for price nor reward," are people saved from sin. "If the Son makes you free, you shall be free indeed" (John 8:36).

Lord, thank You for the freedom found in and through Jesus Christ.

Mark Lashey, LifeHouse Church, Townsend, DE

WEEK 50—WEEKEND

Jesus Is in Charge

For since by man came death, by Man also came the resurrection of the dead. For as in Adam all die, even so in Christ all shall be made alive. But each one in his own order: Christ the firstfruits, afterward those who are Christ's at His coming. Then comes the end, when He delivers the kingdom to God the Father, when He puts an end to all rule and all authority and power. For He must reign till He has put all enemies under His feet.

1 CORINTHIANS 15:21-25

During His earthly ministry, Jesus declared and displayed His authority. People were astonished because He spoke as "one having authority" (Matthew 7:29). He healed a paralyzed man to validate His authority "to forgive sins" (9:6). He calmed a raging storm and established that "even the winds and the sea obey Him" (8:26-27). He declared, "All authority has been given to Me in heaven and on earth" (28:18). Jesus is to be preeminent in all things (Colossians 1:17–18).

However, Jesus' authority is not always recognized. As foretold by Isaiah, it was even despised (Isaiah 53:3). After driving merchants out the temple, and as He was teaching and preaching there, the religious leaders questioned His authority (Luke 20:2). "He came to His own, and His own did not receive Him" (John 1:11).

Nevertheless, Jesus makes it clear that it will not bode well for those who reject His authority (Luke 20:18). There will come a time when every knee (not some, but every knee) will bow before Him (Philippians 2:10).

....

Lord, I want You to be preeminent in every area of my life.

Heaven, Life, and the Resurrection

WEEK 51—MONDAY

Ultimate Game Changer

I make a decree that in every dominion of my kingdom men must tremble and fear before the God of Daniel. For He is the living God, and steadfast forever; His kingdom is the one which shall not be destroyed, and His dominion shall endure to the end. He delivers and rescues, and He works signs and wonders in heaven and on earth, who has delivered Daniel from the power of the lions.

DANIEL 6:26–27

Some people are specially gifted at creating momentous change—business leaders such as Google founders Sergey Brin and Larry Page, who radically altered the way we discover information, or athletes like Tom Brady, who not only throws the ball with unbelievable accuracy but also knows how to motivate his teams. Game changers can turn around seemingly impossible situations. And our God is the master game changer. By His sovereign power, He can transform our greatest problems in order to glorify His name.

Under pressure from wicked advisers, King Darius threw Daniel into the lions' den. Miraculously, God protected Daniel by shutting the lions' mouths. In response, King Darius commanded people throughout his kingdom to "tremble and fear" before the living God. He knew that if God could deliver Daniel, He was worthy of everyone's reverence. Today, remember that God will work in your life as you seek to honor Him. Just as He proved His power on Daniel's behalf, the Lord can deliver you for His glory.

> Dear Lord, I praise You for Your ability to turn around impossible circumstances. Use my faith in You to show those around me that You are alive and that Your power can accomplish anything. In Jesus' name, amen.

Dr. Stephen Rummage, Bell Shoals Baptist Church, Brandon, FL

WEEK 51—TUESDAY

An Anchor that Holds

I said, "O my God, do not take me away in the midst of my days; Your years are throughout all generations. Of old You laid the foundation of the earth, and the heavens are the work of Your hands."

PSALM 102:24-25

The website for a nautical gift company showed a photo of a beautiful anchor for sale. The anchor featured two sturdy-looking prongs and a massive chain. It looked as though it could dig firmly into the sea floor. But this anchor only appeared impressive and heavy. It was actually made of Styrofoam! We often try to secure our lives with things like Styrofoam anchors—our health, education, success, money, or friendships—but those anchors won't hold, especially when the greatest storms come. The only secure anchor for our lives is the Lord.

The psalmist understood that God alone offered stability and security. God lives forever, beyond all the generations of history. He established the things that seem most enduring, such as the earth and the heavens. So the psalmist cried out, "O my God, do not take me away in the midst of my days." In fact, even the earth on which we stand and the heavens above us will one day wear out, but our eternal God provides His redeemed people with security forever. Through faith in Jesus, you can depend on God to anchor your life and sustain you, not only throughout your life on earth but for eternity.

> Dear Lord, thank You for the promise of eternal life that You have given me through Jesus Christ. Help me look to You for my strength and security today, trusting that You alone can sustain my life. In Jesus' name, amen.

Heaven, Life, and the Resurrection

WEEK 51—WEDNESDAY

Trusting the Shepherd

As the Father knows Me, even so I know the Father; and I lay down My life for the sheep. And other sheep I have which are not of this fold; them also I must bring, and they will hear My voice; and there will be one flock and one shepherd. "Therefore My Father loves Me, because I lay down My life that I may take it again. No one takes it from Me, but I lay it down of Myself. I have power to lay it down, and I have power to take it again. This command I have received from My Father."

JOHN 10:15-18

A writer spent time with a shepherd on the Texas plains. One night, the shepherd built a fire and the sheep gathered close. Coyotes howled in the distance, and the sheep began bleating. The shepherd tossed logs onto the fire. As flames shot up, the writer looked out and saw four thousand tiny lights—the fire reflected in the eyes of two thousand sheep. With enemies all around, the sheep looked trustingly toward their shepherd.

God's people are like sheep in many ways. We tend to wander from the fold. We can be helpless in the face of predators. We may have trouble getting along with other sheep. But most importantly, we are totally dependent on the Shepherd. Jesus, our loving Shepherd, laid down His life for the sheep. Because He paid such a high price for you, you can trust in Him completely.

> Lord Jesus, You are my perfect Shepherd. You have given Yourself for me. You will guide me where I should go. Give me ears to hear Your voice and a heart to follow You. In Your name, amen.

Dr. Stephen Rummage, Bell Shoals Baptist Church, Brandon, FL

WEEK 51—THURSDAY

Idol Removal

For the LORD is great and greatly to be praised; He is to be feared above all gods. For all the gods of the peoples are idols, but the LORD made the heavens. Honor and majesty are before Him; strength and beauty are in His sanctuary.

PSALM 96:4-6

I was waiting to preach as guest speaker for a church in Malaysia when an announcement in the bulletin caught my attention: "Idol Removal Service," followed by place and time. When I asked the pastor, he said people in their church often came to Christ from a life of idol worship. When they became Christians, they would drag their idol statues to the curb, smash them into pieces, and leave the rubble to be taken away with the trash. Removing the idol was a public testimony of new faith in Christ.

The Hebrew word for "idol" means "an empty thing." We often allow spiritually empty things to occupy a place in our hearts that only Jesus deserves to occupy. Those things can be harder to identify and destroy than a statue of wood, stone, or metal, but they are idols nonetheless. They can be fully removed only if replaced by something greater: worship of the true, living God. You can join the psalmist today in coming before the Lord in worship, offering Him the highest praise, most reverent fear, and deepest honor for His majesty, strength, and beauty.

....

Lord God, You alone are worthy of my life and loyalty. Forgive me for putting other things where You alone deserve to be. Remove the idols in my life, and replace my love for empty things with pure love for You. In Jesus' name, amen.

Heaven, Life, and the Resurrection

WEEK 51—FRIDAY

Light for Darkness

Then Jesus spoke to them again, saying, "I am the light of the world. He who follows Me shall not walk in darkness, but have the light of life."

JOHN 8:12

Years ago, families would often put up their Christmas trees on Christmas Eve and then light small candles on the branches. They would admire the lights for a few minutes, then blow them out. Candles on a Christmas tree could set the entire house on fire. In 1882, Edward Johnson created something safer, the first string of colorful, electric Christmas tree lights. A set of bulbs had just eight lights. They were very expensive at first, and few homes could afford them. But eventually the price came down, and the rest is history. It's amazing how a small strand of tiny Christmas lights can transform a dark place. When darkness is the greatest, light means the most.

Whether candles or electric, Christmas lights beautifully symbolize the light of Jesus. As the radiance of God's glory, Jesus came to a dark world. His light has only one message for darkness: Leave immediately! Spiritual darkness makes life on earth chaotic and discouraging. But His light overcomes darkness in every life He touches. It penetrates the darkness of our sin and expels the murkiness of uncertainty and confusion. As we follow Jesus, we stop stumbling in the dark and begin walking in the light of eternal life.

....

Lord Jesus, I give You praise for Your light. Thank You for the gift of eternal life You have given me. When my heart is overwhelmed by the darkness of this world, give me grace to look to You and see Your light. In Your name, amen.

Dr. Stephen Rummage, Bell Shoals Baptist Church, Brandon, FL

WEEK 51—WEEKEND

Fully Pleasing to God

For He received from God the Father honor and glory when such a voice came to Him from the Excellent Glory: "This is My beloved Son, in whom I am well pleased." And we heard this voice which came from heaven when we were with Him on the holy mountain.

2 PETER 1:17-18

Only through Jesus Christ can we please God. Imagine God's law as a delicate piece of glass given to each person to protect. Any act of disobedience is like throwing a rock at that glass, and an impact at any point shatters it. One moment of impurity, one hateful act, one failure to obey, and the glass is irreparably broken. Truth is, we are born with that glass already in shards. As David wrote, "I was brought forth in iniquity" (Psalm 51:5).

Now imagine Jesus, from His virgin birth through His temptation in the wilderness, through every moment of His perfect life, carrying that delicate glass without breaking or even smudging it. He kept it so perfectly that His Father could speak from heaven and proclaim, "In My Son I am well pleased." At the cross, Jesus laid down His perfect life and was pierced through with every vicious shard of our sinfulness so we could be redeemed from our sin by his blood and brought into God's family. Because Jesus paid the penalty for your sin, you can be pleasing to God.

> Lord Jesus, I give You glory for who You are and what You've done in my life. Thank You for Your perfect life. Thank You for Your sacrificial death that makes me pleasing to God. Grant me grace to live for You today. In Your name, amen.

Heaven, Life, and the Resurrection

WEEK 52—MONDAY

The Danger of Beauty

And take heed, lest you lift your eyes to heaven, and when you see the sun, the moon, and the stars, all the host of heaven, you feel driven to worship them and serve them, which the Lord your God has given to all the peoples under the whole heaven as a heritage. But the Lord has taken you and brought you out of the iron furnace, out of Egypt, to be His people, an inheritance, as you are this day.

DEUTERONOMY 4:19-20

Our God is a God of beauty, so what He creates is beautiful. As creatures made in His image, we are drawn to beauty. But the beauty that was meant to direct our attention toward God (Psalm 19:1) can often take our attention from Him.

Moses reminded Israel of times when they had given too much attention to something other than God, and it cost many lives. God wants you to acknowledge His glory through what has been made but not replace Him with it. This can happen even with good things, like Christmas, family, or patriotism. As you see beauty, be sure to let it inform your worship of God, not dilute your worship of God.

....

> Father, I love You and am so thankful for all You give me. Even if You give me nothing more, You are worthy of all of my praise. God, forgive me for times when I give the praise You deserve to another. The greatest expression of Your love is the love we see in Jesus, and there is no other name by which we may be saved. Draw me closer to You I pray, in Jesus' name, amen.

Brian Boyles, First Baptist Church, Snellville, GA

WEEK 52—TUESDAY

Our Merciful Warrior

I will cry out to God Most High, to God who performs all things for me. He shall send from heaven and save me; He reproaches the one who would swallow me up. God shall send forth His mercy and His truth. . . . Be exalted, O God, above the heavens; let Your glory be above all the earth.

PSALM 57:2–3, 5

If you live long enough, you will have enemies. In this passage, the great warrior David was running from his enemies. While David in this instance was innocent, the evil we battle may sometimes result from our own actions. Whether you are guilty or innocent, praying for God to help you is an important response.

Many people first try to solve problems themselves. You may think it is good to show boldness when God wants you to show humility (Matthew 26:62–63). You may think it is good to speak up when God wants you to be silent so others can speak for you (Proverbs 27:2). Although our culture praises those who fight with their hands and their mouths, God's people are compelled to do battle on our knees with our prayers. The God who made the heavens and the earth is able to help, protect, preserve, and rescue you. And He can do all of it in a way that gives the glory to Him. Trust God and let Him help you.

> Father, I want to be a warrior for Your kingdom. Help me see that You can win even the hardest battles and that my greatest weapon is on my knees in prayer. In Jesus' name I pray, amen.

Heaven, Life, and the Resurrection

WEEK 52—WEDNESDAY

Boldness in Fear

"Let it be known to you all, and to all the people of Israel, that by the name of Jesus Christ of Nazareth, whom you crucified, whom God raised from the dead, by Him this man stands here before you whole. This is the 'stone which was rejected by you builders, which has become the chief cornerstone.' Nor is there salvation in any other, for there is no other name under heaven given among men by which we must be saved."

ACTS 4:10-12

It can be intimidating to speak the name of Jesus in a hostile crowd. Peter was under arrest and outnumbered by people who could keep him in prison, cause physical pain, or worse. Yet he had the courage to give credit to Jesus and to proclaim the gospel. The same Peter who cowered as Jesus was being beaten was now willing to lay down his life to direct people to Jesus. The event that made the difference was Jesus' resurrection.

When you are intimidated, afraid to speak Jesus' name, recall the resurrection of Jesus and the love of your Father in heaven, who is able to protect you. The people who seem powerful and able to cause you harm may be the ones God wants you to reach with the gospel. If you are afraid, you are probably trusting your own ability. Instead, place your trust in what God can do through you.

Father, You are powerful, and I am weak. You are mighty, and I am small. You are sovereign, and I am uncertain. Help me trust Your strength through me and give me boldness when I feel afraid. In Jesus' name I pray, amen.

Brian Boyles, First Baptist Church, Snellville, GA

WEEK 52—THURSDAY

Happy to Be Humbled

Thus says the LORD: *"Heaven is My throne, and earth is My footstool. Where is the house that you will build Me? And where is the place of My rest? For all those things My hand has made, and all those things exist," says the* LORD. *"But on this one will I look: On him who is poor and of a contrite spirit, and who trembles at My word."*

ISAIAH 66:1-2

The more we consider God's majesty, the more amazing it is that He loves us. He tells of His greatness, yet words seem incapable of capturing its true scope. Though the earth is large, He could rest His feet on it. Though the heavens are unreachable, His throne is there. Though we construct buildings that scrape the sky, no structure could house Him. God does not say these things to boast but to keep us from the sin of pride. He is God, He loves us, and He wants to keep us from sin.

So what does God look for in you? This passage gives the answer: He wants you to be poor spiritually so you'll come to Him to fill you. He wants you to be humble so you'll avoid pride. He wants you to tremble at His Word so you'll live in a way that honors Him. It is comforting to be loved and protected by the God of the heavens and the earth.

....

Lord, You alone are great, wonderful, good, and mighty. You are God, and we are Your people. Forgive me for my pride. Help me be humble and love You enough to follow Your Word. It is like honey on my lips. In Jesus' name I pray, amen.

Heaven, Life, and the Resurrection

WEEK 52—FRIDAY

Ability Is Secondary

"Behold, I give you the authority to trample on serpents and scorpions, and over all the power of the enemy, and nothing shall by any means hurt you. Nevertheless do not rejoice in this, that the spirits are subject to you, but rather rejoice because your names are written in heaven."

LUKE 10:19-20

Christians can fall to the sin of pride in what God has given us in Jesus. A man named Simon was so captivated by what the apostles did that he offered to pay them to teach him how to do it (Acts 8). He was captivated by their power but allowed it to become a distraction. This may happen to us when we put more emphasis on the music of a church than the gospel proclaimed there, or focus on the appearance of the preacher rather than the doctrine he delivers.

In this passage, Jesus was concerned that His followers might relegate the gospel's power to second-tier status behind something as fascinating as the ability to overpower evil. Let nothing take priority over the truth and power of the gospel of Jesus Christ. It is only the gospel that cleanses a soul, restores a relationship with God, and makes the dead live again. Anything else comes in a distant second place. For these things we rejoice because any who come to Christ in faith have their names written in the Lamb's book of life.

> Father, I rejoice because Jesus has set me free and taken my place on the cross. Because He died for me, I get to live with Him in heaven. Nothing will ever compare to that. In Jesus' name I pray, amen.

Brian Boyles, First Baptist Church, Snellville, GA

WEEK 52—WEEKEND

Prayerful Prayer

Confess your trespasses to one another, and pray for one another, that you may be healed. The effective, fervent prayer of a righteous man avails much. Elijah was a man with a nature like ours, and he prayed earnestly that it would not rain; and it did not rain on the land for three years and six months. And he prayed again, and the heaven gave rain, and the earth produced its fruit.

JAMES 5:16–18

We're told to confess our mistakes to one another for the purpose of intentional prayer. Before you think your sins are too great and prayer would make no difference, God gives us the example of Elijah, whose prayer affected the weather. Some may think Elijah was different, but God says he had a nature like ours. Yet Elijah's prayer was more than a quick sentence in God's direction. He prayed earnestly, or prayed prayerfully.

Do you pray prayerfully? Elijah's prayer took place in 1 Kings 18. God told him He would send rain, yet Elijah still prayed for God to send rain several times. He continued praying until God sent the rain He had already promised to send. This is praying prayerfully. Whatever you are going through, whatever fear or addiction or problem you face, pray for God to help you. And pray prayerfully until He does.

> God, I know You hear my prayers. Help me pray to You more and to pray to You prayerfully. Let me not simply toss up a doubt-filled sentence but send up a faith-filled pleading for Your will to be done. In Jesus' name I pray, amen.

Heaven, Life, and the Resurrection

Contributors

Dr. Chris Aiken, Englewood Baptist Church, Rocky Mount, NC . . . . Week 29
Jamie Altman, Bethlehem Community Church, Laurel, MS . . . . Week 26
Tim Anderson, Clements Baptist Church, Athens, AL . . . . Week 17
Steven Blanton, Ebenezer Baptist Church, Hendersonville, NC . . . . Week 18
Dr. J. Kie Bowman, Hyde Park Baptist Church, Austin, TX . . . . Week 31
Brian Boyles, First Baptist Church, Snellville, GA . . . . Week 52
Dr. Kelly Bullard, First Baptist Church Summerfield, Summerfield, NC . . . . . . Week 48
Chad Campbell, Mount Pisgah Baptist Church, Easley, SC . . . . Week 27
Dr. Frank Cox, North Metro Baptist Church, Lawrenceville, GA . . . . Week 35
Steven Cox, Peace Baptist Church, Whiteville, NC . . . . Week 49
Jeff Crook, Christ Place Church, Flowery Branch, GA . . . . Week 37
Tim DeTellis, New Missions, Orlando, FL . . . . Week 36
Chris Dixon, Liberty Baptist Church, Dublin, GA . . . . Week 20
Dr. Adam B. Dooley, Englewood Baptist Church, Jackson, TN . . . . Week 38
Dr. David Edwards, DaveEdwardsSpeaks.com, Oklahoma City, OK . . . . Week 39
Dr. Grant Ethridge, Liberty Live Church, Hampton, VA . . . . Week 40
Dr. Steve Folmar, Covenant Church, Houma, LA . . . . Week 41
Brian Fossett, Fossett Evangelistic Ministries, Dalton, GA . . . . Week 42
Dr. Robby Foster, Northside Baptist Church, Valdosta, GA . . . . Week 15
Jerry Gillis, The Chapel at Crosspoint, Getzville, NY . . . . Week 34
Dr. Chad Grayson, Life Community Church, Jamestown, NC . . . . Week 30
Dr. Sam Greer, Red Bank Baptist Church, Chattanooga, TN . . . . Week 4
Dr. Alex Himaya, BattleCreek Church, Broken Arrow, OK . . . . Week 3
Mark Hoover, NewSpring Church, Wichita, KS . . . . Week 2
Dr. Johnny Hunt, North American Mission Board, Alpharetta, GA . . . . Week 1
Dr. Steven Kyle, Hiland Park Baptist Church, Panama City, FL . . . . Week 16

Mark Lashey, LifeHouse Church, Townsend, DE........................... Week 50

Roy G. Mack, Grace Fellowship Church, Niles, OH .... Week 43

Jeremy Morton, First Baptist Church Woodstock, Woodstock, GA .... Week 5

Mike Orr, First Baptist Church Chipley, Chipley, FL....................... Week 25

Dr. Jim Perdue, Second Baptist Church, Warner Robins, GA .... Week 21

Dr. Jim Phillips, North Greenwood Baptist Church, Greenwood , MS .... Week 22

Dr. Robert C. Pitman, Bob Pitman Ministries, Muscle Shoals, AL........... Week 23

Marc Pritchett, NorthRidge Church of Thomaston, Meansville, GA.......... Week 19

Paul Purvis, Mission Hill Church, Temple Terrace, FL..................... Week 44

Rocky Purvis, Northside Baptist Church, Lexington, SC................... Week 46

Dr. William Rice, Calvary Baptist Church, Clearwater, FL .... Week 45

Dr. Stephen Rummage, Bell Shoals Baptist Church, Brandon, FL............ Week 51

Cary Schmidt, Emmanuel Baptist Church, Newington, CT .... Week 6

Dr. Jeff Schreve, First Baptist Church Texarkana, Texarkana, TX .... Week 7

Tim Sizemore, Lighthouse Baptist Church, Warner Robins, GA................ Week 8

Billy Smith, Christ Chapel Community Church, Zebulon, GA............... Week 24

Dr. Bryan E. Smith, First Roanoke Baptist Church, Roanoke, VA .... Week 33

Joel Southerland, Peavine Baptist Church, Rock Spring, GA................ Week 28

Mike Stone, Emmanuel Baptist Church, Blackshear, GA .... Week 9

Brent Thompson, Heflin Baptist Church, Heflin, AL...................... Week 47

H. Marshall Thompson Jr., Riverstone Community Church, Jacksonville, FL.. Week 14

Dr. Ted H. Traylor, Olive Baptist Church, Pensacola, FL .... Week 10

Dr. Mike Whitson, First Baptist Church Indian Trail, Indian Trail, NC....... Week 11

Dr. Brad Whitt, Abilene Baptist Church, Martinez, GA.................... Week 12

Dr. Don Wilton, First Baptist Church, Spartanburg, SC..................... Week 13

Dr. Danny Wood, Shades Mountain Baptist Church, Birmingham, AL .... Week 32

Heaven, Life, and the Resurrection

Scripture Index

GENESIS
Genesis 1:1–2 149
Genesis 2:4–5 41
Genesis 2:7–9 191
Genesis 3:22–23 98
Genesis 15:4–6 107
Genesis 22:17–18 100
Genesis 28:16–17 89

EXODUS
Exodus 16:4–5 261
Exodus 20:11–12 30

DEUTERONOMY
Deuteronomy 3:24–25 268
Deuteronomy 4:7–9 36
Deuteronomy 4:19–20 310
Deuteronomy 6:4–7 155
Deuteronomy 10:12–13 190
Deuteronomy 17:18–19 200
Deuteronomy 26:14–15 272
Deuteronomy 30:15–16 213
Deuteronomy 30:19–20 202

JOSHUA
Joshua 1:5–6 274

JUDGES
Judges 16:28–30 132

1 SAMUEL
1 Samuel 1:10–11 218

Heaven, Life, and the Resurrection

1 KINGS
1 Kings 3:11–12 179
1 Kings 8:22–23 10
1 Kings 8:39–40 184

1 CHRONICLES
1 Chronicles 29:11–12 295

2 CHRONICLES
2 Chronicles 1:11–12 194
2 Chronicles 6:14 264
2 Chronicles 6:29–30 287
2 Chronicles 7:14 226

ESTHER
Esther 7:3–4 146

JOB
Job 10:9–12 238
Job 11:17–20 58
Job 24:22–24 246
Job 33:1–4 227
Job 33:26–28 171
Job 33:29–33 112

PSALMS
Psalm 8:3–5 69
Psalm 11:4–5, 7 104
Psalm 14:2–3 282
Psalm 19:1–5 114
Psalm 20:6–9 144
Psalm 21:3–6 68
Psalm 23:4–6 206
Psalm 27:1–3 4
Psalm 30:3–5 105
Psalm 33:4–6 217
Psalm 33:12–15 123

Psalm 34:11–14	154
Psalm 36:5–7	205
Psalm 36:7–9	35
Psalm 42:6–8	189
Psalm 50:4–6	131
Psalm 53:2–3	156
Psalm 54:4–7	130
Psalm 57:2–3	279
Psalm 57:2–3, 5	311
Psalm 57:9–11	289
Psalm 61:5–8	76
Psalm 63:3–5	297
Psalm 68:32–34	158
Psalm 72:12–14	51
Psalm 73:25–26	60
Psalm 76:7–9	224
Psalm 85:10–13	255
Psalm 86:2–5	260
Psalm 89:11–14	237
Psalm 91:14–16	165
Psalm 96:4–6	307
Psalm 96:11–13	78
Psalm 102:17–19	219
Psalm 102:24–25	305
Psalm 103:1–5	178
Psalm 103:10–12	9
Psalm 103:17–19	278
Psalm 104:1–2	75
Psalm 108:3–6	170, 266
Psalm 113:4–8	147
Psalm 115:1–3	87
Psalm 115:14–16	236
Psalm 119:49–50, 54–56	201
Psalm 119:89–91, 93	181
Psalm 119:93–96	223
Psalm 119:107–109, 111–112	284
Psalm 121:1–3	228

Heaven, Life, and the Resurrection

Psalm 123:1–2 300
Psalm 124:6–8 133
Psalm 128:2–5 24
Psalm 133:1–3 16
Psalm 134:1–3 241
Psalm 135:5–7 292
Psalm 136:1–3, 26 177
Psalm 136:2–5 267
Psalm 139:7–10 37
Psalm 144:3–5 79
Psalm 146:5–8 22
Psalm 147:7–9, 11 111
Psalm 148:1–4 61
Psalm 148:13–14 129

PROVERBS
Proverbs 23:4–5 250
Proverbs 30:4–5 27

ISAIAH
Isaiah 34:4–5 230
Isaiah 37:16–17 273
Isaiah 42:5–6 42
Isaiah 43:3–4 8
Isaiah 44:21–23 207
Isaiah 45:7–8 55
Isaiah 45:12–13 302
Isaiah 45:18 50
Isaiah 48:12–13 34
Isaiah 51:6 242
Isaiah 51:15–16 276
Isaiah 55:8–9, 11 182
Isaiah 55:10–11 209
Isaiah 65:17–19 119
Isaiah 66:1–2 313
Isaiah 66:22–23 174

JEREMIAH
Jeremiah 10:12–13 150
Jeremiah 14:20–22 142
Jeremiah 23:23–24 245
Jeremiah 31:37–38 38
Jeremiah 32:17–18 127
Jeremiah 51:15–16 138
Jeremiah 51:47–48 97

LAMENTATIONS
Lamentations 3:40–42 210

DANIEL
Daniel 2:17–19 88
Daniel 4:24–25 106
Daniel 4:31–32 116
Daniel 4:34–35 .... 125, 301
Daniel 6:26–27 304
Daniel 7:26–27 29

HOSEA
Hosea 2:19–21 291

HABAKKUK
Habbakkuk 3:3–4, 6 115

MALACHI
Malachi 3:10 247

MATTHEW
Matthew 3:16–17 293
Matthew 4:17–20 14
Matthew 5:1–5 269
Matthew 5:10–12 281
Matthew 5:18–19 204
Matthew 5:43–45 134
Matthew 6:19–21 212

Heaven, Life, and the Resurrection

Matthew 6:25–27 163
Matthew 7:7–8, 11 45
Matthew 7:21–23 222
Matthew 8:10–11 122
Matthew 10:7–9 66
Matthew 10:32–33 262
Matthew 11:11–12, 15 203
Matthew 11:25–27 162
Matthew 12:48–50 92
Matthew 13:31–32 33
Matthew 13:44–46 57
Matthew 13:47–50 74
Matthew 14:19 235
Matthew 16:17–19 143
Matthew 16:21–23 103
Matthew 16:24–27 151
Matthew 18:1–3 6
Matthew 18:10–11 140
Matthew 18:18–20 .... 216, 239
Matthew 19:13–15 121
Matthew 19:16–17 48
Matthew 19:23–24 188
Matthew 20:1–4 128
Matthew 20:17–19 94
Matthew 22:30–32 249
Matthew 23:9–12 288
Matthew 24:29–30 25
Matthew 24:32–35 176
Matthew 24:36–37, 40–42 93
Matthew 26:64 265
Matthew 27:50–53 169
Matthew 28:2–4 26
Matthew 28:18–20 80

MARK

Mark 1:9–11 91
Mark 6:41–44 175

Mark 8:31–33 192
Mark 8:36–38 64
Mark 9:30–32 65
Mark 9:33–35 258
Mark 10:21–22 109
Mark 11:25–26 81
Mark 13:24–27 229
Mark 13:32–34 32
Mark 14:61–62 49
Mark 16:19–20 44

LUKE
Luke 2:11–14 270
Luke 2:15–16 85
Luke 3:21–22 13
Luke 6:22–23 73
Luke 9:16–17 95
Luke 9:22–24 7
Luke 10:19–20 314
Luke 11:2–4 120
Luke 11:11–13 96
Luke 12:22–25 86
Luke 12:31–34 254
Luke 14:12–14 161
Luke 15:20–21 43
Luke 15:7 280
Luke 17:24–26 108
Luke 17:33–36 99
Luke 18:21–22 221
Luke 18:31–33 139
Luke 21:10–12 299
Luke 21:31–33 56
Luke 22:42–44 135
Luke 24:50–53 62

JOHN
John 1:50–51 234

John 3:12–13 31
John 3:14–16 157
John 3:26–28 5
John 3:30–33 240
John 4:13–14 187
John 5:20–22 199
John 5:26–29 90
John 6:26–27 252
John 6:32–34 198
John 6:38–40 193
John 6:41–44 168
John 6:50–51 102
John 6:56–58 72
John 6:62–63 286
John 8:12 308
John 10:9–11 159
John 10:15–18 306
John 11:1, 3–4 110
John 11:17, 21–23 12
John 11:24–27 256
John 12:26–28 21
John 12:49–50 277
John 17:1–3 84

ACTS

Acts 1:9–11 271
Acts 2:1–4 19
Acts 2:19–21 70
Acts 2:30–32 275
Acts 4:1–4 183
Acts 4:10–12 312
Acts 4:32–33 118
Acts 7:48–50 166
Acts 7:54–56 101
Acts 9:3–5 53
Acts 10:9–11 285
Acts 14:14–15 294

Acts 17:23–25..63
Acts 22:6–8..231
Acts 24:15–16...225

ROMANS
Romans 1:1–4..67
Romans 1:18–20..17
Romans 6:5–8..77

1 CORINTHIANS
1 Corinthians 8:4–6...52
1 Corinthians 15:12–14.......................................233
1 Corinthians 15:21–25.......................................303
1 Corinthians 15:26–28.......................................257
1 Corinthians 15:42–45.......................................211
1 Corinthians 15:47–49.......................................195

2 CORINTHIANS
2 Corinthians 5:1–2...18
2 Corinthians 5:3–5..197
2 Corinthians 5:5–7...83

EPHESIANS
Ephesians 1:3–4..298
Ephesians 1:9–10..71
Ephesians 1:19–21..263
Ephesians 2:4–7..186
Ephesians 3:9–10...196
Ephesians 3:14–17..232
Ephesians 6:5, 8–9..82
Ephesians 6:10–13..173

PHILIPPIANS
Philippians 2:9–11...290
Philippians 3:7–9..152
Philippians 3:17, 20–21......................................141

COLOSSIANS
- Colossians 1:3–5 243
- Colossians 1:15–17 39
- Colossians 1:19–22 47
- Colossians 1:21–23 136
- Colossians 4:2–3 185

1 THESSALONIANS
- 1 Thessalonians 1:9–10 214
- 1 Thessalonians 4:16–18 283

2 TIMOTHY
- 2 Timothy 2:20–22 251
- 2 Timothy 4:17–18 172

HEBREWS
- Hebrews 1:8–10 11
- Hebrews 3:1–4 167
- Hebrews 4:14–16 296
- Hebrews 6:1–3 20
- Hebrews 6:4–6 137
- Hebrews 7:26–27 215
- Hebrews 8:1–2 220
- Hebrews 9:11–12 54
- Hebrews 9:23–24 244
- Hebrews 10:34–36 46
- Hebrews 12:1–2 208
- Hebrews 12:22–24 126

JAMES
- James 5:11–12 160
- James 5:16–18 315

1 PETER
- 1 Peter 1:3–4 28
- 1 Peter 1:10, 12 124
- 1 Peter 3:21–22 148

2 PETER
    2 Peter 1:17–18 309
    2 Peter 3:5–7 117
    2 Peter 3:10–11 40

1 JOHN
    1 John 5:6–8 253

REVELATION
    Revelation 3:12–13 113
    Revelation 4:1–2 259
    Revelation 5:1–3 59
    Revelation 5:11–12 248
    Revelation 10:5–6 180
    Revelation 11:15–16 164
    Revelation 11:17, 19 23
    Revelation 12:7–9 145
    Revelation 12:10, 12 15
    Revelation 20:5–6 153